UNDERSTANDING AND TEACHING
HOLOCAUST
EDUCATION

SAGE was founded in 1965 by Sara Miller McCune to support the dissemination of usable knowledge by publishing innovative and high-quality research and teaching content. Today, we publish over 900 journals, including those of more than 400 learned societies, more than 800 new books per year, and a growing range of library products including archives, data, case studies, reports, and video. SAGE remains majority-owned by our founder, and after Sara's lifetime will become owned by a charitable trust that secures our continued independence.

Los Angeles | London | New Delhi | Singapore | Washington DC | Melbourne

UNDERSTANDING AND TEACHING
HOLOCAUST
EDUCATION

PAULA COWAN | HENRY MAITLES

Los Angeles | London | New Delhi
Singapore | Washington DC | Melbourne

Los Angeles | London | New Delhi
Singapore | Washington DC | Melbourne

SAGE Publications Ltd
1 Oliver's Yard
55 City Road
London EC1Y 1SP

SAGE Publications Inc.
2455 Teller Road
Thousand Oaks, California 91320

SAGE Publications India Pvt Ltd
B 1/I 1 Mohan Cooperative Industrial Area
Mathura Road
New Delhi 110 044

SAGE Publications Asia-Pacific Pte Ltd
3 Church Street
#10-04 Samsung Hub
Singapore 049483

Editor: James Clark
Assistant editor: Robert Patterson
Production editor: Nicola Marshall
Copyeditor: Audrey Scriven
Proofreader: Jill Birch
Indexer: Silvia Benvenuto
Marketing manager: Lorna Patkai
Cover design: Naomi Robinson
Typeset by: C&M Digitals (P) Ltd, Chennai, India
Printed and bound in Great Britain by Ashford
Colour Press Ltd

© Paula Cowan and Henry Maitles 2017

First published 2017

Apart from any fair dealing for the purposes of research or
private study, or criticism or review, as permitted under the
Copyright, Designs and Patents Act, 1988, this publication
may be reproduced, stored or transmitted in any form, or
by any means, only with the prior permission in writing of
the publishers, or in the case of reprographic reproduction,
in accordance with the terms of licences issued by
the Copyright Licensing Agency. Enquiries concerning
reproduction outside those terms should be sent to the
publishers.

Library of Congress Control Number: 2016940953

British Library Cataloguing in Publication data

A catalogue record for this book is available from
the British Library

ISBN 978-1-4739-1933-4
ISBN 978-1-4739-1934-1 (pbk)

At SAGE we take sustainability seriously. Most of our products are printed in the UK using FSC papers and boards.
When we print overseas we ensure sustainable papers are used as measured by the PREPS grading system.
We undertake an annual audit to monitor our sustainability.

TABLE OF CONTENTS

ABOUT THE AUTHORS

Paula Cowan, PhD, is Senior Lecturer in Education at the University of the West of Scotland. She researches, publishes and teaches in the area of school-based Citizenship and Holocaust Education. She was commissioned by the Scottish Executive to write teaching resources for primary and secondary schools to accompany the introduction of a national Holocaust Memorial Day and is a founding trustee of the UK Holocaust Memorial Day Trust. She is a UK delegate on the International Holocaust Remembrance Alliance and a member of the Holocaust Memorial Day (Scotland) Steering Group. In 2015 Paula was awarded an Outstanding Achievement Award for her work in Holocaust Education from the Children's Identity and Citizenship Europe Association (CiCeA), a research association that focuses on Citizenship Education and identity formation in young people.

Henry Maitles is Professor of Education and Assistant Dean in the School of Education at the University of the West of Scotland. He researches, publishes and teaches in the area of citizenship and values and in particular the impact of citizenship initiatives, such as the Holocaust, in schools. He was a member of the Scottish Executive Review Group, which drew up the proposals for Education for Citizenship which is a policy priority in all Scottish schools. He is on the editorial boards of the *Journal for Critical Education Policy Studies* and *Citizenship Teaching and Learning*. He is a former President of CiCeA and an Executive Member of Children's Identity and Citizenship in Europe, an EU Jean Monnet-funded research network.

The authors' co-edited book, *Teaching Controversial Issues in the Classroom*, (Continuum, 2012) includes several chapters on teaching the Holocaust.

ACKNOWLEDGEMENTS

Holocaust Education has defined both our careers. Our professional interest in Holocaust Education began when we were teachers in the 1990s. At that time school-based Holocaust Education was in its infancy, and an insertion in the (Glasgow) *Herald* newspaper that Prime Minister Tony Blair was proposing a National Holocaust Memorial Day could easily be missed. Since then school-based Holocaust Education has developed in ways we could never have imagined.

The first conference Paula attended as a junior lecturer in education was the Legacy of Holocaust Survivors' conference at Yad Vashem in 2002 where the late Elie Wisel said, 'Whoever listens to a witness, becomes a witness.' This places a lot of responsibility on Holocaust educational researchers like ourselves, who have been privileged to meet Holocaust survivors and eyewitnesses. Their testimonies have informed our thinking of the Holocaust and of Holocaust Education. Hence, we express our gratitude to these individuals, some of whom have contributed to school-based Holocaust Education by regularly visiting schools and engaging with students and teachers and others who have spoken to us privately.

We would like to convey our thanks to our colleagues at the University of the West of Scotland. We are grateful to them, wider colleagues and friends who have commented on draft chapters of this book and to the teachers and students who shared their insights with us in Chapters 7 and 8. Our most sincere thanks to the team at Sage Publications, particularly Robert Patterson and James Clark, for their helpful comments, consistent encouragement and patience.

Our final special mention is to our families; their love and support are essential to our research, thinking and writing. Our partners, Stephen and Clare have consistently supported us. Holocaust Education is meaningless without the next generation, so thanks to Elliot, Naomi, Gemma, Laura and Hannah for making our work meaningful.

TIMELINE OF HOLOCAUST EDUCATION

1947	*The Diary of Anne Frank* first published in the Netherlands
	Auschwitz-Birkenau Memorial Museum (also known as the Auschwitz-Birkenau State Museum) created by the Polish Parliament
1951	Yom HaShoah designated by the Israeli Parliament
1952	*Anne Frank: The Diary of a Young Girl* first published in English
1961–62	The trial of Adolf Eichmann
1979	Auschwitz-Birkenau Memorial Museum becomes a UNESCO World Heritage Site
1988	*March of the Living* programme established
1990	The Organisation for Security and Co-operation in Europe (OSCE) first condemns antisemitism; this includes Holocaust denial
1992	Art Spiegelman wins the Pulitzer Prize for the graphic novel *Maus*
1993	Film *Schindler's List* released; International School for Holocaust Studies at Yad Vashem, Israel, established
1998	International Holocaust Remembrance Alliance established
1999	Lessons from Auschwitz programme established by the Holocaust Educational Trust
2000	Stockholm Declaration
2001	Holocaust Memorial Day introduced in the UK
2005	International Holocaust Remembrance Day designated by the United Nations General Assembly

1

INTRODUCTION

Learning Objectives

- To provide a general background to, and current contexts of, Holocaust Education, remembrance and research
- To demonstrate the complexity in defining the Holocaust
- To discuss the different meanings of antisemitism
- To provide authors' definitions of the Holocaust and antisemitism
- To provide an outline of the following chapters

It is now more than fifteen years since 46 government representatives, including 23 heads of state and prime ministers, attended the Stockholm International Forum on the Holocaust (2000), and discussed the importance of Holocaust Education, remembrance and research in the twenty-first century. Their discussions led to the Stockholm Declaration, which recognised the unprecedented nature and magnitude of the Holocaust, and that this should never be forgotten. Committed to this Declaration, the intergovernmental organisation, the International Holocaust Remembrance Alliance (IHRA), formerly known as the Task Force for International Co-operation on Holocaust Education, Remembrance and Research, is committed to encouraging the political commitment of governments to support education, remembrance and research of the Holocaust and to fostering international co-operation in this area by developing multilateral partnerships amongst its member countries. Before the establishment of this organisation in 1998, the Holocaust was principally of interest to people who had obvious connections to it; the IHRA brought about a shift in expectations that conveyed the relevance and remembrance of the Holocaust to a far wider international audience.

One approach to impacting on collective memory is the establishment of an annual day of Holocaust Remembrance. Prior to the establishment of this Day, Holocaust remembrance had, since the 1950s, been principally commemorated by Jewish communities and individuals worldwide on *Yom HaShoah*. Established in the UK in 2000 and adopted by the United Nations in 2006, Holocaust Remembrance (or Memorial) Day, which falls on 27 January (the date, in 1945, of the liberation of Auschwitz-Birkenau), has contributed significantly to Holocaust Education in schools, colleges, universities and in other institutions such as prisons, libraries, and corporate organisations. Today the Holocaust is remembered and taught in a wide range of innovative and engaging ways, in different languages by people of different religions, cultures, and ethnicity. This provides sound evidence that the Stockholm Declaration's objectives continue to be taken seriously.

Yet the politicisation of the Holocaust is not beyond criticism. For example, Peter Novick (1999) accused the US government of hypocrisy when former US President Bill Clinton spoke of the lack of help given to victims of the Holocaust, at the opening of the state-funded United States Holocaust Memorial Museum in Washington DC in 1993, but as Head of Government did not intervene to stop the genocide of the Tutsis in Rwanda in 1994. In the UK, Mark Levene (2006) criticised the intentions of former Prime Minister Tony Blair's decision to establish a national Holocaust Memorial Day. Levene claimed that this was an attempt to bring together shared Western values after the Cold War, conveniently avoiding the UK's failure to prevent recent genocides and the controversies of providing financial support to genocidaires, most notably Saddam Hussein in the 1980s, when hundreds of thousands of Kurds were murdered in Iraq.

Similarly is the recognition that in the early twenty-first century while Holocaust Education and remembrance has been developing worldwide, there has been little intervention from world states and the United Nations with regard to the ongoing genocide in Darfur which, to date, has claimed the lives of some 400,000 people, and displaced nearly three million since 2003. While questioning the agendas of governments and political leaders is healthy, these agendas do not necessarily negate governmental contributions to developing Holocaust Education and remembrance. The authors' experiences of learning about the Holocaust in Scotland in the 1960s, 70s and 80s were that it was very infrequently taught in schools. Even students who chose History as one of their subjects, and studied the Second World War, found that their programme focused on the causes of the War. Students who studied Judaism in

Religious and Moral Education programmes were more likely to learn about the Holocaust and did so, though from a religious and/or philosophical perspective, i.e. without the assurance of a historical foundation. Hence an understanding of the Holocaust for generations of young Scots was heavily reliant on individual personal interest that occurred outside schools. We, the authors, therefore share the Holocaust historian Yehuda Bauer's view (2002) that the contribution of politicians to the Holocaust Education effort is necessary. In the UK, governmental support in the form of subsidising the national Holocaust Memorial Day ceremony and resources for schools and wider communities to support this (see for example DfEE, 2000; LTS, 2000, 2002b; Gathering the Voices, 2012) has impacted on Holocaust Education and remembrance across the country. Our research findings demonstrate that Holocaust Education has the potential to impact on young people's values and attitudes towards minority groups (Maitles et al., 2006). Today's young people are tomorrow's politicians and government officials. It is possible that by applying an open and engaging attitude to Holocaust Education, the next generation of politicians and government officials will be better equipped than their predecessors to address topics of prejudice and genocide.

The Process of the Holocaust

It is now more than seventy years since the liberation of Auschwitz-Birkenau, a place that was inconceivable eighty years ago but today has become synonymous with evil and the worst example of man's inhumanity to man. Archive footage and images of the Holocaust are hard for people, irrespective of their age and/or heritage, to digest. Similarly, words such as annihilation and extermination may not be commonly referred to on Holocaust Remembrance Day, or in a classroom, yet are important in understanding the destructive process of European Jewry.

Hilberg (1985) categorised six sequential stages of the Holocaust process:

1. definition
2. expropriation
3. ghettoisation
4. mobile killing units
5. deportation
6. death camps

The definition of Jews was achieved through the Nuremberg Laws (1935) which deprived German Jews of their citizenship. Prior to this, antisemitic legislation had been passed (1933–34) in Germany restricting the number of Jewish students in German schools and universities, and Jews from working in the medical and legal professions. Also, confiscation of Jewish property and possessions began at this time and continued until 1945. Although Jews were forced to emigrate, expansion of the Third Reich in central and western Europe, and the unwillingness of countries to open their doors to Jews, together with immigration policies that did not allow massive immigration to Palestine, meant that they found it increasingly difficult to leave Germany and German-occupied countries. Jews were initially deported to ghettos as an interim arrangement before their deportation to camps. One year before the discussion and finalising of the 'The Final Solution of the Jewish Question' at the Wannsee Conference (1942), the systematic annihilation of Jews had already begun, with mobile killing units, the *Einsatzgruppen*, murdering more than 1.3 million Jews in the newly German-occupied Soviet Union. As effective and efficient instruments of the 'Final Solution', the death camps were killing factories that were designed to exterminate Jews. They were fitted with gas chambers and crematoria, and employed techniques of mass production. It is worth noting that commanders of the *Einsatzgruppen* included Dr Otto Rasch, an intellectual with two PhDs, an economist and lawyer, Otto Ohlendorf, and that Dr Josef Mengele (who had a PhD in physical anthropology in addition to an MD) was one of 23 German doctors at Auschwitz. This summary serves to highlight the unprecedented nature of the Holocaust.

The above summary explains the following question that we were asked after presenting a paper at a national educational research conference on senior school students' responses to visiting the camps at Auschwitz. One member in the audience commented that the questions in our research about the impact of the visit on students' understanding of the Holocaust, genocide, the Second World War and human rights were deeply flawed as 'understanding' was too subjective. He explained that irrespective of what he read, or what he saw, because of its complexity, he could never really *understand* the Holocaust. He claimed that if *he* could not understand this, how can we, or anyone else, expect school students to do so? We argued then, as we do so in this book, that it is precisely because of the complex nature of the Holocaust, this 'ungraspable nature of the Holocaust' that Ruth Gilbert refers to (Gilbert, 2010), that not only should teenagers study the Holocaust in their junior and senior years, but that Holocaust learning should also begin at primary school. We also argued that the Holocaust is not the only complex area of learning in a school's curriculum. Teachers may consider child obesity, and the current treatment and plight of refugees, to be equally difficult to understand. While we are resolute in this issue, it is worth reflecting that if this audience member is correct, then what can the purpose of Holocaust Education and remembrance possibly be?

The Holocaust led to the adoption of the term 'genocide' (1944), the UN General Assembly's declaration of genocide as a crime under international law (1946), the *UN Declaration of Human Rights* (1948), the *Convention on the Prevention and Punishment of the Crime of Genocide* (1948), and the establishment of the UN High Commissioner for Refugees (1950). Our opinion is that Holocaust Education and Holocaust remembrance can help learners, young and old, understand the past, as well as contribute to their understanding of the historical event that has become known as the Holocaust. While it is inappropriate for young learners to study each of Hilberg's stages, we consider that teachers should have this understanding and that it should inform their teaching. Feedback that we have received from teachers suggests that teacher knowledge and pedagogy are serious barriers to teaching the Holocaust. As the title of this book suggests, our focus is on teacher pedagogies and practice. Readers who would like to develop their knowledge of the Holocaust should refer to our suggested Further Reading texts at the end of this chapter.

Defining the Holocaust

The literal meaning of the word 'holocaust', a 'burnt offering' or a 'sacrifice by fire', is problematic, as these biblical connotations suggest that the genocide of the Jews, under Nazi rule in what has become known as the Holocaust, was a sacrifice, which it clearly was not. A sacrifice can be a loss of something one gives up usually for the sake of a better cause. The connotation that the murder of European Jews could be explained by achieving a 'greater good', or a better society, is repugnant. This is one reason why the word 'Shoah' is often preferred, and has been adopted in several countries such as Israel and France. Meaning 'catastrophe', this word conveys a sense of the horror and devastation that ensued. Yet the murder of European Jews was not a catastrophe in that it was not a natural occurrence, a tsunami or an earthquake, that humans could not foresee or control. This man-made catastrophe could have been prevented. We (the authors) will adopt the usage of the capitalised word 'Holocaust' as this is the word that is commonly used in the UK, where Holocaust (not Shoah) Memorial Day is annually commemorated, and where the Holocaust (not the Shoah) is included in the school curriculum in England.

The central aim of this book, as its title suggests, is to support teachers and educators in their teaching of the Holocaust in schools. One of the first pieces of advice offered by the IHRA to teachers is to 'define the term Holocaust' (IHRA, n.d.), yet this presents challenges as definitions are influenced by cultural and historical narratives. While the Holocaust was a catastrophe for Jews, it is also considered by many Muslims, and in particular Arab Muslims, as a catastrophe for Palestinians, which they call the Nakba. Many Palestinians consider that the Holocaust led to the displacement of nearly one million Palestinians as a result of the United Nations approving the establishment of the State of Israel in 1947 (Werbner, 2009). Other historical sources provide different definitions.

The IHRA provide the following two definitions on their website.

Definition 1

The Holocaust refers to a specific genocidal event in twentieth-century history: the state-sponsored, systematic persecution and annihilation of European Jewry by Nazi Germany and its collaborators between 1933 and 1945. Jews were the primary victims – 6 million were murdered; Gypsies, the handicapped, and Poles were also targeted for destruction or decimation for racial, ethnic, or national reasons. Millions more, including homosexuals, Jehovah's Witnesses, Soviet prisoners of war, and political dissidents, also suffered grievous oppression and death under Nazi tyranny.

(From the Imperial War Museum, London)

Definition 2

The Holocaust was the murder of approximately six million Jews by the Nazis and their collaborators. Between the German invasion of the Soviet Union in the summer of 1941 and the end of the war in Europe in May 1945, Nazi Germany and its accomplices strove to murder every Jew under their domination. Because Nazi discrimination against the Jews began with Hitler's accession to power in January 1933, many historians consider this the start of the Holocaust era. The Jews were not the only victims of Hitler's regime, but they were the only group that the Nazis sought to destroy entirely.

(From the United States Holocaust Memorial Museum, Washington, DC, USA)

It is hardly surprising that these definitions are strikingly similar as they are both historically accurate. They agree that the year when the Holocaust began was 1933: not 1939 when the Second World War began; not 1941 when the mobile killing squads began wiping out entire Jewish communities; and not 1942 when the implementation of the Final Solution was agreed. The above definitions also agree on the number of Jews murdered, acknowledge that the perpetrators or victimisers were Nazis (or Nazi Germany) and their collaborators, and that Jews were the primary victims. Aside from obvious age-appropriateness issues in teaching this to young learners which can be challenging for teachers, there are significant differences between these definitions.

Definition 1 identifies the main groups of people who were targeted by the Nazis and their collaborators; definition 2 acknowledges the murder of other groups of peoples but only names the Jews. This clearly emphasises the distinctive treatment of the Jews, although some may consider that this marginalises the treatment meted out to many other victims. Definition 1 also includes the term 'state sponsored' to emphasise that such actions and behaviour were national policy. Another difference is their conveying the genocidal nature of the event. In definition 1 this is the first feature of the Holocaust to be brought to the reader's attention, and the point is made explicitly. In contrast, this point is made at the end of definition 2 where the genocidal nature is described but not labelled as such. Of the two, we prefer Definition 1 as we consider Jews to be the major victims of the Holocaust and that the systematic and barbaric way in which they were treated is crucial to understanding and teaching the Holocaust. This does not diminish the persecution and murder of other groups of victims but serves to understand the tragedy of what has become known as the Holocaust.

One aspect of the Holocaust which is overlooked in Definition 1, and not as well documented as the Jewish genocide, is the genocide of the Roma and Sinti (sometimes referred to by others as Gypsies). Also referred to as *The Forgotten Genocide*, it has taken decades for this genocide, also known as Porajmos, to be recognised, with scholarly estimates of 220,000–500,000 Romani people murdered. The nature of this genocide, like all genocides, was distinctive but similar to that of the Jews: they were systematically persecuted when the National Socialists came to power in 1933; defined by the Nuremberg laws in 1935 as 'enemies of the race-based state', and murdered in the gas chambers alongside Jews in death camps such as Auschwitz. The other group who were systematically murdered were children and adults with mental and/or physical disabilities. This was the Nazis' first programme of mass murder which began in 1939, and though officially stopped in 1941 due to protests by the Catholic Church and victims' parents, continued in secret. It is estimated that 200,000 people were murdered through this programme of euthanasia which was known as 'T4'. For these reasons, the definition of the Holocaust that we adopt in this book is not identical to Definition 1, as our definition includes recognition of the genocide of the Roma and Sinti and the systematic murder of the disabled.

Another aspect is that the Holocaust was not an exclusively European tragedy. While not included in the above definitions, hundreds of thousands of Jews living under colonial rule in North Africa were also victims of the Nazis. At that time, 400,000 Jews lived in Morocco, Algeria and Tunisia under the Vichy regime, and 30,000 Jews lived in Fascist Italian-controlled Libya. Of these, Tunisia was the only country to be Nazi occupied. Because Morocco was a protectorate and not a colony of France whose citizens were not considered to be French citizens, the implementation of anti-Jewish laws was not as extreme there as it had been in Algeria. Algerian Jews were stripped of their rights, lost their jobs, expelled from schools, and required to wear a distinguishing mark: approximately 2,000 Algerian Jews were sent to labour and concentration camps in Algeria; 2,100 Moroccan Jews were sent to work camps in Morocco; and around 5,000 Tunisian Jews were sent to labour camps in Tunisia. In Libya, anti-Jewish laws had been enforced since 1938. Thousands of Libyan Jews were sent to concentration camps in Libya and camps in Europe, most to Bergen-Belsen. Hence thousands of North African Jews died from hunger, punishment, exhaustion and disease in labour and concentration camps that were not on European soil.

It is clear from evidence from previous research (Russell, 2006; HEDP, 2009) that many teachers' definitions are quite different from the ones we have presented, and there is a lack of consensus amongst teachers as to what they perceive to be the Holocaust. In a study carried out by the Holocaust Education Development Programme (renamed the Centre for Holocaust Education in 2012) into teaching the Holocaust in English secondary schools, teachers were presented with a list of seven statements about the Holocaust and asked to select one that best presented their understanding. More than 50% of the teacher respondents (n = 1,976), indicated that the definition which reflected their understanding was significantly different from both the definitions we have presented. The definition that they selected was as follows:

> The Holocaust was the persecution and murder of a range of victims perpetrated by the Nazi regime and its collaborators. They were targeted for different reasons and were persecuted in different ways. Victims included Jews, Gypsies, disabled people, Poles, Slavs, homosexuals, Jehovah's Witnesses, Soviet prisoners of war, Black people, and other political and ethnic groups. (HEDP, 2009: 65)

This suggests that there is a difference between teachers' popular perceptions of the Holocaust and its historical definitions. We carried out a similar online exercise with our Professional Graduate Primary and Secondary teachers (n = 200) and their views were remarkably similar to those in the HEDP findings. Although several students understood the specific targeting of the Jewish people in the Holocaust, they considered the inclusion and acknowledgement of every group who were persecuted by the Nazis and their collaborators as vitally important. What we consider as worrying is that many teachers do not regard Nazi policy towards the Jews as substantively different from that for the other groups of people. We consider the distinctive treatment of the Jews to be fundamental to understanding the Holocaust, and are concerned as to the impact that the above perception has on school-based Holocaust Education.

Before the success of Amazon and online shopping, if you wanted to buy a book on the Holocaust in a bookshop in my home town in Scotland, it was located under Jewish History or Jewish Studies and not European History or Second World War (Cowan, 1994). While today there are fewer bookshops on the high street, it is accepted that Holocaust literature is not exclusively about Jews or Jewish history. Yet if the common understanding of the Holocaust is that Jews suffered in the same manner as other groups of people such as homosexuals, communists or Jehovah's Witnesses, then fundamental truths of the Holocaust are being ignored.

Our students were able to read each other's comments and saw that some had changed their initial views after reading more about the Holocaust and discussions with their peers. The following comment highlights other factors that impact on teachers' understandings of the Holocaust:

> 'The thing that I cannot get away from is that I see the views of each post and can understand why they [each of the different definitions] are believed by other people – it truly depends on the society you live in, and your own links or experiences with the Holocaust.'

One example of this is the United Kingdom, where in 1945, when the concentration and death camps were liberated, there were few explicit references in broadcasts, newsreels or press articles towards the Jews. It is worth noting that the BBC refused to use leading broadcaster Richard Dimbleby's script in his report from Bergen-Belsen as it referred 'explicitly to the Jewishness of the victims' (Kushner, 2006: 193), yet two-thirds of the survivors at this camp were Jewish. In more recent times, the destruction of the Jews during the Holocaust has been deliberately ignored in Soviet historiography (Dumitru, 2008). One-quarter of the six million Jews murdered in the Holocaust were on Soviet territory, yet the Holocaust was not regarded as a special phenomenon, and it was not until perestroika in the 1980s 'that the Holocaust gained attention among historians and other scholars' (Dumitru, 2008: 52). This explains why the victims of the Holocaust in Latvia were usually referred to as 'Soviet civilians' prior to its independence in 1991, thereby carefully omitting the antisemitic nature of the Holocaust. Competing perspectives of Holocaust remembrance will be discussed later in this book. These examples also demonstrate how time is a factor that impacts on one's understanding and definition of the Holocaust.

The word Holocaust is sometimes used as a general term for all the atrocities perpetrated by the Nazis and their collaborators. We consider this to be a misuse of the term 'Holocaust', as its lack of recognition of the fundamental truths of the Holocaust is disrespectful to the victims, to the horrors of antisemitism, racism and genocide, and indeed to history. This misuse may be a naïve consequence of over-simplifying the Holocaust, with educators exclusively focusing on universal lessons of tolerance, diversity and humanity that have general appeal, and ignoring the unique lessons of Holocaust history. Another example of its misuse is the term 'Bombing Holocaust' (in German, *Bomben-Holocaust*) that refers to the Allied bombing of Dresden in the Second World War in 1945. This term obfuscates the meaning of the Holocaust as it suggests that the bombing of Dresden was part of the Holocaust and that German civilians were the principal victims of this.

Further misuses of the word include its highlighting and sensationalising singular issues, unrelated to the Second World War or Nazi ideology, which are regarded by some to be evil: for example, Holocaust on Your Plate, a (2003) campaign organised by People for the Ethical Treatment of Animals (PETA), which compared modern agricultural practices and eating meat to the Holocaust; and an anti-abortion group, Survivors of the Abortion Holocaust, whose name arouses people's attention. These misuses are offensive to the victims of the Holocaust and the families of those victims. They also trivialise the magnitude, horror and heroism of the Holocaust, and challenge the unprecedented nature of its character.

It is now two years since four Jewish people were shot dead and fifteen others held hostage in the Hyper Cacher kosher deli in Paris, and after the copycat murder where one Jewish man was shot outside a synagogue in Copenhagen. In the UK, 2015 began with a heightened realisation that antisemitism in Europe was not restricted to mainland Europe and was a subject of focus in the media. For the first time in our lifetime, in the UK, antisemitism dominated the headlines of television and radio news, was a topic for phone-in discussion programmes and the leader article in some newspapers, and featured in magazines. This interest was additionally sparked by the publication of two reports on antisemitism in the UK. The first was the *Annual Antisemitism Barometer* (Campaign Against Antisemitism [CAA], 2015) which reported the results of a survey on people's attitudes towards British Jews; the second was *The All-Party Parliamentary Inquiry into Antisemitism* (All-Party Parliamentary Group Against Antisemitism [APPGAA], 2015) which included a review of the state of antisemitism in the UK.

Both the above reports included references to the Holocaust in the reviews and analysis of their findings. In the first report, which contained data from more than 3,000 participants, one of the findings was that 13%

believed that 'Jews talk about the Holocaust too much in order to get sympathy' (CAA, 2015: 4). The second report provided an insight into the contribution of social media on antisemitism, one example being the Twitter hashtag 'Hitler was right'. Other examples of the link between current antisemitism and the Holocaust in 2015 were the daubing of Jewish cemeteries with swastikas and the decision by two cultural institutions in Iran, the House of Cartoon and the Sarcheshmeh Cultural Complex, to hold their second Holocaust International Cartoon Contest, a prizewinning competition that satirises the genocide of the Jews.

Defining Antisemitism

At this point it is important to clarify our meaning of the word antisemitism as the origins of this word can obscure its true, though not universally accepted, meaning. Its biblical origin comes from the the Book of Genesis where 'semites' were the descendants of Shem (the second of Noah's three sons) who was an ancestor of Salah; linguistically, the Semitic category of languages includes several languages such as Hebrew and Arabic. It follows then that 'Semites' are then not exclusively Jews, and 'antisemitism' can refer to hatred of or hostility towards all Semites, which includes Jews, Arabs and other peoples. We, the authors of this book, do not subscribe to this meaning as there is no such thing as 'Semitism', and the only group of people who have ever been included in the hatred and prejudice denoted by antisemitism are Jews. Cowan has previously recognised that the coining of the word antisemitism has been attributed to Wilhelm Marr (1819–1904) by naming his organisation 'The League of Anti-Semites' (Cowan in Cowan and Maitles, 2012). Marr used the word *antisemitism* to clearly distinguish between the historical religious hatred towards Jews, and a new racial hatred, in the late nineteenth century, that was emerging towards this same group of people. We have therefore adopted the meaning of antisemitism as a certain perception of Jews which can be expressed by a hatred of, hostility towards, or discrimination against, Jews. This definition is similar to definitions in the Oxford and Merriam-Webster dictionaries, and the working definition used by the European Union Monitoring Centre on Racism and Xenophobia (EUMC).

In addition, because inserting a hyphen in the spelling of antisemitism (i.e. anti-Semitism = opposing or being against Semitism) reinforces the notion of 'Semitism', which unlike racism in 'anti-racism' and sectarianism in 'anti-sectarianism' as stated above does not exist, 'antisemitism' is consistently unhyphenated in this book. It follows that those who do not recognise this definition of antisemitism will have difficulties in engaging with Holocaust Education, as Nazi antisemitism was directed exclusively at Jews.

Outline of this Book

Holocaust Education is not universal and the research and experiences that we refer to in this book are predominantly from English-speaking countries, Europe and Israel. We hope that it will be of interest and relevance to teachers and educators from the above countries where Holocaust Education is well established, as well as teachers and educators from countries in Europe, South East Asia, South America, Africa and India, where Holocaust Education is in its infancy. It aims to inform readers of the development of Holocaust Education in the contexts of today's world and broaden readers' understanding of the Holocaust as a controversial issue. It focuses on a number of issues in Holocaust Education that are being discussed in today's primary and secondary schools. These issues include curricular considerations relating to the contribution of Holocaust Education, principally within History, Citizenship Education, and Religious and Moral Education, and pedagogical approaches such as the use of survivor testimony, role play, fiction, visits to memorial sites and interdisciplinary learning.

We have inserted learning objectives at the beginning of each chapter to provide readers with clear expectations as to their content and structure, and suggested Further Reading for readers' interest. Chapters 1–5 focus on theoretical issues; Chapters 6–11 focus on pedagogical and practical issues. We hope that this book will prove useful to teachers and educators who have experience of teaching the Holocaust, to those who have recently entered the teaching profession, to student teachers who plan to teach the Holocaust, to other educators in the wider community who include the Holocaust in their educational programmes, and to international educators and academics who plan teaching programmes or conduct research in this area.

This introductory chapter has provided a background context for these forthcoming issues, as clarity on the meanings of 'Holocaust' and 'antisemitism' is essential in understanding and teaching Holocaust Education. It follows that clarity as to the meaning of Holocaust Education is similarly important, and Chapter 2 discusses the difficulties in defining this and attempts to provide readers with a suitable definition. This identifies the lessons of learning *about* the Holocaust and learning *from* the Holocaust. Chapter 3 focuses on the connection between Citizenship and Holocaust Education by examining ways in which Holocaust teaching can contribute to citizenship values. This considers the lessons from sociology and psychology about the circumstances in which perpetrators, bystanders and rescuers were found.

Although this introductory chapter defines antisemitism, this is developed further in Chapter 4 where the authors consider the contribution of teaching about antisemitism in school-based Holocaust Education. As a means of supporting teachers in their understanding of Nazi antisemitism, the chapter provides a summary of the history of antisemitism. It also identifies various forms of antisemitism and includes expressions of antisemitism that have recently emerged.

Chapter 5 focuses on the collective memory of the Holocaust. While this has expanded in many ways in recent years, it cannot be taken for granted. This chapter identifies competing perspectives on Holocaust remembrance in Europe, and the alternative forms of Holocaust remembrance. It also discusses the challenges of Holocaust commemoration in primary and secondary schools.

Chapters 6–8 focus on broad teaching approaches. Chapter 6 identifies and explains key words in Holocaust Education and discusses the importance of political and emotional literacy; Chapter 7 examines teaching pedagogies that assist in effective Holocaust teaching and recognises ways in which teachers can address the diverse needs of their students; Chapter 8 justifies teaching the Holocaust to students in the upper stages of primary school and provides teachers with support and themes that are suitable for these students.

Chapter 9 focuses on classroom teaching approaches. It explores issues that accompany the use of literature, role play and simulations, and online survivor testimony in Holocaust Education. Chapter 10 focuses on school visits to the Auschwitz-Birkenau Memorial and Museum. It discusses the rationale for such visits, and analyses the educational experience provided at the museum.

Chapter 11 summarises the development of Holocaust Education and discusses the legacy of the Holocaust. This concluding chapter also explores the challenges for Holocaust educators, and provides a glimpse into the future by presenting student teachers' responses as regards addressing intolerance in schools and learning about the Holocaust.

The word Holocaust has dark connotations, and this alone explains why teachers who are not required to teach it will never engage in Holocaust Education. Unfortunately this book cannot remove this darkness. We consider historical content to be at the core of effective Holocaust Education, and hence teachers and educators are required to be true to historical events and the process of the Holocaust. This book provides constructive and practical advice for those who are willing to rise to the challenge, and informs readers of the developments in Holocaust Education in today's ever-changing world.

Further Reading

Dawidowicz, L.S. (1990) *The War Against the Jews 1933–45*. London: Penguin.

Gilbert, M.G. (1989) *The Holocaust: The Jewish Tragedy*. London: HarperCollins.

Marrus, M.A. (2000) *The Holocaust in History*. Toronto: Key Porter.

Supple, C. (2005) *From Prejudice to Genocide: Learning About the Holocaust*. Stoke-on-Trent: Trentham.

2

THE NATURE OF HOLOCAUST EDUCATION

Learning Objectives

- To justify school-based Holocaust Education
- To clarify the meaning of genocide
- To demonstrate the difficulties in defining Holocaust Education that arise from countries' contrasting experiences
- To provide authors' definitions of Holocaust Education
- To define controversial issues and explain the controversial nature of the Holocaust

---

Rationale

There are many reasons why the Holocaust should be a core feature in a school programme. Firstly, it demonstrates how unprecedented crimes, unspeakable acts of cruelty towards Jews, Roma and Sinti, the disabled and many other ethnic and minority groups, were committed as 'normal' routine. Hannah Arendt referred to this behaviour, executed by ordinary, civilised and educated individuals and not deranged fanatics or monsters, individuals who did not think about or reflect on their actions, as the 'banality of evil' (Arendt, 1963). This phrase was coined in response to the answers that Adolf Eichmann, the Chief of the Jewish Office of the Gestapo, who was responsible for transporting Jews from all over Europe to killing sites in occupied Poland and occupied Soviet Union to implement the Final Solution, gave in court at his trial in 1961. According to Arendt, a crime against humanity was 'banal' if the crime had become accepted, routine and implemented without questioning or resistance by the perpetrators. This perspective is relevant in today's society where new unspeakable crimes occur, such as the abduction and kidnapping of more than 200 schoolgirls in Nigeria in 2014, and sexual violence in conflict towards children in the Democratic Republic of Congo.

Secondly, the Holocaust demonstrates how a civilised, cultured, technologically advanced country used its scientific and industrial innovations for the mass extermination of people. Bauman (1989) argues that the decisive factor that made the mass murders possible was not Nazi racial policy per se, but modernity itself. This explains how 10,000 Jews on average were murdered daily at Auschwitz–Birkenau between May and September 1944 and the 'success' of this, and other atrocities, can be attributed to the efforts of scientists, medical professionals, architects, engineers, industrialists and businessmen. This also justifies why the Holocaust cannot be exclusively interpreted as a specifically *Jewish* affair and recognised primarily as a part of Jewish history, but acknowledged as a concern for human civilisation with its existing and emerging new technologies.

The consequences of the normality of evil and the dangers of modernity are effectively demonstrated in the following letter to educators written by an unknown Holocaust survivor. Raising serious questions about the value of education, the survivor's request emphasises the importance of promoting social justice and moral behaviour in achieving humane and responsible citizens:

> *'I am a survivor of a concentration camp. My eyes saw what no person should witness: gas chambers built by learned engineers. Children poisoned by educated physicians. Infants killed by trained nurses. Women and babies shot by high school and college graduates. So, I am suspicious of education.*
>
> *My request is:*
>
> *Help your children become human. Your efforts must never produce learned monsters, skilled psychopaths or educated Eichmanns. Reading, writing, and arithmetic are important only if they serve to make our children more humane'.* (Ginott, 1972; and available online at The Center for Holocaust Humanity Education website)

Thirdly, the Holocaust is the paradigmatic genocide. As identified in the previous chapter, it led to United Nations' legislation and the concept 'genocide' which was coined by Raphael Lemkin (1900–1959). Article II of the *Convention on the Prevention and Punishment of the Crime of Genocide* (1948) defines genocide as:

> Any of the following acts committed with intent to destroy, in whole or in part, a national, ethnical, racial or religious group, as such:
>
> (a) Killing members of the group;
> (b) Causing serious bodily or mental harm to members of the group;
> (c) Deliberately inflicting on the group conditions of life calculated to bring about its physical destruction in whole or in part;
> (d) Imposing measures intended to prevent births within the group;
> (e) Forcibly transferring children of the group to another group.

Criticisms of this definition include that it protects national, religious, racial and ethnic groups against destruction but lacks inclusivity by not considering other groups such as political groups and social classes as target groups. The phrase, *'intent to destroy ... as such'* is ambiguous, and in practice, as the form of intent is difficult to prove and because the legal definition of genocide does not define genocide exclusively as the total annihilation of a group, intent to destroy part of a group is also a genocidal crime. Helen Fein (2009: 54) attempts to address this in her definition:

> Genocide is sustained purposeful action by a perpetrator to physically destroy a collectivity directly or indirectly, through interdiction of the biological and social reproduction of group members, sustained regardless of the surrender or lack of threat offered by the victim.

Stanton's ten stages of genocide (2013) are helpful in understanding and identifying genocide. With reference to the Holocaust and more recent genocides, these stages can be explained as follows:

1 Classification (distinguishing between *us* and *them*, e.g. Aryans and Jews, Hutus and Tutsis in Rwanda, with clear identification of the 'others')
2 Symbolisation (when names and/or symbols are used to support the classification, e.g. the yellow star)
3 Discrimination (denying the rights of the 'others', e.g. the 1935 Nuremberg Laws)
4 Dehumanisation (comparing the 'others' to animals, not part of humanity, e.g. Jews were 'vermin', Tutsis were 'cockroaches')
5 Organisation (organised usually by the state or trained military to support denial, e.g. the Janjaweed in Darfur)
6 Polarisation (broadcasting of propaganda, e.g. the Nazis used pamphlets, newspapers and posters to spread their antisemitic ideology, the National Revolutionary Movement for Development (MNRD) used the radio and other media to spread Hutu ideology)
7 Preparation (planning the murders of the 'others', by for example training people to be perpetrators, amassing weapons, etc.)
8 Persecution (stripping the 'others' of their property and belongings, segregating; e.g. ghettos)
9 Deporting (e.g. camps) or confining them to a famine region
10 Extermination (mass killings) and denial

This last stage, *denial*, leads us to the fourth reason why the Holocaust should be taught in schools. The word was first named by Lemkin in 1933, in a paper he presented to the League of Nations that described the methodical massacres and atrocities perpetrated against Armenians living in the Ottoman Empire, by the Ottoman Turkish government between 1915 and 1923. It is estimated that more than one million Armenians were murdered in these attacks, which is recognised by scholars, governments and the general public to be the first major genocide of the twentieth century. Yet to this day this remains a contested genocide as the Republic of Turkey has consistently rejected that this constituted genocide. It claims that there was no intent to destroy Ottoman Armenians and that these deaths occurred within the context of First World War brutality and/or the civil unrest between Armenians and Turks. Had the atrocities against the Armenians been recognised as genocide at that time, it would not have been unlawful, as the United Nations did not recognise genocide as a crime under international law until some thirty years later. However, it is the denial of the Armenian genocide that has been credited with inspiring Hitler to carry out the atrocities and genocides that led to the Holocaust. In a statement to his commanding generals, one week before the invasion of Poland in 1939, he is alleged to have said, 'Who, after all, speaks today of the annihilation of the Armenians?' At that time the fate of the Ottoman Armenians may well have been fading into oblivion. In 1941 'genocide' was still, as Winston Churchill broadcast, 'a crime without a name'.

Genocide deniers are not an homogeneous group of people. They include perpetrators, perpetrator governments, non-perpetrators who are attracted to fascism, bigotry and racism, and well-intentioned non-perpetrators who are upright citizens and not bigots. Most deniers will have something to gain from their denial and all will seek scholarly recognition and acceptance. In the context of the Holocaust, without knowledge, young people's understanding of this event will be overly reliant on the media and the internet, which are sources for both Holocaust Education and Holocaust denial. This can be confusing for new learners and result in more misconceptions about the Holocaust than genuine understanding. Educators may consider such a denial or distortion of established facts of one of the most documented events in history as outrageous, and quickly dismiss such claims. We consider that the best strategy for addressing Holocaust denial is providing effective, age-appropriate, school-based Holocaust Education. Individuals of all ages can only dismiss Holocaust deniers when they have the knowledge and understanding of facts that are supported with established evidence; without this, individuals are more likely to allow deniers centre stage. The question that Hitler raised about the Armenians in 1939 still has resonance today, especially when society is driven by the third generation of the Holocaust and few people who were directly involved in it are still alive. Holocaust Education can impact on young people 'speaking' today of the Armenians, Jews, Roma, Bosniaks, Tutsis and all victims of genocide. (Holocaust denial is discussed in more detail in Chapter 4.)

Our research findings provide further reasons for school-based Holocaust Education. Our 2004 longitudinal study into the impact of Holocaust Education on students' citizenship (or civic) values and attitudes, through exploring the student perspective, compared primary students' values and attitudes before and immediately after they had studied the Holocaust (Phase 1). We compared this core group's values and attitudes ten months later, when they were in the first year of secondary school, with their earlier data and with their secondary peers who had not studied the Holocaust (Phase 2). The findings from Phase 1 demonstrated several positive gains in students' attitudes, in particular in their attitudes towards Gypsy/Travellers[1] and refugees (Cowan and Maitles, 2005). Findings from Phase 2 demonstrated that the core group maintained positive gains in relation to minorities, and in particular to Gypsy/Travellers, that the core group tended to have stronger positive values and attitudes than those who did not, and were more tolerant and more disposed to active citizenship by their understanding of individual responsibility towards racism than their peers, who had not had the opportunity to study the Holocaust at school (Cowan and Maitles, 2007). These findings provide evidence that learning about the Holocaust at school can be a contributing factor in developing students' positive values and attitudes about minority groups and towards responsible citizenship. This strengthens the case for teaching the Holocaust in primary and secondary (high) schools, by demonstrating that its learning has both an immediate and longer-term impact on students' attitudes.

Findings from our research into the views of students who participated in the first Lessons from Auschwitz Project (LFAP) in Scotland in 2007 further justified school-based Holocaust Education (Cowan and Maitles, 2011). Although this project involved learning opportunities outside school, in particular a day visit to the Auschwitz-Birkenau Memorial and Museum (ABMM), it is still defined as school-based as it is a programme for schools that encourages students to share their learning with their school peers. Findings showed that students perceived that their visit to the ABMM contributed to their Citizenship Education as well as to their understanding of the Second World War, with higher student gains in understanding human rights and genocide than in the Second World War. Further, when student participants returned to their schools, their active citizenship involved their leading informal and formal activities with their peers in a range of subject classes, comprising discussions of the Holocaust, discrimination, antisemitism, racism, and other genocides. In some cases students spoke outside their schools, to church groups, college students, and primary school teachers, in their community. The following student comments show how they considered this experience had contributed to their personal values.

---

1 Gypsy/Travellers is the term used to describe Scotland's travelling communities.

Student 1

'It has made me more aware of other things that are going on in the world. It has changed my attitude towards genocide. I am a lot more aware of it now than I was before. I think that it helped me a lot to understand how it must have felt to have been Jewish at the time and what it would have been like not to be Jewish, and either be at risk of supporting Jewish people or just going along with the crowd. I think going into the camp helped me understand the mass scale it was on.'

Student 2

'It definitely made me think that things like separation on racial grounds are not acceptable and things like sectarianism … You hear a lot of jokes about it and that is fair enough but afterwards I definitely had more of a view that these things can escalate to extreme levels. It definitely made me less accepting towards things of this nature.'

Student 3

'I am slightly more likely to be more assertive if someone makes an offensive comment. When people say things like that I do say to them, "Hang on …".'

(Cowan and Maitles, 2011: 14–15)

We concluded that the LFAP contributed significantly to developing personal responsible citizenship. In particular, there was evidence of personal growth in terms of students' understanding of European history, and in developing citizenship values related to prejudice and discrimination and respect for others. Findings of the larger-scale evaluation of the LFAP in England supported this by reporting a development in students' general attitudes, priorities and values, with an appreciation of individual responsibility and the need to challenge prejudice (Institute of Education, 2010: 9). This further justifies young people learning about the Holocaust at school.

Emergence and Development of Holocaust Education

Although it has been more than seventy years since the end of the Second World War, school-based Holocaust Education is a relatively new initiative. The first influential Holocaust school educational resource was *The Diary of Anne Frank* which was published in Dutch in 1947. This was translated into English in 1952, adapted into a Pulitzer Prize-winning play in 1956, and made into a film in 1959. Yet the immediate years following the Second World War are often referred to as the 'silent years' for their absence of interest and scholarship in the Holocaust. Other notable exceptions to this were the establishment of the Auschwitz-Birkenau Memorial and Museum (1947) and Yad Vashem, the Holocaust memorial and museum in Jerusalem (1953).

The next wave of commemorative Holocaust awareness came as a consequence of the above-mentioned televised trial in Jerusalem of Adolf Eichmann. After this trial large numbers of Holocaust survivors began to talk openly about their experiences, and this resulted in a growth in Holocaust scholarship by survivors, historians, survivor–historians, museum curators: the establishment of new, independent, state-funded, and non-governmental organisations whose aims demonstrated a strong commitment to Holocaust Education.

In 1993 the Oscar winning film *Schindler's List*, directed by Stephen Spielberg and based on the book *Schindler's Ark* by author and Booker prizewinner Thomas Keneally (1982), generated new global interest in Holocaust Education. The impact of this film contributed to the rationale of the Stockholm International Forum (see p. 1), and indeed inspired the authors of this book in their commitment to school-based Holocaust teaching and Holocaust Educational research. We agree with Landau's views that after being reduced to a footnote to the Second World War, the Holocaust currently has 'its own distinctive history' and above all is a recognisable 'historical event' (Landau,1998: 1–2). At the time of writing this book, Holocaust educators and researchers are engaged in a race against time in collating and digitally recording first-hand Holocaust survivor testimony for school and university students, as well for the wider community, and simultaneously ensuring developments in our digital and technological world are effectively used to develop young people's knowledge and understanding of the Holocaust.

Defining Holocaust Education

As indicated in our research on the LFAP, school-based Holocaust Education can extend beyond the classroom to memorial sites, as well as to museums, documentation centres and synagogues. Such outdoor learning opportunities can provide learners with memorable learning experiences which place learning that is taught in the classroom into meaningful contexts. Outdoor learning can bring classroom teaching alive, by allowing students to see and sometimes handle real and high quality replica artefacts. Furthermore, students who struggle with classroom learning are often able to access ideas and emotions in non-verbal ways in museums.

If Holocaust Education is first and foremost concerned with teaching *about* the Holocaust, then its content will largely be determined by one's definition of the Holocaust. It follows from our definition that Holocaust Education should focus on the years between 1933 and 1945, and clarify the distinction between the Nazi treatment and targeting of Jews, Roma and Sinti, and the disabled from each other, as well as from the other groups of people who were persecuted and/or murdered. While Hilberg's six stages (see p. 3) are a useful reference for teachers, they are confusing for teachers as they are not consistently chronological. Also, ending the process with death camps/killing centres is bleak and inaccurate, as the Holocaust did not end at this stage for those who survived it.

We advocate a more suitable approach for young learners which consists of the following stages:

- alienation
- segregation
- deportation
- extermination (or annihilation)
- liberation

This approach is consistently chronological, ends on a more positive note, encourages teachers and educators to address young learners' misconceptions that *all* the Jews were murdered in the Holocaust, and raises questions about the needs of refugees and world relief.

We consider historical content to be at the core of Holocaust Education. We acknowledge that other disciplines can form and contribute to excellent Holocaust Educational programmes, and discuss the benefits of this and interdisciplinary teaching later in this book (see Chapters 3 and 8), but these benefits can only be achieved by placing the Holocaust securely in its historical context. We think that all school learning programmes on the Second World War should include, at the very least, *some* meaningful reference to the Holocaust. Lindquist writes that the first goal of Holocaust Education is that pupils understand 'that the Nazis' attempt to annihilate European Jewry was an official state policy' (2011: 27). This emphasises the importance of students developing an understanding of Nazi racist, antisemitic ideology which cannot be done without placing history at the forefront of any Holocaust teaching.

Bage (2000) considers that history can play a central role in developing young people's understanding of society's values. We accept that a study of the Holocaust in history can stimulate discussion of religious, political, moral and ethical issues, but remain committed to its roots belonging in the discipline of history. We consider this to be relevant to all Holocaust Education providers and discuss this further in Chapter 3. As well as schools this includes national education providers, museums, NGOs, memorial sites, libraries, community youth groups, colleges and universities. This is particularly relevant to history teachers who prefer to emphasise the moral lessons rather than the history of the Holocaust in their teaching (Russell, 2006: 3), and to schools where teachers of citizenship are responsible for teaching the Holocaust. Secondary schools that provide Holocaust Education annually at each stage, such as *Hauptschules* in Bavaria (schools ending at ninth grade; see Ortloff, 2015), or teach the Holocaust at selected stages, such as in France, are justified in adopting thematic approaches which are based on other disciplines or curriculum areas, but only *after* their students have been taught the history of the Holocaust. Historical knowledge and understanding are also integral to Holocaust remembrance (see Chapter 5).

One may assume that teachers and educators who share our definition of the Holocaust or indeed one that is similar to Definition 1 (see p. 6) will agree with Lindquist's statement as to what teachers' basic learning intentions should be. Findings from a comparative analysis of IHRA member countries, demonstrated an alternative definition that impacted on Holocaust Education (Balodimas-Bartolomei, 2012). These findings were that eight countries (Argentina, Denmark, Germany, Greece, Israel, Lithuania, the Netherlands and Norway) excluded the other victim groups and referred only to the extermination of the Jews in their definition, and that seven countries included other groups (Austria, Croatia, France, Sweden, Switzerland, the UK and USA). This inevitably impacts on school-based Holocaust Education, and explains the significant variations in what comprises Holocaust Education across the globe.

UNESCO's study into the status of the Holocaust in the secondary curriculum in 135 countries identified three different types of curricula that contained Holocaust Education. These were 'direct reference', which used the term 'Holocaust' or 'Shoah', or alternative terminologies such as 'genocide against the Jews' or 'Nazi persecution of minorities'; 'partial reference', where Holocaust Education achieved a learning aim that was not primarily focused on the Holocaust but illustrated another topic such as aspects of Human Rights Education; and 'context only', where curricula referred to the Second World War or National Socialism without referring explicitly to the Holocaust as a term or an event (UNESCO, 2015: 12). This provides further explanation of the significant variations in what comprises Holocaust Education across the globe.

Variations can be further justified by Gundare and Batelaan's (2003) claim that Holocaust Education is influenced by each country's involvement in the Second World War. For example, countries which Snyder (2011) refers to as the 'bloodlands', and whose indigenous population suffered under Nazi and Soviet occupation (such as Belarus, Estonia, Latvia, Lithuania, Poland and Ukraine) have particular challenges in teaching the Holocaust as a singular event as their Second World War context is complex. Findings from a national survey in Poland, the country where the death camps were located, showed that 'young Poles have a sense that Polish suffering during the Second World War might not be acknowledged enough if Jewish suffering is highlighted' (Ambrosewicz-Jacobs and Szuchta, 2014: 283). In an earlier study in Poland in 2008, students' responses to the question *Who were the largest group(s) of victims at Auschwitz?* were that 38% indicated the Jews, 43% indicated 'it isn't important which group – they were simply people who died', and 10% indicated the Poles (Ambrosewicz-Jacobs, 2011). Further, findings from a study of 60 Polish teachers in 2010 showed that more than half the participants stated that they wanted to 'illuminate, misremember, unknown or falsified facts' in their teaching of the Holocaust (Gross, 2013: 115). This demonstrates how established cultural and historical narratives of the Holocaust, in a country with a troubled history, can have a limited and potentially negative impact on Holocaust Education, and that good quality Holocaust Education may involve teachers and educators 'unlearning' their previous learning.

Gundare and Batelaan's claim also explains the variation in Holocaust Education amongst countries with less complex histories than that of Poland. For example, in Sweden the successful efforts of the diplomat Raoul Wallenberg in saving thousands of Jews in Hungary from deportation to the camps will feature in Holocaust Education, as will the story of the *Kindertransport programme* ('children's transport'; see p. 104) in the UK, the rescue of the Danish Jews in Denmark, and the experiences of people in hiding, such as Anne Frank and her family, in the Netherlands. While these stories are relevant and significant, teachers and educators should ensure that Holocaust Education does not focus exclusively on these, as doing so will prove too narrow. Achievement of the first goal of Holocaust Education, as referred to earlier in this chapter by Lindquist, should be teachers' first priority.

In addition, Holocaust Education is influenced by each country's experience of genocide and racism. For example, teaching the Holocaust to young Bosnian Muslims (Bosniaks) and Croatian civilians, whose parents, families and friends suffered or were murdered by Bosnian Serb forces in the ethnic cleansing and subsequent Bosnian genocide (1992–95), can assist in their understanding of reconciliation and tolerance. This is supported by Miles' assertion (2004) that Holocaust Education in Third World countries is related to their history of decolonisation, and Xin's (2009) assertion that the Holocaust allows the Chinese to re-examine the Nanjing massacre or the Rape of Nanking, which was perpetrated by Japanese forces in the period 1937–38. It follows that Holocaust Education is not taught in isolation in Africa where it relates to slavery, in South Africa where it would relate to this country's history of apartheid, or in Northern Ireland where it would relate to this country's history of sectarianism.

This explains and justifies why Holocaust Education involves wider learning *from* the Holocaust. The premise for this is that these lessons provide opportunities to study issues such as genocide, social intolerance, anti-racism, antisemitism, human indifference, and human rights. The above issues are aspects that are relevant in Citizenship education (see Chapter 3) and the findings of many researchers (e.g. Brown and Davies, 1998; Rathenow and Weber, 1998; Claire, 2005; Cajani, 2007; Jordan et al., 2012) acknowledge the benefits of combining history and citizenship lessons. One common assumption is that this form of interdisciplinary learning (see Chapters 3 and 7) makes history lessons more relevant for school students; less commonly assumed are the benefits this has in teaching citizenship. Skills that are essential to historical inquiry, such as document analysis and comparison of controversial interpretations, are beneficial in developing and exercising citizenship (Cajani, 2007).

Controversial Issues

A controversial issue can be defined as an issue that elicits conflicting views from individuals or groups 'for which society has not found a solution that can be universally accepted', that 'arouses protest', and in short, 'divides teachers, pupils and parents' (Fraser, in Stenhouse, 1971: 161). In the UK, the TEACH report (*Teaching Emotive and Controversial History 3–19*) stated that:

> The study of history can be emotive and controversial where there is actual or perceived unfairness to people by another individual or group in the past. This may also be the case where there are disparities between what is taught in school history, family/community histories and other histories. Such issues and disparities create a strong resonance with students in particular educational settings. (The Historical Association, 2007: 3)

At one level, one may consider that the Holocaust is not controversial as there is a universal consensus that it was a terrible tragedy that incurred the most hideous hate crimes. Yet we have already identified several ways in which the Holocaust meets the above criteria: its varying definitions; the alternative meaning attributed to antisemitism that many Arab Muslims view the Holocaust in terms of the suffering and dispossession of the Palestinians in 1948; and Holocaust denial, the attempt to negate the Holocaust by Holocaust deniers. These contrasting interpretations and views justify its categorisation as a controversial issue. The above TEACH report recognised the Holocaust as an emotive and controversial issue, because it has continued to have contemporary significance or personal resonance for students (2007a: 11).

In his writing on controversial issues John Stenhouse (1971) emphasised the importance of a value judgement in teaching controversial issues, and arguably teachers who teach in schools where the Holocaust is not mandatory and choose to teach it, exercise a value judgement in their consideration of the Holocaust as an issue of school importance. Stenhouse promoted the teaching of controversial issues in schools and provided guidelines to assist teachers in their teaching (see Chapter 7). The benefits of teaching controversial issues include developing students' independent critical thinking with a growing awareness of multiple perspectives and bringing real-life contexts into the classroom. On the one hand, identifying the Holocaust as a controversial issue is beneficial for Holocaust Education, as it provides a further opportunity to bring the Holocaust into the classroom, and can contribute to teachers developing their skills in teaching students about the Holocaust. In our ever-changing world, controversial issues remains an area of constant growth: few primary and secondary teachers who teach History and/or Citizenship Education can avoid this area, especially when discussing issues such as human rights and racial prejudice. On the other hand, not all teachers will approach controversial issues with enthusiasm and confidence as facilitating classroom discussions, and managing lively discussions on conflicting issues, can be particularly challenging. Findings from the above TEACH report indicated that it was not uncommon for teachers to be uncertain about the best strategies to apply when addressing emotive and controversial historical topics. The following quote from research in Scotland into student primary teachers' perceptions of teaching human rights and Human Rights Education (HRE), in schools where they were placed during their initial teacher education programme, demonstrates the caution of one teacher as regards addressing a controversial issue, and highlights the natural contribution of Holocaust Education to HRE:

> One student had planned an integrated topic to introduce human rights issues to a primary five class (aged 9 years), but her supervising teacher consulted a colleague and decided that it was 'a bit controversial', and despite the student having assured the class teacher that she knew what she was doing, the discussion between the two colleagues led to the student undertaking a 'non-controversial' topic. The student stated that she 'may have shied away from it [HRE] until I realised – after the Holocaust Memorial Day – just how easily the children were able to talk about it. (Cassidy et al., 2014: 27)

Parents too require to be considered. Primary teacher participants in our continued professional learning (inservice) courses, who have taught, or are keen to teach the Holocaust, share a consensus that the priority is to avoid parental concern or upset. One exception to this was the following parental complaint in a school where the Holocaust was being taught in one primary 7 class (pupils of 11 years) as part of their topic on the Second World War, but not in the other. Pupils in the class where it was taught had a rich learning experience, in that they were given opportunities to access special resources at the university and listen to a Holocaust survivor speaker. This parental complaint was made by a parent whose child was in the class that were *not* studying the Holocaust: the parent considered that their child should have this opportunity and was, in effect, missing out on a meaningful learning experience. This demonstrates the two sides of parental concern and upset in Holocaust Education, but we consider this an exception. It is far more likely that due to alternative perceptions of Jews and the Holocaust that schools will teach the Holocaust cautiously. One of these perceptions is that Holocaust Education encourages young people to be sympathetic to Jews and to Israel, and that Holocaust Education is promoted by Jews for this specific purpose. This may be underpinned by ignorance, prejudice or political and/or racist ideology. Nonetheless, it emphasises the controversial nature of school-based Holocaust Education.

Conclusion

In this chapter we have provided sociological and educational reasons for justifying school-based Holocaust Education. We have restated that Holocaust Education's first place is in a History curriculum, but if history is its heart then the contemporary citizenship lessons that young people can learn from its study make up its very soul. We have explained the reasons for variations in the content of Holocaust Education across countries and continents. Further, if one considers the number of Holocaust memorial sites, it is clear that students in Germany and Poland have easier access to a choice of sites than students from northern Europe.

One additional key factor is the curriculum. In England, the Holocaust is mandatory in the secondary school History curriculum for 13–14 year olds (although this does not apply to Academy schools). In France the Holocaust is mandatory in primary and secondary schools, and like Germany is taught at more than one stage in secondary. It follows that school-based Holocaust Education will be quite different in these countries than in those countries where pupils only study the Holocaust for a couple of hours during their entire school life. Teachers in countries where the Holocaust is taught at school more than once require to ensure that their teaching of the Holocaust is progressive and balanced and that their students maintain an interest in learning; teachers in England require to prioritise and select what they consider to be the most important points that students should learn about the Holocaust in the limited time they have available. Findings from our own research were from Scotland where the Holocaust is not mandatory in primary or secondary schools. While school-based Holocaust Education may not be widely taught across Scotland, it is taught by teachers who, in the main, choose to teach it and not by those who 'have' to teach it, or at worst, are coerced into its teaching. It is worth reflecting whether the excellent quantity of school-based Holocaust Education achieved by its mandatory status in the national curriculum is matched in quality.

Further Reading

Save the Children (2013) *Unspeakable Crimes Against Children*. London: Save the Children Fund.

The Transcript of the Trial of Adolf Eichmann, online The Nizkor Project, www.nizkor.org/hweb/people/e/eichmann-adolf/transcripts/Sessions/ (last accessed 13 October 2016).

3

CITIZENSHIP AND HOLOCAUST EDUCATION

Learning Objectives

- To clarify the relationship between Citizenship Education and Holocaust Education
- To provide authors' definition of Citizenship Education
- To justify the approach of learning *about* and *from* the Holocaust
- To show through a case study how Citizenship Education and Holocaust Education can impact on students' attitudes

---

What is Citizenship?

Almost all democracies now accept citizenship as a legitimate goal of education. That is not to suggest that there is much agreement about what it means, other than that it is a 'good thing'. The debate tends to be around maximal and minimal interpretations of citizenship. Evans (1995: 4–5) summarised these as:

> Minimal interpretations emphasise civil and legal status, rights and responsibilities ... The good citizen is law-abiding, public-spirited, exercises political involvement through voting for representatives ... Maximal interpretations, by contrast, entail consciousness of self as a member of a shared democratic culture, emphasise participatory approaches to political involvement and consider ways in which social disadvantage undermine citizenship by denying people full participation in society in any significant sense.

Faulks (1998, 2000) identifies three main types of definition of citizenship: firstly, legal definitions of citizenship stress nationality, rights of residence and duties; secondly, philosophical definitions are determined as being the relationship between the role of the state in providing for needs and the duties of the individual to the state. It has been argued (Gardner, 1994;

Turner, 1993; Faulks, 1998, 2000; Maitles, 2009) that this definition misses out a central issue of the modern world, that of inequalities in society. The third interpretation, socio-political, is defined by Turner as 'that set of practices (juridical, political, economic and cultural) which define a person as a competent member of society, and which as a consequence shape the flow of resources to persons and social groups' (1993: 2).

All definitions tend to stress the nature of the relationship between the individual and the state. Yet it would be fair to say that although discussed by policy makers, these debates rarely impinge on the way the discussions are framed in educational establishments.

This trend towards a larger role for education for citizenship has been global, shown, for example, by calls from the European Ministers of Education every year at their standing conference that there is a need for a more coherent and sustained approach by schools to education for democratic citizenship. Further, in central and Eastern Europe, the ending of communist one-party rule in the early 1990s has put the issue of education for democracy to the fore. Outside Europe mass movements, such as the movement for democracy in China and their demonstrations in Tiananmen Square, and in the early 1990s the overthrow of the racist apartheid regime in South Africa, gave rise to inspiring moments. The 38 countries across the world involved in the International Civic and Citizenship Education (ICCS) study (Schultz et al., 2011) all had developed programmes in place, albeit a wide range of understandings were found. From New Zealand where activity is stressed as the key message (Wood, 2012), to south Asia where the concept of nation dominates (Ghosh, 2012), to the Citizenship and Tolerance agenda in Santa Barbara in the USA (Jennings, 2015), the diversity is striking. However defined, most countries have citizenship as a compulsory element in their curricula (Crick, 2000; Osler and Starkey, 2005; Print, 2007; Kiwan, 2008; Schultz et al., 2011).

Across the world, it is fair to say that education for citizenship is seen as having three distinct strands – although the emphasis on each varies: political literacy, community involvement and the development of positive values. Problems, however, begin to develop as soon as the strands of education for citizenship are defined: there are almost as many definitions as there are people discussing them! Nonetheless, the political literacy strand has perhaps two main themes: knowledge as an understanding of the society in which we live, and skills relating to the ability to critically evaluate information, weigh up evidence, and draw conclusions. Community involvement, however 'community' is defined, can be wide ranging and both social and political. Occasionally the mixture of political literacy and community involvement can have interesting consequences as young people involve themselves in protests. We should not see these as problems but as natural developments in understanding society. As Crick and Porter (1978: 2) put it: '... *if we want citizens we have to tolerate some of the unpredictable inconveniences of action and participation*': indeed, perhaps the word 'tolerate' should be changed to 'encourage'. Again, there is little agreement, other than in very general terms, about the types of attitudes we would want an education system to foster. Even in something as relatively uncontroversial as 'positive' political attitudes (never mind moral values), research suggests that the most difficult thing is a definition of positive political values (Maitles, 1998, 2000, 2010b; Cowan and Maitles, 2006, 2007).

It must be noted that there is no universal agreement as to the value of political literacy and activism in schools per se. There are worries across most democracies about a sense of apathy amongst young people, although recent experiences in Greece, Spain and Scotland suggest that this is not a universal truth. For example, in the September 2014 Scottish referendum on independence, the average turnout was more than 85% (in some places over 90%) and involvement by young people (aged 16–24) in the campaigns was very high. Yet even where it is shown to be correct, there is also evidence that although young people are alienated from formal politics, they are active and interested in single issue, environmental, political and animal welfare issues. For many, activism is a necessary prerequisite of democracy (Advisory Group, 1998; Hannam, 1998; Kerr, 2003; Ross and Roland-Levy, 2003) and yet it can lead to support for fringe organisations outside the democratic process.

It is our contention that the nature and logic of democracy needs a citizenship educated population, with an understanding of how democratic institutions work and their importance, and knowledge of how to participate. There is evidence, certainly from across Europe over the last twenty years (Angvik and von Borries, 1997; Hahn, 1999; Maitles, 2000, 2009; Torney-Purta et al., 2001; Schultz et al., 2011), that there is much ignorance over basic political issues amongst school students. This reinforces a feeling that the political apathy felt by many young people, the perceived decline in the moral base of society, or the rebellion shown in events over the last forty years, is born, at least partly, out of ignorance of political rights and responsibilities and a lack of understanding of the consequences of inactivity; that indeed socialisation requires citizenship.

Citizenship Education and Human Rights Education

Some citizenship agendas had human rights as a founding principle (Advisory Group, 1998; LTS, 2002a), and across the world there is usually included some Human Rights Education (HRE) in the citizenship agenda;

the ICCS study of 2010 found that 35 of their 38 countries involved HRE in the citizenship programmes, and that only Guatemala, Hong Kong SAR and the Russian Federation did not. Within this, a study of the Holocaust shows the impact that abuses of human rights can lead to.

Our working definition, therefore, is to see HRE Education as a crucial part of Citizenship Education, as it is in most countries, and to also see Citizenship Education as an area of the curriculum that has the development of knowledge, critical skills and values as well as activism as key parts of the democratic citizen. The role of Holocaust Education within this should be central, whether the area is developed through History or in a broader Citizenship context.

Learning *about* and *from* the Holocaust

The pedagogy of Holocaust Education (HE) and its relationship to other areas of the curriculum, and in particular Citizenship Education (CE), can be presented as more problematic than they need to be. That the policies of the Nazis were a terrible attack on the citizenship rights of the Jews (and indeed of others, including many non-Jewish Europeans) is undeniable. And that there was a serious infringement of the human rights of the Jews and tens of millions of other individuals is equally clear. HE through a CE programme can thus provide a suitable context for learning in many key areas such as human rights, the need for mutual respect, tolerance and understanding of a diverse and multi-cultural, multi-ethnic society.

Indeed it is our contention that firstly HE should be a central (but of course not the only) factor in CE, that aspects of CE are central to an understanding of the lessons learnt from the Holocaust, and that HE needs to be put in an interdisciplinary model that crucially draws in aspects of Religious Studies and History, as well as Geography, Social Studies, Science, Art, Music and English. By interdisciplinary learning we are using a model (Chettiparamb, 2007; Harvie, 2012) which suggests using a number of disciplines to develop understanding of a subject or problem that extends beyond the scope of any single discipline: 'Learners integrate and develop information, concepts, methodologies and procedures from two or more disciplines to gain new knowledge, understanding and skills, and commonly also to explain or solve problems' (Graham et al., 2014: 2–3). Secondly, that the *United Nations Declaration on Human Rights* and the *United Nations Convention on the Rights of the Child* can be a positive impetus for introducing lessons *from* the Holocaust. We contend that this is the best way forward for Holocaust Education. The logic of seeing *about* and *from* as distinct is that they miss what is arguably the central aim of this aspect of education, namely humanity. It is not to argue that to 'understand' the Holocaust is to 'understand' citizenship and/or human rights, rather the areas that can be developed in the overlap begin to raise issues of 'Never Again', a phrase strongly associated with the Holocaust as a moral call to action, as other genocides can then be examined in light of our understanding. Indeed, the survivor's request (see p. 16) sums up a strand of the case for linking HE and CE.

However, it is incorrect to assume that all educators see the Holocaust in this way. For example, Pettigrew (2010) and Salmons (2010) argue that one looks for too much out of Holocaust Education and that it cannot be used as a substitute for in-depth examinations of moral and ethical issues. Salmons goes further and argues that the Holocaust should not be used to preach moral lessons as this can diminish its historical significance. Nicholas Kinloch (1998) expresses this line of argument succinctly when he argues that teachers should not concern themselves with attempting to promote specific behaviours nor moral development amongst students, and that teaching about the Holocaust should 'start and end with what happened and why; with the Shoah as history' (1998: 44). While we emphasised the importance of historical content in Holocaust Education in the previous chapter, it is possible that school-based lessons *from* the Holocaust are not counter to learning *about* it, rather that there is a dialectical relationship between the two. In other words, students may learn about and from the Holocaust at the same time; they impact on each other. Salmons' (2010) title, 'Universal Meaning or Historical Understanding?', epitomises a dichotomy that does not need to exist: why does it have to be one or the other? Why not both universal meaning AND historical understanding? We contend that, depending on the correct pedagogical structures, that learning about the Holocaust in an interdisciplinary citizenship context, as long as there is strong historical context, can be just as effective as learning about the Holocaust through History, with citizenship contexts added.

It is wrong to decontextualise the Holocaust and use it to shock, but equally we would argue it is wrong not to develop the universal lessons that emerge from its study. The juxtaposition is in reality a pedagogical problem. It can be acute in countries (such as England) where the main learning about the Holocaust is in the subject area of secondary History, and primarily for time issues, there is severe restriction in going beyond the history and that teachers can feel constrained about developing learning both about and from the Holocaust. The Holocaust Education Development Programme survey of teachers (HEDP, 2009) found that because of time issues, some teachers skipped over historical understanding to spend time on citizenship lessons, while others did the former without the latter. However, to argue that, because of these constraints, learning should be historical enquiry, is only, it seems to us, to make a virtue out of a necessity. Furthermore, in places where secondary History is not the main delivery area, for example in Scotland, where most learning about the Holocaust is in upper primary or in secondary schools which opt to include an interdisciplinary approach, other pedagogical models are also feasible, which have a strong HRE and CE emphasis.

Indeed, even amongst those who feel that it is valuable to teach controversial social, political and historical issues to young people, there is often an uncertainty about whether the concentration should be on content or skills. This is not a new debate: in the 1960s and 1970s there were differences about the goals of future Citizenship Education. For some, it was about imparting knowledge regarded by society as significant; for others, it was about imparting the skills to analyse society and encouraging young people to engage in the political process. In our opinion in some ways it is a non-debate, in that content cannot be effectively taught without analysis and skills need content to have relevance. As Salmons (2010) argues, the use of historical photographs, for example (in this case a photograph from 1944 showing the burning of bodies), raises all kinds of questions not only about the Holocaust but also about humanity and is thus a central aim of CE, as we have defined above.

Yet it could be that one needs to think beyond the abstract and introduce stronger pedagogical models into one's thinking. Eckmann (2015), for example, contends that as well as thinking about learning *about* and *from* these areas, we need to think also of learning *within* the paradigms. This means that school-based HE should reflect aspects of the values (democracy, rights, respect, anti-racism, anti-homophobia) that it is argued should be developed in learning *about* and *from* the Holocaust and that particular pedagogical understandings (active learning, self study and peer support) are key in developing this. In terms of these kinds of classroom approaches, there is evidence that, when asked, students prefer active learning opportunities (Ritchie, 1999; Save the Children, 2000, 2001; Burke and Grosvenor, 2003; Maitles and Gilchrist, 2003, 2006; Rudduck and Flutter, 2004). This is nothing new. John Dewey (1915: 3) argued approximately one hundred years ago that 'give the students something to do, not something to learn; and the doing is of such a nature as to demand thinking; learning naturally results'.

Whilst there are many positive aspects to these kinds of pedagogies, conducive to deeper learning within schools, there is also the thorny issue (taking Eckmann as a starting point) of whether democratic ideas and values can be effectively developed in the fundamentally undemocratic, indeed authoritarian, structure of the current typical school, where many teachers, never mind students, feel that they have little real say in the running of their school. It has been argued that this is not possible (Arnstine, 1995; Levin, 1998; Puolimatka, 1995). Indeed, Rooney (2007) states that to believe that these kinds of initiatives can be developed in the current school system undermines the very nature of education, and makes teachers responsible for the ills of society.

Maitles (2013) found in his interviews with school subject leaders of political and social studies in secondary schools that the problem was acknowledged. As one teacher put it:

> *'Yes, it is a bit awkward ... you keep telling them that they should be questioning things, they should be challenging things and there are ways to do it ... you are trying to get them to do these things and they feel they are getting nowhere, then it can be very counter-productive ... no matter how patient they are, they very often feel that they are getting nowhere. So they come back to you, shrug their shoulders and say "What's the point? We've tried what you said." It's a pity.'*

Yet, most of the teachers interviewed felt that it could, indeed must, be attempted. One teacher actually claimed that he used the school system as an example of democracy or lack of it and another said:

> *'There will be some tension between the inevitable dictatorship of the classroom and the sort of ideas that you are preaching ... it would be a good example for them [the students] of what's wrong with a dictatorship.'*

Complex Holocaust Questions in Citizenship Education

The importance of involving HE in CE is seen by the very complex universal questions that are raised by the Holocaust and by genocides since. Most of these can be disturbing and uplifting at the same time. Amongst the many issues raised in classrooms are the following:

- The very act of surviving the Holocaust has been called a 'symbolic resistance' (Rings, 1982), a phrase that Michael Marrus describes as 'a refusal to be habituated to terror in everyday life, a determination not to accept this as the "normal" state of things' (1995: 83). LaCapra puts it that 'Indeed those who survived extreme conditions might in a legitimate sense be said to have resisted a state of affairs designed to destroy them even if they did not take part in uprising or sabotage' (1994: 197).
- Nonetheless, strong feelings of guilt, best explained by Italian Auschwitz survivor Primo Levi, are reported from survivors. In a chilling phrase, Levi writes that the law in the camps, amongst starving prisoners, was 'eat your own bread, and if you can, that of your neighbour' (1989: 166), and claims that even after liberation, the bestial struggle for survival stayed and there was

no relief from the law of the jungle even as the Germans fled. The survivors fought over scraps, would often refuse help to each other, and were 'further from the model of thinking man than the most primitive pygmy or the most vicious sadist' (Levi, 1989: 171). The victims were so degraded by the experience that they were ashamed they could not or did not behave better. Levi explains it in terms of a shame:

... which the just man experiences when confronted by a crime committed by another, and he feels remorse because of its existence, because of its having been irrevocably introduced into the world of existing things, and because his will has proven non-existent or feeble and was incapable of putting up a good defence. (Levi, 1993:12)

- There is debate around responsibility. Goldhagen (1997) argues that Germans per se were responsible for the Holocaust; others that Nazism was responsible (Browning, 1993; Maitles, 1997; Finkelstein and Birn, 1998). It is complex, in that if Germans were responsible, then Levi's suggestion that 'It can happen anywhere' is not necessarily correct and we need not worry about 'Never Again' – the juxtaposition of events is unlikely. This, it seems to us, could be dangerous. It seems to miss the impact of ten years of Nazi rule on the psyche of perpetrators and bystanders. Hilberg (1992) and Sagall (2013) take up these questions of killers and bystanders and the mixture of sociological and psychological factors that impact on the ability to act, including terrorising the population through threats of concentration camps such as Dachau and Sachsenhausen. Having said this, many Europeans did try to help and rescue Jews: from individuals in Berlin and elsewhere who hid people; to the rescue operation in Denmark (where Jews were ferried en masse to Sweden); to Amsterdam, where on the day of the arrests, there were protests and a general strike, brutally and violently repressed; to the inspiring Oskar Schindler and his rescue of nearly 1,000 Jews (indeed there are more descendants of the 'Schindler Jews' than Jews currently living in Poland).
- Aspects of citizenship, 'reconciliation' and 'forgiveness' are worth a special mention as they are common to recent genocides, and often go unnoticed. For example, in April 2015, 81 year-old Eva Mozes Kor, who with her identical twin sister Miriam had survived the genetic experiments under Josef Mengele at Auschwitz, testified against 93 year-old Oskar Gröning, a former SS officer who faced charges of being an accessory to the murder of 300,000 Auschwitz prisoners while he worked at the camp. Eva's sister, Miriam, had died in 1993 of a rare form of cancer, brought on by the unknown medical experiments and injections which she had been subjected to. Eva herself had suffered from miscarriages and tuberculosis. At Gröning's trial she demonstrated forgiveness in her testimony and accepted a kiss and a hug from Gröning. She explained:

In my testimony, I told him [Gröning] Forgiveness is an act of self-healing, self-liberation and self-empowerment. I do not need anyone's approval or acceptance. Reconciliation takes two people, that is why it is so difficult ... I also call forgiveness the best revenge against the perpetrator. And everyone can afford it. It is free ... I forgave the Nazis, not because they deserve it but because I deserve it. (Kor, 2015)

Eva Kor was criticised by other Holocaust survivor plaintiffs for her actions. Not every Holocaust survivor shares her forgiveness of Mr Gröning. Yet this provides further insight into citizenship and highlights an issue that is relevant to young people today. For example, in Rwanda, among Hutus and Tutsis, where perpetrators and victims live side by side, there have been many reconciliation initiatives at grassroots levels over the years to encourage their reconciliation. The same can be said of Cambodia and Srebrenica. Genocides may become consigned to words and pages in history books, but people who were directly involved, whether as perpetrators or victims, have to move on with their very concrete and real lives.

Case Study of Holocaust Education in a Citizenship Education Programme

There have been a number of studies examining whether learning about the Holocaust, either as part of a study on the Second World War or as part of a citizenship programme in primary and secondary, impacts on young people's values and attitudes (Short and Carrington, 1991; Carrington and Short, 1997; Short, 2003; Cowan and Maitles, 2007; Maitles, Cowan and Butler, 2007; Maitles, 2010b). The Primary studies have previously been outlined in Chapter 2. In one case study, Maitles (2010a) evaluated the impact of learning about the Holocaust in a CE framework at a secondary school in the West of Scotland. The project in this school was called *One World* and involved a number of activities and events for the students. The entire S1 student body, aged about 12 years, was taken off timetable for 12 days and immersed in citizenship activities. Active learning was to be at its core. The first two days involved workshops around motivation, leadership and peer pressure issues – entitled 'What it means to be human'. They were led by representatives from external organisations and also involved the associated primary schools. Days 3 to 6 were spent in subject departments and every department in the school took responsibility for developing citizenship from the perspective of the subject discipline. For example: Mathematics developed work around percentages using the 'small earth' project, designed to develop awareness of global sustainability; English focused on supporting students to research and write about inspirational figures of their choosing; Science examined global warming and environmental issues. Days 7 and 8 involved activities around the UN Convention on Human Rights, in particular a day with Unicef speakers organising workshops on global inequalities and human rights. Days 9 and 10 used trips and workshops outside school relating to Scotland, diversity and racism. Days 11 and 12 covered genocide and Holocaust awareness, involving drama, music, the Anne Frank Trust, Rwanda, stages of genocide and workshops on Nazism. The students had some prior learning about the rise of the Nazis in Germany and the events leading to the Holocaust.

A values and attitudes survey was devised, building on the work of research into social values (Angvik and von Borries, 1997; Hahn, 1998; Lister et al., 2001; Torney-Purta et al., 2001; Kerr et al., 2001; Whiteley, 2005; Maitles et al., 2006; Cowan and Maitles, 2007; Maitles, 2009, 2010b; Schultz, 2011). It attempted through a series of questions with a three-point Likert scale to examine student attitudes towards diversity/multi-ethnicity, immigration/racism, and responsibility for tackling racism. The questionnaire was issued immediately before the initiative started and very soon after it ended. The pre-questionnaire involved 111 students (55 male and 56 female), the post-questionnaire 107 students (53 male and 54 female). This strategy has a strength of ensuring anonymity and encouraging honest answers, but its use meant that individual targeted follow-up interviews would not be possible.

Findings/results
Diversity
We asked a number of questions to assess attitudes to diversity, using future potential voting attitudes, primarily as the school had recently engaged in a major mock election exercise, involving these students, around the 2011 Scottish Parliamentary elections. Following the CE and HE initiative, in almost all areas there was improvement, and in the cases of Jewish, Muslim, Catholic and English people and Women, substantial improvement. In the other two cases, Black and Disabled people, it was virtually the same before and after the initiative. Attitudes towards gay people, whilst more tolerant after rather than before the programme, were lower overall. This supported our previous findings (Maitles et al., 2006; Cowan and Maitles, 2007) which showed that students in transition from primary 7 to secondary 1 were more tolerant towards minority groups after learning about the Holocaust.

The picture was more complex with regard to immigration/asylum seekers. Whilst the students' attitudes towards full rights for black people improved slightly and there was some increased support for refugees, there was no increase in positive welcoming attitudes towards asylum seekers and economic immigrants, although we were not in a position to find out whether students understood the difference between the two categories. Clearly, the impact of both the recession and media and political calls for 'British jobs for British workers', and supposed concerns of immigration into Britain, will be hard for school education programmes to challenge, if they wished to do so. More than 80% in both surveys felt that it was wrong to make racist jokes.

Responsibility for Racism

The attempt here was to gauge the attitudes towards both collective and individual responsibility for dealing with racism. The results were positive. In particular, there was a large increase in the percentage believing that society as a whole should challenge racism and a welcomingly high response to individual responsibility in both surveys.

There can be issues when examining this kind of evidence of HE and CE as to whether one sees the glass as half full or half empty. For example, should we be pleased that over three-quarters of the students felt that they had personal responsibility for challenging racism, or worried that 25% think that racism has nothing to do with them? Overall, there was evidence of a general improvement in values and attitudes after the students undertook the initiative, although in most issues (excepting attitudes towards gay and English people) there was a high(ish) level before the citizenship initiative. Nonetheless, the fact that in the vast majority of categories students were more positive after than before, suggests that these initiatives were worthwhile.

However, the research can be of best value as we try to evaluate the development of citizenship ideas in young people. The involvement of many subjects in a school can take HE and CE Education out of a potential isolation and place its understanding at the heart of the school. This allows for cross-curricular/active learning experiences for deeper learning and more interesting (and potentially longer lasting) learning experiences. For example in Maitles (2010b), in the students' genocide awareness days, the impact of the speaker from Rwanda and the workshop by two senior students at the school outlining their experiences of Auschwitz as part of the LFAP, the Anne Frank workshops and diverse and active music and drama, were powerful for the students and helped their understanding of some of the issues, reflected in the results of the survey reported above.

Conclusion

There is real debate about the pedagogy surrounding HE and its relationship to CE. Where the Holocaust is embedded in the curriculum, generally through the subject discipline of History, there is a clear advantage to learning about it – albeit with the time constraints and lack of interdisciplinarity as key drawbacks. In curricula where the Holocaust is taught as part of a CE programme, there can be interdisciplinary activities and learning related to the citizenship areas inherent in HE, with the proviso that the historical events leading up to the Holocaust must play a central role. For us, there is no dichotomy between the two. It is not in the interests of developing HE to argue that it can only be adequately or properly done through History. Where we can mix the historical knowledge of the events with a strong focus on its evils, and that this is the end to which things the students see about them, such as stereotyping and racist behaviour, can lead to, young people learn both *about* and *from* the Holocaust.

Further Reading

Eva Moses Kor, www.auschwitz.dk/eva.htm (last accessed 14 October 2016).

4

ANTISEMITISM

Learning Objectives

- To discuss the use of the term 'Judeophobia'
- To present a brief summary of the history of antisemitism
- To identify the different expressions of antisemitism
- To explore issues relating to antisemitism in educational establishments

---

We pointed out at the beginning of this book (in Chapter 1) that due to the biblical origin of the word 'antisemitism', this word is perceived by some as applying to other groups of people in addition to Jews. This provides one reason why the term 'Judeophobia' is often preferred, as it is unambiguous and explicit as to whom the word is targeted at. First coined in an essay to his fellow Jews, entitled *Auto-Emancipation* (1882), Leon Pinsker wrote that 'Judeophobia ... is not peculiar to particular races but is common to the whole of mankind' and 'a psychic aberration'. Pinsker's views were challenged by others such as Deutscher (1968) as neglecting the social conditions that give rise to antisemitism and in being defeatist by suggesting that antisemitism cannot be challenged.

Another reason why 'Judeophobia' is preferred is because that words with the suffix 'ism' suggest an opposition to an ideology or specific ideas, and this legitimises hatred of an entire group of people. It is worth pointing out that while the origin of 'phobia' is Greek, meaning 'irrational fear', over time it has come to be used to form nouns that convey a hatred of particular people, such as 'homophobia', 'xenophobia' and 'Islamophobia'. Yet Isaac (2004: 443) argues that 'Judeophobia' emphasises the fear aspect and ignores the delusional and hostile nature of antisemitism. 'Xenophobia' and 'Islamophobia' similarly ignore the hostile nature of ethnicity and racism. This explains why 'antisemitism' and 'Judeophobia' are sometimes used interchangeably.

Hannah Arendt (1951) viewed 'Judeophobia' and 'antisemitism' as two distinctive concepts, and pointed out that 'Judeophobia' denies Jews their equal rights to citizenship, whereas 'antisemitism' is a genocidal ideology that denies them their right to exist. Our problem with this interpretation is that there is no evidence to suggest that the genocide of European Jewry was conceived when the word 'antisemitism' was first coined. In Chapter 7 we assert that it is important to use this word in a Holocaust teaching context (see p. 92). This is because a study of the Holocaust lends itself to a discussion of Nazi antisemitism through the alienation, segregation, incarceration, extermination and attempted genocide of the Jews. Interestingly the avoidance of teachers in referring to the term 'antisemitism' in the classroom was not because they favoured the use of 'Judeophobia', but because of a preference to subsume 'antisemitism' into the larger term of 'racism' (Short and Reed, 2004).

While we acknowledge the merits of the term 'Judeophobia', we prefer that teachers and educators consistently use the word 'antisemitism' in school-based Holocaust Education. Our justification for this is that the word 'antisemitism' is most commonly used by politicians, the media and social media, and in school textbooks. Following the murders at the kosher supermarket in Paris (2015), UN Secretary-General Ban Ki-moon expressed solidarity to fight against *antisemitism*, and referred to the treatment of Jews in the Holocaust in his address to the General Assembly. Also, the findings of a European Union report on antisemitism (European Union Agency for Human Rights, 2015: 6) stated '*antisemitism* remains an issue of serious concern which demands decisive and targeted policy responses to tackle this phenomenon'. Further, in the UK, there is an All-Party Parliamentary Group Against Antisemitism that has produced two reports (2006, 2015). The first includes in its conclusions an acknowledgement of the 'relative neglect of antisemitism as an issue in diversity training', and a need to explain the history of antisemitism to school students (2006: 49); the second includes in its terms of reference:

> To identify and review the effectiveness of existing legal and other frameworks for addressing antisemitism in the UK with a view to avoiding the extreme anti-Jewish violence in Europe that resulted from the conflict [in Gaza, 2014]. (All-Party Parliamentary Group Against Antisemitism, 2015: 2)

If 'Judeophobia' is referred to in class, teachers should avoid confusion of this term and make clear to students that this is another word for 'antisemitism'. Both are examples of bigotry and both reflect a hatred of Jews, on the basis of who (or what) they are or are perceived to represent.

The following discussion of the different expressions of antisemitism is presented chronologically as an attempt to support teachers and educators in their understanding of the history of antisemitism, and address the above conclusion made by the All-Party Parliamentary Group Against Antisemitism. Knowledge of this historical aspect will support students who study the Holocaust to understand that antisemitism was not a German phenomenon, and that persecution of Jews has taken place for centuries across the globe. It will also demonstrate that:

> Antisemitism is a complex historical virus. And like any such organism is composed of a variety of strains: ancient and modern, racialist and religious, left-wing and right-wing. (Schoenfeld, 2004: 4)

One word that is useful in understanding antisemitism is 'pogrom'. This is a Russian word, defined as 'an attack, accompanied by destruction, the looting of property, murder and rape and perpetrated by one section of the population against another' (*Encyclopaedia Judaica*, 1971c: 694). These attacks were nearly always sponsored or initiated by the state. This particularly applies to the hundreds of attacks or massacres by the Christian population on Jews in Russia between 1881 and 1921, yet as you will read later in this chapter, such massacres on Jews were not confined to Russia alone.

The Expressions of Antisemitism

Before Christianity

Like 'genocide', 'antisemitism' existed before the word was coined. In the pre-Christian world, antisemitism was based on tensions between the Jews, observing their religion and the social customs of the day. Cicero (106–43 BCE) and Ovid (43 BCE–17/18 CE) wrote unfavourably of these differences. Jews' belief in one God and their refusal to make sacrifices to other gods, their eating in accordance with Jewish dietary laws, their abstinence from work on the seventh day, *Shabbat*, and their marrying within the faith created suspicion and prejudice of the majority toward Jews who were a minority. This also restricted the assimilation of Jews into the wider community.

The first reference to an antisemitic act was in the fifth century BCE, when the Jewish people narrowly escaped destruction in Persia. This is recorded in the Bible as the story of *Purim* in the Book of Esther (see Chapter 8 for more information on this). In 19 CE, in the reign of the Roman Emperor Tiberius (42 BCE–37 CE), Sejanus deported 4,000 Jews to the island of Sardinia and ordered the Jews to leave Italy unless they abandoned their religious practices. This demonstrates that antisemitism in classical times was characterised by Judaism itself, and this continued with the advent of Christianity.

The Christian World

Religious intolerance toward Jews developed from their being regarded as responsible for the crucifixion of Jesus Christ, and a growing perception that they were evil. The origins of Christian antisemitism can be found in the actions of the Church Fathers, who in the fourth century introduced legislation that denied Jews full citizenship by restraining their religious practices, limiting their political, social and economic rights, and putting pressure on Jews to abandon their religion. As Christianity developed, so too did vilifying the Jews. Christian convert Justin Martyr (100–165) criticised the Jews for rejecting and killing Jesus, and claimed that they were a group of people who needed more laws. St John Chrysostomos (347–407) condemned the Jews in his sermons and writings for murdering Christ and publicly called them outcasts and morally degenerate.

During the Crusades (1096–1272) thousands of Jews were murdered by Christians in Europe in massacres across France, Spain, Germany and Bohemia for refusing to be baptised into Christianity. On arrival in Jerusalem, the first group of crusaders (or knights) murdered Jews alongside their Muslim neighbours for being infidels.

While England had taken little interest and no part in the first two Crusades, King Richard I (1157–1199), also known as Richard 'the Lionheart', decided to participate in the third. At this time Jews in England were officially protected by the king and some were moneylenders to Christian nobles who had incurred heavy debts. Indeed, it was precisely because of discrimination and the fact that many trades and professions were closed to them, that Jews became key moneylenders. Under these circumstances, state-supported antisemitism could be very useful in getting such debts dissolved (Leon, 1971; Gilbert, 1986). In 1190, after massacres on Jews in the northern towns of Norwich, Lincoln and Stamford, the city of York caught or was set on fire and Jews were targeted as being responsible. Homes of Jews in York were attacked and 150 fled to the royal castle, Clifford's Tower, for protection. The castle was attacked by an angry mob led by local knights and clergy. Most of the Jews chose to commit suicide in the castle rather than renounce their faith and surrender to forced baptism or death at the hands of the mob. Those who did not commit suicide were killed when the castle was set on fire or murdered by the rioters. The massacre of the Jews of York is sometimes referred to as the York pogrom.

Alienation by identification

In thirteenth-century France Jews were ordered to wear a round sign, a wheel, on their outer clothing. This badge could either be yellow or red and white, and had to be worn by Jews from either age 7 or age 13. It was normally worn on the breast although some additional regulations required a second sign to be worn on the back. King Philip IV (1268–1314), also known as 'Philip the Fair', collected revenue from the purchase of these badges from royal tax collectors. This was not the first time Jews had been ordered to wear a mark of distinction. Such practice originated in Islam when Caliph Omar II (717–720) ordered every non-Muslim to wear clothing of a different colour for each minority group in order to distinguish people not belonging to the religious faith of the majority. Jews wore one distinctive mark, Christians another. This practice continued across the centuries. In the thirteenth century, Jews in Spain were required to distinguish themselves from Christians by wearing a yellow badge on their clothing, and in England, King Edward I (1239–1307) ordered Jews over the age of seven years to wear a yellow badge in the form of the Tablets of the Law. In the sixteenth century, Jews living in the Italian Duchy of Ferrara were ordered to wear the 'Jews' badge', which at that time was an 'O' with an orange-yellow stripe a handbreadth wide, for the same purpose. Whilst we may think this would be impossible now, in the very week of Holocaust Memorial Day in 2016, it was reported in the UK that refugees in Middlesbrough were to have their doors painted red, and in Cardiff, refugees were to wear identifying wristbands (*Guardian*, 2016a).

Blood libels

During the Middle Ages, Jews were falsely accused of murdering Christians and non-Jews, especially Christian children, for the purpose of obtaining blood to make *matzah* (unleavened bread) for the Jewish festival of Passover. These 'blood libels' originated in the twelfth century in medieval England, when the local Jewish community was accused of the murder of 12 year-old William of Norwich (1132–1144). Six years later, Thomas of Monmouth, a Benedictine monk, wrote that local Jews had crucified the boy as part of a ritual. Similar false allegations spread across Europe and justified the maltreatment, violence against, and murder of Jews. Blood libels were another expression of antisemitism and resurfaced over the centuries in Damascus (1882) and Kiev (1911). The creation of this widespread myth supported Nazi antisemitic policy.

In addition to the blood libels, Christians accused Jews of causing the Black Death or bubonic plague (1348–1352) which caused the deaths of an estimated fifty million people. Although Jews also died in this pandemic, they became scapegoats. There were many murderous attacks or pogroms on Jews across Europe. One example of these occurred in Strasbourg where 2,000 Jews were burnt to death.

Judensau sculptures

Originating in the thirteenth century, *Judensau* (literally meaning 'Jew pig/sow') sculptures dehumanised Jews by depicting them in various obscene activities with a pig, a symbol of filth. Commonly placed in the interiors of churches and cathedals across Germany, they communicated to the general public that Jews were barely human and beast-like, and were a warning to Christians. Jews were distinguished in these sculptures by their wearing a pointed hat, sidelocks and a beard. In the following centuries *Judensau* sculptures were placed on the exterior of religious and public buildings, and provided an opportunity to make fun of Jews. The *Judensau* sculpture in Wittenberg is one of the most famous and is described as follows:

> The Jew of Wittenberg grabs the sow's behind with both hands, with one hand lifting the animal's right hind leg, with the other lifting or holding the tail. His head is lifted to the side, and there can be no mistaking as to where his gaze is directed: right at the sow's anus. (Wiedl, 2010: 340)

Several, like the one on the cathedral in Regensburg, depicted Jews suckling from a pig. Although Christians ate pig meat, pig or sow's milk was not considered clean enough to consume. Yet *Judensau* sculptures depicted Jews 'feeding from the very part that was not fit for (human) consumption' (Wiedl, 2010: 338). These anti-Jewish images alienated Jews further from society. There are isolated examples of *Judensau* sculptures elsewhere in Europe, e.g. in Austria, Belgium, France, Poland, Switzerland and Sweden. These sculptures were symbols of European antisemitic culture and many are on view to this day, with the oldest surviving one situated at the cathedral in Brandenburg (see Further Reading at the end of this chapter).

The German priest Martin Luther (1483–1546) encouraged the building of *Judensau* sculptures. He regarded Jews as a threat and that they could only be saved by converting to Christianity. Gilbert (1986: 19) states that Luther advised the following:

- Their synagogues should be set on fire
- Their homes should be destroyed
- They should live under one roof
- They should be stripped of their belongings
- They should be driven out of the country

Expulsion of Jews was common policy in medieval times. Jews had been expelled from England (1290), France (1306), Lithuania and Portugal (1483), Spain (1492) and Bohemia (1541), and later from Italy (1593).

Ghettos

Ghettos were Jewish residential areas or 'quarters', which in general were surrounded by a wall shutting its residents off from the rest of the city. While the first ghetto was officially established in Venice, Italy, in 1510 (see Chapter 6, pp. 80–82), separate Jewish quarters which had the walled features of a ghetto existed from the twelfth century in several cities in Spain, in Constantinople and Prague, and from 1462 in Frankfurt. Hence, like the word 'antisemitism', 'ghettos' existed before the actual word was coined. Following a Papal decree, a ghetto in Rome was established in 1555 to isolate Jews from Christians. This put pressure on the rulers of other Italian states to do the same and ghettos across Italy began to be established (e.g. in Tuscany, 1570–71; Verona, 1599; and Ferrara, 1624). These were justified on the grounds that Christians were providing better protection to Jews, although in reality, they segregated Jews from their Christian neighbours.

In Muslim countries, Jewish quarters were different from the ghettos in Christian countries in that 'they were not surrounded by a wall and did not have a gate, which was closed at night, on the Sabbath or on the (Jewish) Festivals' (*Encyclopaedia Judaica*, 1971b: 83). Exceptions to this included the quarter in Morocco which was surrounded by high walls and where, in the fifteenth century, all the Jews of Fez were ordered to live.

Emancipation

In the nineteenth century, emancipation allowed Jews citizenship rights and more opportunities to assimilate into wider society and achieve respectability across Europe. Yet the most assimilated Jews became the subject of traditional religious stereotypes as a political and nationalistic antisemitism emerged in which Jews were perceived as a race. Based on a politics that flowed from the ideological justifications for the slave trade, this meant that although Jews could rise to high positions and enter trades and professions, the racism was just as pernicious. This was demonstrated by the antisemitism that the Prime Minister Benjamin Disraeli, himself a baptised Jew, and the Rothschilds, who were German Jewish bankers, were subjected to (Davis, 1996). They and other prominent assimilated Jews were ridiculed and caricatured in the press, and there was an increase in antisemitic political caricatures in the German newspaper *Der Stürmer*. The myth of the presence of a Jewish conspiracy whose purpose was global domination was also widely communicated and believed.

Jews continued to be negatively portrayed in English literature. The 25-year-old Charles Dickens had never met any Jews before he wrote about the grotesque and evil 'Fagin the Jew' in *Oliver Twist*. This creation was based on a dominant culture of the time and, Dickens claimed, on Ikey Solomons (1785–1850), a well-known Jewish criminal in London. Yet Dickens portrayed Fagin as a devil, holding a toasting fork, and having red hair, and referred to him as 'the merry' or 'playful' old gentleman. Like centuries before when Shakespeare penned the moneylending Shylock in *The Merchant of Venice*, and Marlowe *The Jew of Malta*, Dickens transmitted the cultural antisemitism of the time.

The philosopher and political theorist Hannah Arendt (1951) wrote that the Dreyfus affair was 'a kind of dress rehearsal' for Nazi antisemitism. This expression of antisemitism took place in France, the country that had recognised Jewish equality in its *Declaration of the Rights of Man and of the Citizens* in 1791. Captain Alfred Dreyfus (1859–1935), a Jewish artillery officer, was accused and found guilty of treason. The handling of this case from its early stages in 1894, when Dreyfus was denied the right to examine the 'secret' evidence against him and first found guilty, to his public humiliation when he was stripped of his rank in 1895, found guilty again in 1899 though pardoned later that year, and exonerated in 1905, demonstrated antisemitism in the French press, the army, and in the general public. Dreyfus was not guilty of treason but he was guilty of being Jewish. Early publicity against him came from antisemitic groups and the newspaper *La Libre Parole,* and included the accused's contribution to the mythical international Jewish conspiracy.

The myth of Jews conspiring against the state was developed further in 1905 when another form of libel emerged. In *The Protocols of the Elders of Zion*, each 'protocol' or chapter reported on the alleged minutes of meetings of Jewish leaders, that demonstrated how Jews would achieve global domination by controlling the media, manipulating the economy, and fostering religious conflict and disharmony. First published in Russia, the purpose of this publication was to incite and/or justify hatred towards Jews. It was soon widely circulated around Europe, the USA, South America, and Japan. Though, since 1920, it has been proven to be a forged fictional document, this antisemitic publication continues to find willing readers.

Nazism

It is evident from the following list that Nazism adopted many of the expressions of antisemitism, and imagery that had been employed in Europe centuries before:

- Caricatures of Jews dehumanised and alienated them from society
- The antisemitic language in Hitler's *Mein Kampf* was similar to that of Martin Luther

- Jews were scapegoats; they were blamed for Germany losing the First World War and held as the source of Germany's political, social, economic and ethical problems
- The yellow star distinguished Jews from everyone else
- Forcing Jews into ghettos segregated them further from the wider society
- The attack on Jews across the Third Reich in *Kristallnacht* was similar to the many pogroms against Jews
- Popular myths about Jews were used for their own needs; *Judensau* sculptures were revived and the *Protocols* were used in Nazi propaganda

Concentration camps too had not originated in Germany. These had been built by the British army in the Second Boer War (1899–1902) for Dutch settlers, in South Africa. Thousands of women and children died as a result of their dirty and diseased conditions.

The expression of antisemitism that was central to Nazi ideology was not based on religion per se but on race. This was based on Social Darwinism which asserted that human beings comprised several different races and that some races were superior to others. The Nuremberg Race Laws (see Chapter 6, p. 77) established Nazi racial policy and supported the vision of a pure-blooded Aryan society that was not to be polluted by Jews. This meant that conversion of Jews was futile as it could not change someone's innate 'Jewishness'. This idea of inferior stereotypes was similar to the belief held by many that African Americans were genetically inferior to Whites.

One distinctive expression of antisemitism was the implementation of the Final Solution, i.e. complete annihilation of the Jews. In this the Nazis were supported by antisemites in Germany and from many other European countries. Ghettos were not principally used to separate Jews from the wider society but to hold or contain them until they could be deported to concentration or death camps. The Nazi ghettos were not simply Jewish quarters as they were neither comfortable nor habitable; they were overcrowded and adults and children died from hunger and disease. Another distinctive feature of Nazi antisemitism was the use of modernity to implement the devastation of the Final Solution (see Chapter 2, p. 16, Bauman).

It is also worth noting that Nazism did not totally disappear with the end of the Second World War. Neo-Nazism emerged soon after the demise of the Nazis. This movement is characterised by the racist antisemitic ideology and xenophobic nationalism of the Nazi regime, and Neo-Nazis incorporate Nazi symbols and glorify Nazism.

The World Today

There is one other common feature of Neo-Nazism that could be added to the above list, and that is Holocaust denial. To some this seems bizarre as surely those who glorify Nazism are proud of Nazi achievements, whether they be the racial state or the annihilation and persecution of six million Jews and hundreds of thousands of Roma? Why would those who glorify such human devastation want to deny it? The answer here is that most are involved in trying to build far-right organisations and as such they realise the horrors of the general population who equate Nazi with Holocaust. Thus they attempt to suggest it never happened or that it was only an incident in the war. Their Holocaust denial is another expression of antisemitism.

The IHRA define Holocaust denial as:

> ... discourse and propaganda that deny the historical reality and the extent of the extermination of the Jews by the Nazis and their accomplices during World War II, known as the Holocaust or the Shoah. Holocaust denial refers specifically to any attempt to claim that the Holocaust/Shoah did not take place. (IHRA, 2013)

The first examples of Holocaust denial took place before the end of the Second World War when the Germans and their collaborators concealed evidence of their murder of European Jews at the mass graves at the Belzec, Sobibor, and Treblinka death camps, and destroyed evidence of their mass shooting operations in Eastern Europe (United States Holocaust Memorial Museum, n.d.). By the late 1940s claims circulated 'that the Holocaust was a hoax perpetrated by Jews to secure the establishment of the state of Israel' (Cowan, 2012). As well as receiving support from the Neo-Nazi movement, Holocaust deniers include members of other extreme right-wing parties, white supremacists such as the Ku Klux Klan, conspiracy theorists and radical Muslim activists.

Holocaust deniers prefer to be called 'revisionists', as historical revisionism is a legitimate rethinking of accepted historical facts through analysis of newly discovered authentic information, and being identified as such gives them credibility. However, Holocaust deniers deliberately omit, or fail to acknowledge, significant facts and evidence, and so referring to them as 'revisionists' is misleading. Bergmann (2013) reflects that antisemitism which arises in nation-states that are guilty of having committed crimes during the Holocaust, who are faced with accusations and compensation claims from Jews, can also lead to Holocaust denial.

Though the presence of Holocaust deniers in schools and other educational establishments is not discussed openly, they do nonetheless exist. Examples are Arthur Butz, Professor of Electrical Engineering (USA), Vincent Reynouard, Professor of Maths (France), and former school teacher Bernhard Schaub (Switzerland). What is less known is the extent of Holocaust deniers amongst school students. One isolated example (unpublished) comes from a multi-ethnic primary school in London, where a drama educator reported that a teacher had told her before her lesson on Anne Frank, 'Oh just so you know, there's a boy in your class who is a Holocaust denier.' This suggests that guidance and clarity on how to address Holocaust denial in educational establishments in countries where Holocaust denial is not illegal would be beneficial.

Another form of Holocaust denial is the impiety towards the Holocaust demonstrated in the International Holocaust Cartoon Contests. These have been sponsored by the municipal authorities in Tehran since 2006, with the winner receiving a sizeable monetary prize. These contests encourage political cartoonists to create caricatures denying and trivialising the Holocaust, mocking the Holocaust and Jews, or criticising the West and the state of Israel. The cartoons demonstrate the relationship between Holocaust denial and distortion. The IHRA has identified the following elements of Holocaust distortion which are by no means exclusive.

1. Intentional efforts to excuse or minimize the impact of the Holocaust or its principal elements, including collaborators and allies of Nazi Germany
2. Gross minimization of the number of the victims of the Holocaust in contradiction to reliable sources
3. Attempts to blame the Jews for causing their own genocide
4. Statements that cast the Holocaust as a positive historical event. Those statements are not Holocaust denial but are closely connected to it as a radical form of antisemitism. They may suggest that the Holocaust did not go far enough in accomplishing its goal of 'the Final Solution of the Jewish Question'
5. Attempts to blur the responsibility for the establishment of concentration and death camps devised and operated by Nazi Germany by putting blame on other nations or ethnic groups (IHRA, 2013)

Bergmann's levels of current prejudices against Jews in Europe (2013: 2) demonstrate striking similarities with the historic traditions that we have already described. These comprise: the political level, where Jews are viewed as collectively covertly controlling or strongly influencing the politics of the nation-state; the economic level, where Jews exploit or manipulate the international financial market; the moral level, where Jews exploit the Holocaust by using their victimisation to demand compensation and obtain sympathy; and the religious level, where Jews are perceived as an enemy of Christianity. In 2014, after listening to a talk on citizenship by the authors of this book who were guest speakers at the university for International Week, one Muslim student agreed with the speakers that it was unfair and wrong to say bad things about Jews and privately asked whether this was because they controlled the banks and had so much money. This student was totally unaware of his own prejudice, demonstrating the economic level above.

Short (2013) emphasises that the origin of antisemitism in Muslim communities is religious as the Koran states that 'Jews only deserve shame in this life, and to be banned on the Day of Judgement to the harshest torment' (*Sura* 2: 85). One interpretation of this is that it applied to Jews at a time when the early Muslim community was not well established. Yet Short notes that the above religious writing impacts on religious extremists who exploit this for their political means, and on more moderate Muslims who consider that this applies to all Jews in the world today. It is important to point out that Islam is not an obstacle to antiracism.

Tibi (2008: 124) argues that the 'prevalent form of antisemitism throughout the Islamic world has been imported from Europe and given an Islamic shape', and claims that this expression of antisemitism 'more closely resembles the Nazism in which the Jew is seen as the source of all evil'. This 'shape' Tibi claims, is based on the views of Sayyid Qutb (1906–1966), which combine antisemitism and anti-Americanism and approve the annihilation of Jews. This expression of antisemitism in the Muslim world is a relatively new ideology which is adopted by contemporary Islamist movements such as Hamas and Islamic State (IS). It is this ideology that is an obstacle to antiracism, as in addition to creating divisions between Muslims and other Muslims, it creates divisions between Muslims and non-Muslims, which include Jews.

Tibi also explains that the (Jewish) State of Israel plays a key role in this expression of antisemitism. Israel is either regarded as the '"little Satan" acting in the service of the "big Satan," the U.S.', or as 'the "big Satan"... an executioner of a "Jewish conspiracy" against Islam'. It is thus in the interests of those who subscribe to this ideology, to demonise and vilify Israel. In his address to the House of Lords, the former UK Chief Rabbi Lord Jonathan Sacks spoke of this demonisation by radical Islamist forces:

> The Islamists also know that the only way they can win the sympathy of the West is by demonising Israel. They know you can't win support for Isis, Boko Haram or Islamic Jihad, but if you can blame Israel you will gain the support of academics, unions and the media and you will distract attention from the massacres in Syria and Iraq, the slow descent of other countries into chaos, and the ethnic cleansing of Christians throughout the region. (Sacks, 31 October 2014)

It is important to recognise the distinction between 'antisemitism', which we have previously defined, and 'anti-Zionism', which in broad terms is an opposition to the existence of the State of Israel. Clearly not all anti-Zionists are antisemites, e.g. some orthodox Jews and left-wing Jews are anti-Zionists (see Chapter 6, p. 78), but anti-Zionism can be used to camouflage antisemitism. We have stated previously that one can criticise Israel without being antisemitic, but criticism that leads to the destruction of or violence against Israel and/or Jews in general is abhorrent, unacceptable, and an expression of antisemitism (Cowan, 2012: 195). Thus, even within an anti-Zionist narrative, we need to differentiate between those who, for example, call for Jews to be killed or driven out from Israel (antisemitic) and those who argue for a democratic unitary non-religious state (legitimate political expression).

One needs to oppose unreservedly the targeting of Jewish communal organisations, schools and attacks on Jewish individuals, such as the bombing of the Argentine-Israeli Mutual Association in Buenos Aires (1994) in which 85 people were killed and hundreds injured, and the shootings at Ozar Hatorah school in Toulouse (2012) in which a teacher and three children were killed. During the Gaza conflict in 2014, there was an escalation of antisemitism across Europe and anti-Israel demon-strations, where chants of *Jews to the gas chambers*, and *Death to the Jews* were respectively reported in Germany and France. It is difficult to say whether these or the kidnapping and murders of American journalist Daniel Pearl (2002) and the French salesman Ilan Halimi (2006) were a result of antisemitism or anti-Zionism, or a combination of both. Suffice to say each demonstrates extreme hatred towards Jews. In its guidance to police forces in England and Wales, the College of Policing clearly identi-fies that aspects of anti-Zionism are 'a new antisemitism' and states:

> This form of hostility often blames Jews and/or Israelis for all of the tension in the region. A crime motivated wholly or partially by such hostility should be recognised as a hate crime. (College of Policing, 2014: 36)

The College also provides examples of the ways in which antisemitism manifests itself with regard to the State of Israel. These include:

- drawing comparisons of contemporary Israeli policy to that of the Nazis
- holding Jews collectively responsible for actions of the State of Israel
- applying double standards by requiring behaviour not expected or demanded of any other democratic nation (College of Policing, 2014: 37)

While it is one's legitimate right to protest through boycott, demonstration and other means, the BDS campaign of Boycotts, Divestments and Sanctions against Israel has been accused of being antisemitic by its singling out of one small country which is the Jewish homeland. Some argue that other countries are equally, if not more, deserving of a boycott, in relation to social injustice and inequalities, towards gay men, women, and children, but they are not the subjects of such a target. BDS activists emphasise that they are not antisemitic, and indeed include many Jewish supporters who consider that Israeli cultural and academic institutions 'directly contribute to Israel's violation of Palestinian rights' (BDS, online). This campaign, it is argued, attributes guilt by association to Israeli citizens in sporting, cultural and academic institutions in Israel. It is also argued that the campaign is particularly directed against goods from territories recognised by UN resolutions as occupied, and that cultural or sporting boycotts are not directed at Israeli individuals but at the Israeli government. However, whatever one chooses to believe, it is crucial that the following conclusion from the UK All-Party Parliamentary Group Against Antisemitism is taken very seriously:

> The boycott movement faces challenges of how to put their tactics into effect while not slipping into antisemitism, unlawful discrimination or assaulting valued freedoms. (2015: 114)

We share the above concern that the BDS campaign can threaten valued freedoms such as free speech. So of course can campaigns aimed at stopping BDS. Academics in the UK and elsewhere are frequently required to respond to Freedom of Information requests to provide information on Israeli academic institutions that they collaborate with. While UK academics are required to complete this return (from our experience), the identification of the source of the request is not forthcoming, and some academics are intimidated by the thought of their name being on a particular list. Although Holocaust denial is illegal in many countries (e.g. in Austria, Belgium, France and Germany), we consider that silence is not conducive to debating controversial issues, and support the preservation of academic institutions as environments where individuals can debate political, moral, religious, ethical and scientific issues, free of discrimination and censorship. Whilst there can be, in the same spirit, discussions on whether to boycott Israeli academics, we would argue, in the vein of the quote from the All-Party Parliamentary Group Against Antisemitism above, that tactics need to be developed that are not perceived as themselves racist.

The expression of antisemitism on today's university campuses is commonly associated with the Israel–Palestine conflict. In the UK this is supported by the recognition by the UK All-Party Parliamentary Group Against Antisemitism (2006: 38) that tensions exist between varying student bodies on campuses, and that Jewish students in some campuses were being intimidated and harassed. The election of Malia Bouattia as president of the (UK) National Union of Students (NUS) in 2016 brought new concerns for Jewish students, as Bouattia has faced allegations of antisemitism for comments she made while describing the University of Birmingham, a university which has one of the largest Jewish societies in the UK (*Guardian*, 2016b). These concerns have been heightened by the applause given at the 2016 NUS conference to a delegate who spoke against the commemoration of Holocaust Memorial Day on the grounds that doing so singled out the Holocaust and ignored other global atrocities (*Independent*, 2016b) – a statement that was not only offensive but also factually incorrect, as we show in Chapter 5.

Further tension is evidenced by the jointly organised event by the Israel societies at King's College, London, and London School of Economics (2016), at which the former Chief of Israel's Secret Service was the guest speaker. This event was gatecrashed by members of King's College London's Action Palestine society, who threw chairs, set off fire alarms and called Jewish students 'Nazis' (Firsht, 2016). Police were called and students were evacuated from the building. At the time of writing this book, there is an enquiry into allegations of antisemitism amongst students of the Oxford University Labour Club (OULC). In his resignation speech, Alex Chalmers, co-Chair of this student body, highlighted the problems within the Club:

> Whether it be members of the executive throwing around the term 'Zio' (a term for Jews usually confined to websites run by the Ku Klux Klan) with casual abandon, senior members of the club expressing their 'solidarity' with Hamas and explicitly defending their tactics of indiscriminately murdering civilians, or a former co-chair claiming that 'most accusations of antisemitism are just the Zionists crying wolf', a large proportion of both OULC and the student left in Oxford, more generally, have some kind of problem with Jews. (*Independent*, 2016b)

Further evidence of antisemitic behaviour linked to the Israel–Palestine conflict was the behaviour of Paul Donnachie at St Andrews University (BBC, 2011). Donnachie, a supporter of the Scottish Palestine Organisation, defiled an Israeli flag that hung on the wall of an American Jewish student and called this student a 'terrorist'. After being found guilty of a racial breach of the peace, Donnachie claimed that this ruling was 'ridiculous' as he was a member of an anti-racist campaign.

Conclusion

This chapter has addressed the often neglected issue of antisemitism, with the intention of supporting educators in their understanding of the Holocaust and in their delivery of good quality Holocaust Education. Wistrich (1994) referred to antisemitism as 'the longest hatred', and we have certainly not suggested in this chapter that there are any signs of antisemitism abating. Indeed, like other forms of racism, antisemitism is inextricably linked to the political, social and economic conditions, and in times of crisis comes to the fore. We have shown that traditional expressions of antisemitism which were based on religion and racial ideology continue to exist alongside new manifestations of antisemitism, which are based on political ideologies. Our chapter has not painted a rosy picture of mutual respect and citizenship in universities, although it is important to stress that they are taking these issues seriously. For example, Donnachie (mentioned above) was later expelled from St Andrews University.

It is also worth recognising the collaborative efforts of anti-racist organisations which aim to defeat the politics of hate and extremism. One example of this is the international UN anti-racism day (19 March) which has the slogan 'Refugees Welcome Here: Stand up to racism, Islamophobia, antisemitism & fascism!' (Stand Up to Racism, 2016). Another example is Golders Green Together (GGT), which was launched after a Neo-Nazi rally was planned in 2015 in the London suburb of Golders Green to protest against its 'jewification'. This organisation comprised members of HOPE not Hate and the London Jewish Forum. The rally was successfully moved elsewhere in London, and waving a Palestinian Confederate flag, Neo-Nazi demonstrators, who included members of the Golden Dawn party, were outnumbered by a counter protest from the newly formed GGT.

Holocaust Education will not eradicate antisemitism, but it can play a vital part in addressing young people's misconceptions of Jews and in addressing Holocaust denial and distortion. We consider that teachers' understanding of the history of antisemitism, irrespective of their own beliefs, politics and ideologies, will not only assist their teaching of the Holocaust, human rights and Citizenship Education, but also contribute to their understanding of current and future expressions of antisemitism. One present challenge is that legitimate critique of Israeli policy does not slip into antisemitism. Antisemitism is racism and both are always unacceptable.

Further Reading

For surviving examples of *Judensau* sculpture:
www.concordatwatch.eu/topic-50027.834

For the full transcript of Lord Sacks' address to the House of Lords:
www.rabbisacks.org/every-religion-must-wrestle-dark-angels-today-must-jews-christians-muslims-alike/

5

THE COMPLEXITIES OF HOLOCAUST REMEMBRANCE

Learning Objectives

- To explore the links between Holocaust Education, Citizenship Education and Holocaust remembrance and commemoration
- To explore different forms of Holocaust remembrance
- To identify competing perspectives on Holocaust commemoration

Remembrance, Memory and Commemoration

At one level, the word 'remembrance' is misleading as the act of remembering applies to those with living memory of a specific experience, and very soon there will not be a student or educator with personal experience of the Holocaust. This type of memory, also referred to as 'primary memory', contrasts with 'secondary memory', which arises from criticality of primary memory either by the person who has the living memory of the experience or by another person, such as an historian (LaCapra, 1998: 20). We consider that 'remembrance' applies to both these types of memory and that 'commemoration' is a form of remembrance that principally refers to an act of collective memory at an event.

The above distinction of memory emphasises the significance of the presence and contribution of survivors to Holocaust commemoration events as their living testimonies build on one's knowledge of the Holocaust. The same is true of other eyewitnesses of the Holocaust and other genocides. Welzer's (2010) research findings, from interviews with members of German families, were that narratives changed as they transmitted across generations and 'stories about a grandparent's role during the Nazi regime tended to become more positive as the interviewers spoke to successively younger generations' (see Erll, 2011: 313–14). Erll writes that the younger generation's memory of the Holocaust is a combination of what he refers to as 'cosmopolitan memory' of the Holocaust, a memory which is based on narratives surrounding human rights, justice, tolerance, democracy, anti-racism and antisemitism which are central to citizenship, and global memory which is impacted by cultural and family memories (2011: 315).

Knowledge is integral to remembrance as without this all forms of remembrance lack meaning and truth. In the context of a traumatic event, LaCapra explains that the relationship between history and memory is problematic as such an event is 'repressed or denied and registers only belatedly after the passage of a period of latency' (1998: 9). This is especially true of the Holocaust which has impacted on victims, perpetrators, collaborators, bystanders, resisters, their descendants, and other individuals born in more recent times in Germany, Nazi-occupied countries, and in other nation-states. Yet the troubled relationship between history and memory, and indeed the political priorities of nation-states, makes memory problematic. An example is the dissolution of the Soviet Union in 1991 which can be used to show the complexities that often accompany Holocaust remembrance. After the Second World War, the Soviet Union was interested in remembering and discussing experiences and the suffering of its Soviet citizens and not specifically that of the Jews during the Holocaust. This led to a silence and a lack of knowledge about the Holocaust across the Soviet Union. Hence countries like Ukraine are only now beginning to explore the fate of their Jewish communities, and Holocaust commemorations in countries such as Moldova and Albania are currently in the process of development.

LaCapra's assertion (1998: 3), that memory of the Holocaust often marginalises or downplays some factors at the expense of emphasising others, is relevant to Holocaust commemoration, as indeed it is to all contested history. His examples of emphasis include the banality of evil and industrialised mass murder: examples of marginalisation are the 'glorification of extreme transgressions' and the 'unheard-of excess' in the Nazi treatment of Jews. The narrative around trying to explain the Holocaust in light of the Eichmann trial in 1963, the memoirs of survivors such as Wiesel (1960), Levi (1947) and others, and the sociological explanations of Arendt (1963) and Bauman (1989), suggested that the emphasis on banality, the ordinariness of the perpetrators and modernism developed a clearer understanding than some concept of undefined evil. Levi, for example, argued that the key importance of the memory is that we understand that the 'Final Solution' was neither exclusively German nor exclusively in the past: he claimed 'It happened therefore it can happen again ... it can happen, and it can happen everywhere' (1989: 167). It is clearly inappropriate to focus on the horror in schools as all school-based Holocaust Education requires to be age-appropriate (see Chapter 7). Further, it is unlikely that the general public would be interested in attending a Holocaust commemorative event if its pro-grammes focused on this, as these horrors are unpleasant and disturbing. Yet it can be argued that the representation of the Holocaust that is adopted at commemorative events is a particular representation that appeals to the populace and facilitates an understanding of the Holocaust that, by its concealment of important factors, leads to a perception that the Holocaust was gentler than its barbaric and cruel reality.

Stone (2010) claims that this particular representation is largely a result of the focus by historians on Nazi ideology and the industrial genocide of the Jews which, in light of recent archival evidence from Eastern Europe, needs to be rethought. He explains that since the 1990s, findings in coun-tries where little was previously known about the Holocaust (e.g. Serbia, Belarus, Galicia, Lithuania, Latvia and Estonia) have challenged com-monly held perceptions of the Holocaust. Stone explains that the killings across Europe increased in pace in countries such as Ukraine and Lithuania, where local 'perpetrator groups shared the objective of elimi-nating the Jews' (2010: 464). One of the challenges of Holocaust commemoration in Europe is the acknowledgement by the above Eastern European countries and others to confront their past, with regard to the collaboration that took place in their respective country. If this is not achieved, 'Nazi Germany' and/or nameless others will remain the only perpetrators in narratives at Holocaust commemorations in these coun-tries, and lessons *about* and *from* the Holocaust will never be learned.

Stone cites Romania as an example of a sovereign state that was never occupied by the Wehrmacht, whose regime, under the pro-Nazi dictator Ion Antonescu, tried to 'solve the Jewish question in the Romanian way' (2010: 463). Antonescu was executed in 1946 as a war criminal. Stone explains that Romania's Head of State, 1967–89, Nicolai Ceauşescu, did not want it publicly known that Romanian (excluding northern Transylvanian) and Transnistrian Jews were mostly killed by Antonescu's regime and not by Nazis. This provides further evidence of a disparity between common narratives in Holocaust commemoration and actual events.

Holocaust Remembrance

As the Holocaust is 'a global object of remembrance' (Erll, 2011), this section merely attempts to explore forms of Holocaust remembrance that raise issues about knowledge, memory and Holocaust remembrance. The starting point is memorial sites, museums and memorial museums. The term 'memorial museum' usually describes a museum that is built on a site where a historical event has taken place that contains a collection of associated objects which are memorial in nature. One example of this is the Memorial Museum for Children of Izieu in Izieu, France; one exception is the United States Holocaust Memorial Museum. Museums and memorial museums educate the public on the state's narrative, and as a result there will be significant differences as to what is being remembered transnationally and over time.

Blum (2004) reported that when he visited the Auschwitz-Birkenau Holocaust Memorial and Museum in 1989, this museum's narrative was based on the victimisation of Polish citizens and resistance to Nazism. This did not adequately recognise the distinctive fate of the Jewish and Roma as ethnic groups targeted for extermination. Yet this was clearly addressed when Blum returned to the museum in 2003. This experience highlights the transience of historical remembrance of the Holocaust, and demonstrates the power of the state to ensure a particular interpretation of the Holocaust is conveyed by museum staff to visitors. Gross (2009) additionally claims that museum designers may also want to construct a particular message for their visitors. As museums and memorial museums include growing numbers of online visitors as well as actual ones, museums' narration of historical events now has greater impact than before.

Memorials too come in different forms and we have selected the following four because of the messages they convey. The first is the *Stolpersteines*, which literally means 'stumbling stones', which are cobbled plaques that are embedded into the pavement in front of homes where people lived before they were deported. Each plaque bears a stark text, with the name of the victim, birthdate, date of deportation and, if known, date and place of death. This ongoing project began in 1996 and was created by artist Gunter Demnig. Each plaque is commissioned by a person who wants to commemorate family members, friends and/or neighbours in this way, and the installation is sometimes accompanied by a laying ceremony. To date there are 50,000 *Stolpersteines* in nearly a thousand European cities. First established in Germany, they can now be found in Austria, Belgium, the Czech Republic, France, Hungary, the Netherlands, Norway, Russia and Ukraine. While they are memorials that personalise the Holocaust and inform passers-by that victims of the Holocaust used to live on this street, they were, until recently, prohibited in Munich as its members of the Jewish community claimed that the plaques conveyed a mixed message about Holocaust remembrance. They considered walking over a memorial to be disrespectful to victims' memories. This led to these plaques being dug up in Munich in 2004. However, the city subsequently reversed its decision and approved the *Stolpersteine* project in 2015.

The second memorial is a beautiful five-storey building in Berlin, on Friedrichstraße 17, which, although not open to the public, stands out in the street with a tall placard informing passers-by of the significance of this building to the Second World War. The placard has a black and white photograph of a German SA soldier (a 'brownshirt') aiming his rifle at a group of men whose arms are raised, and is accompanied with the following information, in German and English:

> ***The early concentration camp 'Gutschow-Keller' was located here.*** *The greengrocers Hermann and Paul owned this imposing building in Wilhelminian style in Friedrichstraße 17 on the opposite side of the street. Already in 1932, they placed their warehouse and basement at the disposal of the 'SA-Sturmbann 111/8'. These rooms were located here in the second courtyard of the building in Friedrichstraße 234.*
>
> *From March to May 1933, the place was one of the first concentration camps in Berlin. Prisoners called it 'Bluthburg' (castle of blood). Hundreds of trade unionists, communists, social democrats and Jews were seized in their homes, at their places of work and in the middle of the street and were then abducted to this place. Interrogations, torture and humiliation followed – often for days on end. As these torture chambers of the SA were placed in a large tenement block, the neighbours knew about the imprisonment and maltreatment, for the screams of the prisoners could still be heard on the street.* (Aktives Museum Faschismus und Widerstand in Berlin, 2012)

This provides evidence of the terror that took place in the early days of the Nazi regime and that people living nearby would have known what was happening. It also builds on one's knowledge of a concentration camp as this elegant building has no obvious camp appearance. Further, it provides an example of the willingness of a city to confront its dark past and to encourage its visitors and citizens to engage with its history.

The third memorial is the Shoes on the Danube in Budapest, the city that is home to the largest synagogue in Europe. Erected in 2005, this memorial comprises 60 pairs of old-fashioned shoes of different sizes that are made of bronze and set into the ground at the edge of the River Danube, not far from the Hungarian Parliament. A named Budapest 'attraction' in travel books, this memorial is on the tour guides' lists and visitors with deeper connections with the victims often light candles or leave flowers beside the shoes. Accompanied placards inform visitors that the monument is 'To the memory of the victims shot into the Danube by Arrow Cross militiamen in 1944–45'. This brief caption (written in Hungarian, English and Hebrew) does not inform visitors that the overwhelming majority of victims were Jewish. This is an example of the State conveying the message that Hungarian citizens suffered at the hands of other Hungarians, which while true, ignores the antisemitism that existed in Hungary at that time, and distorts the memory of these murders.

Budapest is an example of a Nazi–occupied city that remembers the Holocaust in many ways. In addition to the above memorial, this includes a statue of Raoul Wallenberg, and the naming of a wharf in his name, and in the name of Jane Haining, a Church of Scotland missionary who worked in Budapest. Both Wallenberg and Haining have been honoured by Yad Vashem as Righteous Amongst the Nation, a title awarded to non-Jews who risked their lives during the Holocaust to save Jews from extermination by the Nazis. That said, the final memorial in this section, the Memorial to the victims of the German invasion, is one that is causing controversy in this city. Erected in 2014 in one of the most famous parks in the centre of Budapest, this statue depicts a bronze German eagle, with '1944' marked on one of its talons (representing the year of the German invasion of Hungary), descending on the Archangel Gabriel (representing a passive 'innocent Hungary'). This has received criticism both from within and outside Hungary. Eggs have been thrown at the statue, and at the time of writing, a small number of Hungarians daily demonstrate against this memorial, and a makeshift counter-memorial has been set up across the road. Though the Hungarian Prime Minister, Viktor Orbán, has stated that this is not a Holocaust memorial, its message that Hungary was a passive victim of Nazism who cannot be blamed for her actions during the Holocaust, has serious implications as to how the Hungarian Government wants the Holocaust to be remembered. The following notice has been tied with a ribbon in the Hungarian colours at the counter demonstration:

'Say no to the falsification of history, the national memory poisoning, the state-level Hungarian Holocaust denial!'

This memorial is included in this chapter to show that the relationship between practices of remembrance and Holocaust history can be fraught and complex; memorials can be a deliberate reconstruction of the past that erases reality and creates new collective memories, and the responsibility of ordinary citizens can be heavy. The pig farm on the site of the Lety concentration camp in the Czech Republic, a camp for Roma families, which during the Holocaust was under the protectorate of Bohemia and Moravia, takes this to a new level. The refusal to provide a fitting memorial for these victims, many of whom were children, is about people's attitudes today, and not about those of the past.

Holocaust Commemoration

In exploring Holocaust commemoration, one should firstly understand the distinction between two principal forms, namely *Yom HaShoah* (see p. 2) and International Holocaust Remembrance Day. *Yom HaShoah* was established by the Israeli government in 1953 and has since become a day commemorated by Jewish communities and individuals worldwide. Its official name is Holocaust and Heroism Remembrance Day, and it takes place on the 27th day of the Hebrew month of Nisan to commemorate the uprising of the Warsaw Ghetto. This Day is a time to reflect on, learn about, and recite *Kaddish* (a prayer recited by mourners usually after the death of a close relative) for the six million Jewish people who were murdered in the Holocaust. In Israel this is a day of unusual solemnity, with a single air-raid siren sounding across the country at 10.00am and people stopping whatever they are doing for a two-minute silence. The Holocaust is a living memory to more than one million survivors, and various memorial events and activities are held on *Yom HaShoah* across the country. Elsewhere in the world, Jewish people will attend a local event (usually organised by an organisation or institution within their Jewish community) on this Day.

In this century, the introduction of an annual international day of commemoration of the Holocaust by the United Nations (see p. 2), is formally recognised by more than 80 states in the United Nations. In the UK, Holocaust Memorial Day is promoted and supported by the Holocaust Memorial Day Trust (HMDT), whose website states that this Day is:

> '... a time for everyone to pause to remember the millions of people who have been murdered or whose lives have been changed beyond recognition during the Holocaust, Nazi Persecution and in subsequent genocides in Cambodia, Rwanda, Bosnia and Darfur.' (HMDT, n.d.)

This explicitly shows that, despite its name, the focus of Holocaust Memorial Day is neither exclusively about the Holocaust nor about the genocide of the Jews. The insertion of 'Nazi Persecution' suggests that a collective memory of those who suffered in the years preceding the Holocaust is encouraged on this Day. This broader model of Holocaust commemoration is adopted by many nation-states as well as by the United Nations and UNESCO. Former UN Secretary-General Kofi Annan spoke to delegates of the UN General Assembly, in his opening address at this session marking the sixtieth anniversary of the liberation of Auschwitz, about

> ... the State of Israel – [which] rose, like the United Nations itself, from the ashes of the Holocaust. (UN, 2005)

This justifies why *Yom HaShoah* continues to be commemorated widely in Israel, although it has, to a lesser extent, commemorated International Holocaust Remembrance Day since 2006. Jewish people around the world continue to commemorate *Yom HaShoah and* International Holocaust

Remembrance Day. The mainstreaming of Holocaust discourse in the media and in schools that has accompanied Holocaust Remembrance Day has encouraged Jewish people of all ages who were previously uncomfortable about developing their understanding of or discussing the Holocaust to do so. One form of collective memory that is closely linked with *Yom HaShoah* is the March of the Living, as it is on this Day that participants walk the three kilometre march, from Auschwitz to Birkenau, and participate in the memorial service at Birkenau. Principally (though by no means exclusively) aimed at Jewish people around the world, participants include Holocaust survivors. Placards are held showing participants' country of residence and many drape themselves in Israeli flags with the star of David, a Jewish emblem and iconic image of the Holocaust. Established in 1988, this form of commemoration is sometimes criticised for being more about strengthening Jewish identity than engaging in historical enquiry and opposing prejudice, racism and other forms of bigotry, and as we point out in Chapter 7, the misunderstanding of the differences between Jew and Israel can be problematic in some circumstances, yet the sight of thousands of young Jewish people marching through Auschwitz is a moving sight, especially given that many of them would not be alive today had Germany won the war.

Secondly, one should be aware of the Day of Remembrance of the Extermination of the Roma and Sinti, which remembers the loss of Roma and Sinti during the Holocaust, in the same way as *Yom HaShoah* is a time for remembering Jewish loss of life. This Day has more recently been established on 2 August, the day on which the 'Final Solution' of the 'Gypsy Family Camp' in Auschwitz-Birkenau was planned. It honours the thousands of Roma people who were murdered in the gas chambers there. Introduced in Poland in 2011, this Day recognises the immensity of the loss and suffering that the Roma and Sinti endured during the Second World War by the Polish State. Similar commemorative days such as Romani Resistance Day are held on this day in the Slovak Republic, Romania and Ukraine, and at different times in the year in Austria and Croatia.

Thirdly, there are additional days of Holocaust commemoration that reflect a country's historical narrative. Examples of these are: National Remembrance Day for Victims of the Nazi Concentration Camps in Poland (14 June), which marks a day in 1940 when hundreds of Poles were taken to Auschwitz; Day for the Victims of National Socialism in Austria, which marks the day of liberation of the Mauthausen concentration camp (5 May); and a commemoration of *Kristallnacht*, the 'Night of the Pogrom' or 'Night of Broken Glass', in Germany, where it took place (9–10 November). *Kristallnacht* is also commemorated in the UK, where hundreds of child refugees from Austria, Czechoslovakia, Germany and Poland went on the *Kindertransport programme*, an operation that was prompted by *Kristallnacht*.

The UK Context

Early research findings (Burtonwood, 2002; Cowan and Maitles, 2002) suggest that the introduction of Holocaust Memorial Day in the UK has significantly contributed and facilitated school-based Holocaust Education. Our findings above demonstrated that in one local educational authority in Scotland, 21 out of a possible 24 primary schools taught the Holocaust in some form during the 2000–2001 school session, while previously only eight of these schools had regularly taught the Holocaust and 14 had never taught it. This supports the principle that remembrance builds on one's knowledge and understanding of the topic of remembrance. Unlike in England where the (UK) Holocaust Memorial Day event has, since 2012, been held in London, there is a tradition in Scotland that the (Scottish) national Holocaust Memorial Day event is hosted in a different town or city each year. The common practice of preceding this event with a schools' event for upper primary and secondary pupils extends the reach of Holocaust commemoration and motivates schools and communities in these areas to get involved.

The following experience demonstrates that teachers do however require support in teaching the Holocaust. A few years after Holocaust Memorial Day was introduced, one promoted primary teacher in Scotland who was keen to teach the Holocaust in the upper primary stages told us that after discussion with his stage partner, a newly trained teacher, on his proposed sequence plan and learning outcomes, in preparation for the programme, the stage partner explained that while she was looking forward to teaching the topic as it looked really interesting and something that her pupils would find engaging, she did however have one question. That question was, 'What was the Holocaust?' Her colleague had mistakenly assumed that his stage partner had this knowledge. Given that until the establishment of Holocaust Memorial Day, the Holocaust had not been taught widely in schools in Scotland, this should be no surprise. A requirement for continued professional development at the most basic level is one unforeseen consequence of Holocaust commemoration. The other requirement, also related to professional development, is the pedagogical considerations that teachers require to make and the skills they need to develop that will support pupil engagement with the Holocaust. These are discussed in Chapters 7 and 8.

Holocaust Memorial Day was, for many years, boycotted by the umbrella Muslim organisation, the Muslim Council of Britain (MCB) (2001–2007, 2009) and by other key Muslim community organisations. The MCB considered that 'Holocaust Memorial Day' was too focused on Jewish suffering, and requested that this be renamed Genocide Memorial Day which would, they claimed, be more inclusive in its acknowledging 'the murders of Muslims in Palestine, Chechnya and Bosnia'. One Muslim reported that calling it 'Holocaust Memorial Day' conveyed that 'western lives had more value than non-western lives', and claimed that Muslims felt 'excluded' from this commemoration (Werbner, 2009: 444). The MCB officially removed this boycott in 2012.

With its broad remit, the programme for a Holocaust Memorial Day (HMD) commemorative event can comprise an even amount of content on the Holocaust and subsequent genocides, or focus heavily on one and marginalise the other. This Day does not therefore guarantee an opportunity for students to learn and/or consolidate the basic facts of the Holocaust as we have presented in this book (see Chapter 2 pp. 21–22). This partially explains the following comment from a man during the UK HMD event in 2003 in Edinburgh. As we waited for Princess Anne and other VIPs to take their seats, he said that he had attended the previous year's (Scottish) Holocaust event, and when asked what he had thought of it, he shook his head and said, 'It was too much about the Jews'. While the preference for Holocaust commemoration to be 'less Jewish' is somewhat disconcerting, at best this was an insensitive comment, and at worst racist, as one would assume that the Jewish experience during the Holocaust would be given a high profile at such an event. It certainly suggested that this invited guest was keen for more content on other victims of the Holocaust and other genocides. In contrast, at another national UK HMD event a few years later, one Jewish invited guest commented that the word 'Jewish' was conspicuous by its absence in the programme. This suggests that people have different expectations of the Day. This is precisely why, as we outline throughout this book, lessons on the Holocaust have to include *about* and *from*.

It is important to understand that while the national commemorative event is central to the Day, Holocaust Memorial Day encourages a plethora of Holocaust and Holocaust-related activities. It is reported that more than 2,400 activities take place each year in schools and local communities across the UK (Cabinet Office, 2015). One unique example was the Anne Frank + You Festival which lasted for three weeks in January 2007 in Fife, Scotland. This developed through the energies of senior pupils from three local secondary schools in partnership with national and local education and cultural services. Overall, more than 7,000 young people actively engaged in learning about Anne Frank, the Holocaust and twenty-first century issues at this 'Festival'. Activities included a debate on the effects of technology on conflict led by Professor Heinz Wolff, a talk by Anne Frank's cousin Buddy Elias (1925–2015), and a workshop on web blogs on how Anne Frank would have written her diary had she been alive today (Cowan, 2008a, 2008b). At the climax and conclusion of this Festival was the hosting of the (Scottish) national commemorative event, which involved more than 1,000 people participating in a candlelight procession that simulated the March of the Living (Fife Regional Council, 2007: 3). Although some may consider the word 'Festival' inappropriate in the context of Holocaust commemoration, this initiative provided high quality events and attracted a large number of young people who had never commemorated the Holocaust before.

Competing Perspectives of Holocaust Commemoration

At the same time as Holocaust commemoration has become a global phe-nomenon, competing perspectives have emerged. One of these perspectives, the Nakba (see p. 6), extends outside Europe, but several are held in Europe. As its name suggests, the Time of Remembrance and Reconciliation for Those Who Lost Their Lives During the Second World War, observed by the United Nations since 2004 on 8–9 May, which coincides with Victory in Europe (VE) day (8 May), is an occasion for people to pay tribute to *all* victims of the Second World War. This large group of people includes some three million German soldiers who were killed in the Soviet Union and Eastern Europe, as well as victims and perpetrators of the Holocaust. While it is clear that many Germans *were* victims of the Second World War, and indeed of the Holocaust, the concern of this commemorative day is that it reinforces the idea that Germans were victims and not accomplices of the cruel Nazi regime, and provides an opportunity for non-German perpetrators to be recognised as victims too. Whilst at one level correct, it is important that we do not confuse perpetrators – those who actively collaborated with the Nazis – with victims.

The controversial notion of German victimisation is illustrated by the response to the visit by former US President Ronald Reagan to Bitburg Military Cemetery, Germany, in 1985. This visit was viewed by many as a part of West German Chancellor Kohl's strategy to rewrite German his-tory, as 49 members of the Waffen SS (the armed force of the SS that rivalled the German army) were buried in this cemetery; Kohl had removed this organisation from a list of right-wing groups that the West German Ministry of the Interior was required to make for reports to Parliament in 1983. Reagan later outraged many people by equating dead German soldiers with the victims of the Holocaust.

Another competing perspective comes from Neo-Nazis and right-wing fraternities. This is shown in the commemoration of fallen soldiers of the German Army in Austria by German right-wing nationalists (8 May), the officially banned Day of Honour in Hungary which commemorates the Hungarian and German soldiers' (that included members of the Waffen SS and the Arrow Cross) failed attempt to stop the Soviet siege of Budapest (11 February), and a march by Neo-Nazis in Ukraine (on Holocaust Memorial Day) to commemorate the creation of the 14th Waffen Division, the Ukrainian version of the SS, that was a volunteer brigade of Galicians, comprising mostly ethnic Ukrainians who briefly served the Nazis against the Red Army.

The Middle East and some radical political positions provide further perspectives. In 2009 the Scottish Palestine Solidarity Campaign hosted Azzam Tamimi, who condoned suicide bombing in Israel, to speak at an event to mark Holocaust Memorial Day. Tamimi was a supporter of Hamas, an organisation that the USA, Canada and other countries recognise to be a terrorist organisation and whose military wing is also recognised as terrorist by the UK and Australia. It has been widely acknowledged that the use of this Day as an anti-Israel campaigning strategy debases and abuses the memory of the Holocaust, and has been widely condemned.

In 2008, the European Union designated 23 August as the European Day of Remembrance for Victims of Stalinism and Nazism. This Day's intention is to promote vigilance against totalitarianism, yet equating Stalinism and Nazism obfuscates the memory of both the Holocaust and the Second World War. Expecting Europeans to unite in remembering victims of Stalinism, some of whom were perpetrators of the Holocaust, has similarities with the above-mentioned UN Time for Remembrance and Reconciliation Day. It is highly contentious, especially when several countries in Eastern Europe have yet to acknowledge and face up to their crimes in the Holocaust. For example, Ephraim Zuroff, director of the Wiesenthal Centre's Israel office, has stated that the Baltic countries' 'prosecution of local Nazi war criminals has been an abysmal failure' (Katz, 2010). His justification for this is that not a single person has been punished for their crimes in the Holocaust in these countries, countries which are recognised as being victims of communism. This Day perpetuates a newly created notion of the equalisation of the evils of Nazism and communism under Stalin, and encourages acceptance of the 'double genocide' model. This is not conducive to Holocaust remembrance, memory and commemoration.

Conclusion

At a meeting, in the late 1990s, to obtain feedback from the Glasgow Jewish community on establishing a national Holocaust Memorial Day, one elderly lady (who was married to an Austrian refugee) commented, 'This sounds a good idea, but what good has ever come from bringing attention to Jews?' Cowan had little idea then of the possible tensions that would be created by this Day or of the range of people's expectations. Cowan replied that this Day had the potential to bring educational benefits as young people in Scotland (at that time) knew very little about the Holocaust.

Establishment of this Day has led to school-based Holocaust Education being more mainstream in both primary and secondary sectors in the UK. The impact of this Day on schools is likely to be at its highest in countries where the Holocaust is not included in the curriculum, as the Day can be a stimulus for teaching the Holocaust. In addition to classroom teaching, Holocaust Education has also contributed to schools' international and outdoor education programmes by students visiting Holocaust museums and memorial sites. Yet the many forms of antisemitism that Jews are faced with today (see Chapter 4), and increasing antiziganism in Europe, suggest that Holocaust commemoration does not eradicate hatred and prejudice towards Jews, or the largest ethnic group in Europe, the Roma.

Holocaust remembrance, memory and commemoration come in many shapes and forms and state support is crucial to their success. This implies that the sustainability of any form of Holocaust remembrance requires state intervention. This is fine when the state is supportive in strengthening and developing an understanding of the Holocaust, and is committed to confronting its own role in the Holocaust. However, it becomes problematic when the state agenda is to remember the Holocaust in a way that is laced with particular beliefs and prejudices, ignores the basic facts of the Holocaust, distorts existing memories, and reconstructs the past by creating new collective memories. This has particular resonance for the commemoration of the European Day of Remembrance for Victims of Stalinism and Nazism.

Further Reading

A three-minute film of the response to the siren in Israel: 'Today is *Yom HaShoah*, the Holocaust memorial day in Israel'. www.youtube.com/watch?v=tYm43CalGSQ

Klarsfeld, S. (1985) *The Children of Izieu: A Human Tragedy*. New York: Harry N Abrams.

Tell Your Children (2007), a five-minute film on the 1945 January mass murders by the Arrow Cross at the Danube bank, director András Salamon. www.youtube.com/watch?v=OKpznsxZews

For pictures of the four memorials in this chapter

Stolpersteine in Berlin:
www.stolpersteine-berlin.de/en

Concentration camp 'Gutschow-Keller':
www.gedenktafeln-in-berlin.de/nc/gedenktafeln/gedenktafel-anzeige/tid/konzen
trationslager/

The Shoes on the Danube Promenade – Commemoration of the Tragedy:
www.yadvashem.org/yv/en/education/newsletter/31/shoes.asp

German occupation memorial completed under cover of darkness:
http://budapestbeacon.com/public-policy/german-occupation-memorial-
completed-under-cover-of-darkness/10320

6

THE IMPORTANCE OF LANGUAGE

Learning Objectives

- To clarify the meanings of key words in Holocaust Education
- To emphasise the concise use of language
- To highlight the issue of gender inclusivity
- To demonstrate the connection between political literacy and Holocaust Education

In the previous chapter we indicated that the use of the word 'festival' in the context of Holocaust commemoration can be considered to be inappropriate (see pp. 66–67). Our justification is that a festival is a day or period of celebration and has connotations of fun and frivolity which do not fit well with the seriousness of the issues of Holocaust Education, remembrance and commemoration. In the Anne Frank + You Festival, the word 'festival' was used by young people to attract young people's engagement, and it is possible that this title contributed to its success. This suggests that in the context of the Holocaust, language can be used in ways that some people may disagree with.

One example that may achieve a greater consensus in its inappropriate use of language is the use of road signs by an authority who hosted the national (Scotland) Holocaust Memorial Day event, that read 'Holocaust' followed by an arrow directing drivers the correct way. On arrival to the car park, the attendant greeted visitors with, 'Are yous for the Holocaust?' While this misuse of language is, on one level humorous and harmless, on another, it may have caused offence to guests, especially Holocaust survivors and their families who were attending the commemorative event. It is because of the impact that language has on one's thinking that we have decided to begin the section on teaching approaches in this book with literacy issues.

It is clear from our experience as teacher educators that teachers are well aware of the importance of the language they use in class. Teacher talk includes asking questions, challenging and encouraging students, explaining concepts and ideas, and summarising facts and events. In Scotland, literacy is promoted by the General Teaching Council for Scotland, the independent professional body that promotes and regulates the teaching profession in Scotland, and emphasises the contribution of literacy in maintaining professional standards by requiring teachers to 'model appropriate levels of literacy in their professional practice' and 'promote competence and confidence in literacy' (GTCS, 2012). It is further highlighted by Education Scotland in their emphasis that all school practitioners, i.e. not just teachers of English language, have the responsibility to develop and reinforce young people's literacy skills. Teachers' use of language is therefore very important, and inconsistent or indeed incorrect use of vocabulary can lead to students' misconceptions of the Holocaust and/or adversely impact their understanding of the Holocaust.

One specific type of literacy, political literacy (see Chapter 3, pp. 30–31), is a key component of Citizenship Education, and a major factor in young people's decisions as to whether they will participate in the state's decision-making process or not. Political literacy is crucial to a young person's evaluation of societal issues and the nature of their participation in society. Davies and Hogarth (2004) claim that political literacy may be the most challenging aspect of Citizenship Education. This type of literacy is dependent on one's application of critical thinking skills which can only be achieved when students have the language of argument. This language includes the skills to: support a point of view through the use of examples and facts; show the difficulties with a specific course of action or policy; and refute counter arguments and persuade others. Political literacy is also dependent on one's knowledge of political concepts, contexts and parliamentary language.

We argue throughout this book that our task is not to impose an ideology onto students but instead to teach them critical thinking and how to evaluate evidence; to step back, gather the facts, and analyse why. The key part of any discussion on the Holocaust is that students analyse the issues and recognise that the rhetoric and language used by others are dehumanising. In this context, language matters. Dehumanisation, often through language (the fourth stage of genocide; see Chapter 2, p. 17), may not always lead to genocide, but is indicative that a problem exists. Dehumanisation allows not only genocide, but also crimes against humanity, war crimes, human rights abuses, and many other forms of violent and non-violent practices. So teachers should always encourage debate and discussion, but should also understand that when they encounter rhetoric that can be construed as dehumanising, they need to stop and analyse and ask why? This is not meant to stifle debate, but to continue the analysis. How and why are central to academic debate, but so is understanding that the use of language contributes to dehumanisation and concepts of hate speech.

Teachers and educators must not underestimate the support that students need with language in this teaching context. Even a discussion of seemingly simplistic words such as 'good' and 'evil' requires a range of language skills. Consistency and accuracy in teachers' use of language are features that teachers, as growing professionals, assume they deliver, yet the reality is that they strive to achieve this. We have already demonstrated that the Holocaust and Holocaust remembrance mean different things to different people, and this justifies a consistency in the concise use of language and clarification of the meaning of words that are commonly used in school-based Holocaust Education and can be easily misunderstood. The remainder of this chapter focuses on such words in an attempt to address this.

(i) Nazis

A Nazi is defined as 'a member of the National Socialist German Workers' Party' (see *Oxford Dictionary Online*, n.d.). There are three features of this word that can be problematic. The first is its political feature pertaining to the meaning of 'Socialist' in this context. One common feature of socialism is equal opportunity yet the Nazis applied this exclusively to racially pure Aryans, who according to Nazi ideology were the superior race. Discrimination, persecution and extermination of people deemed inferior were permitted, and at the peak of Nazi popularity and strength were also encouraged. This form of socialism was not characterised by the absence of private property, as party members stole and expropriated property and possessions belonging to people (that included German citizens) whom they drove from their homes, most industries were privately owned, and trade unions were abolished. This justifies why Nazi ideology is commonly perceived to represent a form of capitalism. The Nazi Party developed a racist and antisemitic ideology, abolished basic freedoms, advocated a right-wing authoritarian government, and established a totalitarian dictatorship. All of the above demonstrates the strong links between Holocaust Education and political literacy.

Today, the word 'Nazi' is also used in a derogatory way to describe 'a person with extreme racist or authoritarian views' (*Oxford Dictionary Online*, n.d.). In 2008, British radio presenter Jon Gaunt called his guest on air a 'Nazi', and a 'health Nazi', for wanting to ban smokers from fostering children. He was suspended from his job and later sacked after losing his appeal. The High Court upheld the complaint under the rules regarding offensive material.

In the Middle East context, Israelis have been compared to Nazis, although we consider this to be an example of the misuse of language commonly associated with the Holocaust. For those who oppose Israeli policies, such as building settlements in the West Bank, it is important that they make it clear that there is not, and has never been, Israeli policy or ideology of the genocide of Palestinians in the Middle East. For those supportive of Israel, Israeli actions toward Palestinians it is argued are based on the necessity to defend the population of Israel (which includes more than one and a half million Israeli Arabs, and about 300,000 non-Arab Christians and Bahais) and respond to threats to Israel's security. Associating the primary victims of the Holocaust (Jews) with its main perpetrators (Nazis) is inflammatory, chilling, and diminishes the significance of the Holocaust. While the actions and behaviour of the State of Israel towards its Palestinian neighbours are not beyond criticism, it is incorrect and provocative to use the worst and most traumatic collective experience of the Jewish people against Jews. As this narrative spreads, teachers must be vigilant. This too emphasises the links between political literacy and Holocaust Education.

The second is its inclusive feature. 'Nazis' is not equivalent to 'Germans', although there is a tendency for educators to use these words interchangeably and/or for the word 'Nazis' to be generalised to apply to all Germans in the armed forces in the Second World War. This is incorrect as not all Germans were members of the Nazi Party. For example, the Wehrmacht, the German armed forces, were comprised mainly of non-Nazi German soldiers, although they were required to swear an oath of allegiance to Hitler. The assumption that all Germans were Nazis flies in the face of evidence suggesting that nearly three million Germans passed through the concentration camps, and indeed, the Nazi Party itself was angry that more Germans could not be made to undertake antisemitic violence.

It was a high-ranking Wehrmacht soldier, Claus von Stauffenberg (1907–1944), who as Chief of Staff attempted to assassinate Adolf Hitler at the Fuehrer's 'Wolf's Lair' headquarters. Armed with explosives in his briefcase, von Stauffenberg placed the briefcase on the floor at a briefing meeting. Although the bomb was detonated moments after he left the room, and four people were killed in the explosion, Hitler was only injured slightly. This became known as the July Plot and shortly afterwards von Stauffenberg was executed by firing squad.

There were also members of the Nazi Party who did not directly support Hitler or Nazi policies. Of these, perhaps the most famous is Oskar Schindler (1908–1974) who joined the Nazi Party in 1939. Through bribery and other means, Schindler prevented more than 1,000 Jews from deportation to the death camps. To strengthen his claim that his Jewish employees were essential for the German war effort, he added an armaments manufacturing division. When relocating this plant to Brunnlitz, Moravia, in 1944, he drew up a list of 1,200 Jews whom he 'needed' to work. This list became known as 'Schindler's List'. Although Schindler was arrested several times on suspicion of giving unauthorised aid to Jews, he successfully tricked the Nazi authorities by presenting bogus production figures, producing very little ammunition and saving more than 1,000 Jews. Less well known is Major Karl Plagge (1897–1957) who joined the Nazi Party in 1931, and saved more than 250 Jews in the Vilnias ghetto, Lithuania. Responsible for repairing military vehicles damaged on the eastern front, Plagge insisted that all the Jews in his repair garage were skilled mechanics and essential to the war effort. Though Schindler and Plagge were exceptional, their actions demonstrate that some Nazis acted against Nazi policy.

The third relates to gender. Gender inclusivity has clear implications for Holocaust Education. One thinks of images of men and women (and of course children) when one thinks of victims of the Nazis, but do they convey a balanced gender representation of Nazis? Educators rarely acknowledge the behaviour of female Nazis, and prefer to focus on the maternal and child-bearing roles of women in Nazi Germany as these are considered important to students' understanding of Nazi ideology. While Josef Mengele, Rudolf Hoess, and Adolf Eichmann are notorious Nazi figures, female Nazis are unknown to most school students. Many death camps had female sections and approximately 10% of the camp guards were female. Interestingly only 5% of these female guards were members of the Nazi Party. Of these were Irma Grese (1923–1945) and Maria 'The Beast' Mandel (1912–1948), both sentenced to death for murder and crimes and atrocities against the laws of humanity. Grese was known as the 'Beautiful Beast of (Bergen) Belsen', and Mandel was the chief guard of the Birkenau women's camp. However, in her study of the role of women in Nazi Germany Lower states,

> The first Nazi mass murderess was not the concentration camp guard, but the nurse. Of all the female professions, she was the deadliest. (Lower, 2014: 120)

Lower justifies this by explaining nurses' participation in the mass murder that followed from the euthanasia programme, and in newly appointed roles to develop the racial state. Perhaps it was because German women were not part of the Nazi leadership that the significance of German women in the Nazi system is sometimes overlooked. Lower states that most secretaries were members of the Nazi Party or active in its organisation. However, not all women who became perpetrators and killers were agents of the Nazi regime; many were mothers, girlfriends, or wives of Nazis. Lower makes two important points about these women's participation: firstly, that none of them had to kill; and secondly, that refusing to kill a Jew would not have resulted in punishment, although helping a Jew was an entirely different matter. This made it easier for women to distance themselves from the Nazi regime, yet

> ... thirty thousand women were certified by Himmler's SS and police as auxiliaries in gendarme offices, Gestapo headquarters and prisons ... and the likelihood of direct participation in mass murder was high. (Lower, 2014: 7)

It is important not to generalise about the role of women in the Reich, or indeed to recognise that sadistic women were the norm. However, we argue that acknowledgement of these women's roles contribute to one's understanding of Nazis and the Third Reich, and should not be overlooked.

Research demonstrates the under-representation and diminished role of females in history textbooks and curricula (e.g. Blumberg, 2007; Fardon and Schoeman, 2010). Kenig (in Cowan et al., 2014) writes that the absence of women is one issue and *how* women are represented is another. In this she states that historical literature reinforces traditional gender roles of women that include being wives and mothers, anonymous victims and impoverished peasants. This, in turn, Kenig argues, reinforces the idea of the superiority of man over woman. This explains why History has been referred to as *His-story* within the feminist critique since the 1960s. Kenig continues that 'History and remembrance become powerful instruments for maintaining the gender asymmetry' (2015: 9). This has clear implications for school-based Holocaust Education and is further discussed in Chapter 8.

(ii) Jews

The word 'Jew' is derived from the Hebrew word *Yehudi*, meaning a member of the tribe of Judah (in Hebrew, *Yehudah*) who was Jacob's fourth son. It is a word that continues to be used in a negative and offensive way. In 2002, during a talk show on Al-Jazeera television discussing the reconciliation of Kuwait and Iraq after the Iraqi invasion of Kuwait (1990), a guest described Kuwaitis 'as the Jews of the Arabs'. The Kuwaitis were insulted and sued the television station. This shows that the word 'Jew' is considered derogatory to some people in the Arab world. More recently there was a report of school students using the word to insult each other in the playground (Rosen, 2011). In this report, charity worker Tamara Pollard, who works in a mainly white non-Jewish area, stated:

A few weeks ago a group of kids, aged about eight or nine were shouting antisemitic insults. They were calling each other 'tight Jew'. I asked the ringleader if he knew any Jews and he said he didn't, so he looked pretty stupid in front of his friends and I thought that was the best way to deal with it.

Last week I heard children aged between nine and 11 saying 'scabby Jew' and 'f***ing Jew'.

This justifies Short's statement that before teachers begin to teach the Holocaust they should 'explore and if necessary challenge their students' perceptions of Jews and Jewish culture' (2015: 456). According to Short, this approach is rarely used.

Of the 14.2 million Jewish people in the world, 43% reside in Israel. It is worth noting that the population of Israel comprises around 75% Jews, 21% Arabs, and 4% of people from other faiths such as non-Arabic Christians and Bahai (Central Bureau of Statistics (Israel), 2015). In addition to European Jews there are Jewish communities in Africa, India, Australia, North and South America and China. As Jewish people live throughout the world, they speak different languages and belong to different races and nations. The two main Jewish cultural groups are Ashkenazi, who are Western Jews (i.e. Jews from France, Germany and Eastern Europe), and Sephardi, who are from Spain, Portugal, North Africa, and the Middle and Far East.

Defining individuals who are Jewish can be complex, as according to Jewish law a Jew is a person whose mother is/was Jewish or who has gone through a formal process of conversion to Judaism. Hence an individual is Jewish irrespective of his lack of observance of any Jewish customs and/or religious laws. While this applies to Orthodox and Reform Judaism, Liberal Judaism additionally recognises an individual with a Jewish father.

Maitles (2012) emphasises that in the Holocaust 'the genocide of the Jews was a result of Nazi racist ideology and not simply religious persecution'. In Nazi Germany, the Nuremberg Laws (1935) defined a 'Jew' as someone who had three or four Jewish grandparents; the individual's religious beliefs or whether they identified themself as a Jew or not were irrelevant. Even individuals whose Jewish grandparents had converted to Christianity were defined as Jews. This included Roman Catholic priests and nuns, and Protestant ministers. This definition was adopted in Germany and Nazi-occupied territories throughout the period of Nazi rule. Children of Aryan and Jewish parents who were born before the Nuremberg Laws were therefore 'half-Jewish', although they had only two Jewish grandparents. These partial Jews or *mischlinge* were never declared Jewish, although according to Jewish law, if their mother was Jewish, then they too were Jews.

Issues over definitions of Jewish identity are further complicated by the persecution of Jews. One example of this was in the late fourteenth to the middle of the fifteenth century in Spain, where laws were oppressive towards practising Jews and conversion was provided as an alternative to death. This led to more than 100,000 Spanish and Portuguese Jews being forced to convert to Christianity to escape persecution, but secretly practising Judaism. These Jews were called *Marranos* or *conversos*. This situation has not been consigned to history, as around 70,000 Jews lived in a similar situation in Ethiopia until the 1970s, when the former Israeli Prime Minister Menachem Begin encouraged the immigration of Ethiopian Jews to Israel. Known as *Beta Yisra'el* (House of Israel), but often referred to as *falashas*, a derogatory term that means 'stranger', one school of thought is that Ethiopian Jews are the descendants of the lost Dan tribe.

Another example was a consequence of the persecution of the Jews by the Nazis. The case of Shmuel Oswald Rufeisen (1922–1998), also known as Brother Daniel, demonstrates another struggle with Jewish identity. Rufeisen was a Polish Jew who fled to Vilna (now named Vilnius) to escape the Nazis, and with a gift for languages had talked his way into a variety of jobs. One of these was in the German military police, and in this role he helped Jews escape from the Mir ghetto in Belarus before its liquidation. Soon after this he too had to go on the run and hid for safety in a convent. Rufeisen converted to Christianity in 1942 and joined the Carmelite Monastery in Krakow in 1945. When he moved as Brother Daniel to Israel in the 1950s to lead the Carmelite monks in Haifa, he asked to be listed as a Jew under the Law of Return which grants every Jew in the world the right to live in Israel. The Israeli rabbinate, i.e. the group of rabbis who comprise the religious governing body in Israel, ruled that Rufeisen should be awarded citizenship as he was a Jew born to Jewish parents. However the Supreme Court did not agree. It ruled in 1962 that an individual could not be both a Catholic priest and a Jew. The complexity of this case was truly exceptional, but the information is presented here with the aim of broadening readers' understanding of this key word.

In Chapter 4 we discussed the synonymity between Zionists and Jews in the context of antisemitism. It is worth mentioning here that while mainstream Judaism (Orthodox and Reform) supports the existence of the Israeli state, there is one small faction of orthodox Jews, the *Neturei Karta* (an Aramaic word, meaning 'Guardians of the City'), who are anti-Zionists. These Jews oppose the State of Israel, as they believe that according to Jewish faith and law the Jewish people are forbidden to have their own state while waiting for the Messiah. These Jews recognise Israel as the Holy Land, and support Jews living there; those living in Israel refuse to serve in the Israeli army. They do believe that Jews have a right to the Land of Israel, but only at the future time of redemption. This explains the pictures on social media sites which show orthodox Jews joining radical Muslims in demonstrations against Israel and burning Israeli flags. Their support of anti-Zionism has nothing to do with the Middle East conflict, and educators should be aware that Jews in these pictures belong to this marginal sect.

(iii) Roma (Gypsies)

We could have easily not included 'Roma' in this chapter on the grounds that if the treatment towards the Roma in the Holocaust is *The Forgotten Genocide* (see p. 7), teachers can be excused for overlooking this in their teaching. As we include the Roma in our definition of the Holocaust, we consider that 'Roma' should be a commonly used word in school-based Holocaust Education, and would therefore seek to clarify this term.

The *Oxford Dictionary* defines a Gypsy as 'a member of a travelling people traditionally living by itinerant trade and fortune telling. Gypsies speak a language (Romany) that is related to Hindi and are believed to have originated in South Asia' (*Oxford Dictionary Online*, n.d.). This meaning is unhelpful in that it perpetuates common stereotypes of Travellers, and does not recognise the diversity within this group of people, or their rich culture. Myers (2012: 201) asserts that 'Gypsy' is a generic umbrella term that 'can describe a lifestyle as well as signify ethnic status'. The Roma were first called 'Gypsies' because Europeans mistakenly believed they had come from Egypt. The word 'Gypsy' is therefore a construct.

During the Second World War, Gypsies came from Sinti and Roma families; Sinti referred to members of the minority living in Western and Central Europe and Roma to those of eastern and southeast European origin. In contrast to the 'half-Jews', the *mishchlinge* above, who had a chance of survival in the Reich, Bauer (2002: 62) writes that in the Holocaust, 'the main assault on the Roma was on the "half breeds", because the danger, from a Nazi point of view was one of penetration of Gypsy blood into the Aryan race'. Bizarrely, Bauer claims that pure Roma in the Reich had a chance of survival, yet it is clear that the Nazis wanted to eliminate the Roma as bearers of an alternative culture to Aryanism.

Today the term 'Roma' is commonly used in EU policy documents although it encompasses Roma, Sinti, and other groups such as Travellers. With an estimated population of ten to twelve million Roma in Europe, they are currently the largest European minority group. Like Jews, they live in different countries and have their own unique culture. In the UK context, the combined term 'Gypsies and Travellers' is often used; 'Gypsies' to refer to the above indigenous communities of Roma (or Romani) Gypsies; 'Travellers' to refer to Scottish and Irish Travellers and other distinct groups, such as Occupational Travellers, Showpeople and New Age Travellers. While these groups may share a nomadic lifestyle, they do not share an ethnicity and have distinctive cultures and subcultures. Like the word 'Jew', the word 'Gypsy' can be used in an offensive and derogatory way.

(iv) Camps and Ghettos

The word 'camps' in the context of the Second World War connotes a range of images, all harsh and cruel, of individuals incarcerated in confinement. They include prisoners of war (POW) camps, detention or transit camps, concentration camps, death or extermination camps, slave labour camps, and displaced persons camps. As we are focusing on the Holocaust, this section will focus on the camp system that the Nazis developed as a means of persecution. But before doing so, it is important to acknowledge that Jews from the Allied countries fought for their country in the armed forces throughout the Second World War, and that some of these were captured and imprisoned in POW camps. For example, around 100 Jewish soldiers were prisoners at Colditz Castle in Saxony. These included Anthony 'Fish' Karpf (1913–1993), a Polish officer born in Rzeszow, and Irish-born Captain Julius Green (1912–1990), a dental officer. Karpf was subjected to a mock execution at Colditz, and eventually escaped (from another camp) and came to live in Scotland; Green worked for MI9 in the prison camp and sent coded letters to his family. So too were there British Jewish soldiers who were imprisoned in the POW camps in the Far East. One of these, Captain Dr Allan Berkeley (1912–1990) from Glasgow, wrote an affidavit on 'The Matter Of War Crimes Committed By Japanese Nationals And In The Matter Of The Ill-Treatment Of Prisoner Of War (Civilian Internees) At Fukuoka' (Berkeley, n.d.).

In teaching the Holocaust, educators must be cautious in their general usage of the word 'camps' as this can be used to refer to all Nazi camps. History texts will often cite the existence of tens of thousands of Nazi concentration camps. While the number of Nazi camps is alarming, such numbers include all the camps and ghettos. Research by Megargee and Dean (Megargee, 2009; Megargee and Dean, 2012) reports on more than 40,000 camps and ghettos, and they are determined that every camp and ghetto should be historically archived, and that knowledge of the scale of the camp system is not confined to a few household names.

Within a year of their existence ... SS chief Heinrich Himmler gained control of the camps (from the police) and established a uniform system regarding the admission and supervision of prisoners. (Baumel, 2001)

Initially built in Germany and Austria, concentration camps extended to Nazi-occupied territories, such as Latvia (e.g. Kaiserwald in Riga), and to countries whose governments were affiliated with Nazi Germany, such as Struthof in Alsace, France, and Jasenovac in Croatia. The Jasenovac complex has been referred to as the *Dark Secret of the Holocaust* as it was not, by definition, a Nazi concentration camp. This is because it was established by the Ustaša authorities of the so-called Independent State of Croatia and not by Nazi authorities; it was staffed by Croatian political police and personnel of the Ustaša militia, which was the paramilitary organisation of the Ustaša movement, not members of the SS. Its victims were Jews, Roma, ethnic Croats, Serbs and Muslims. This demonstrates the influence of the Nazis in Europe and evidence that the camp system led to large-scale torture and murder carried out by fascists outside Nazi Germany.

It follows that it would be good practice for teachers to consistently specify the type of camp in their lessons. This however is not an easy approach to adopt as the term 'concentration camp' itself presents challenges. In addition to being used generically, 'concentration camp' can be defined as 'a camp in which people are detained or confined, usually under harsh conditions and without regard to legal norms of arrest and imprisonment that are acceptable in a constitutional democracy' (USHMM, n.d.). One problem with this definition is that it can virtually apply to all of the above camps! Another problem is that while the Nazi concentration camps were in 1933 initially aimed at political and ideological opponents of the Nazi regime, after 1938 Jews were also targeted for these camps. The forced labour imposed on these prisoners led to the larger concentration camps setting up satellite camps (e.g. Neuengamme, Gross-Rosen at Sachsenhausen), and this explains the interchangeable use of the terms 'labour camps' and 'concentration camps'.

However, the main challenge is that the camp system expanded as the Second World War progressed and the Final Solution was implemented, with many camps changing their status. For example, Majdanek was established as a POW camp in 1941 before it became a concentration camp and then a death camp. Each of the six death or extermination camps were originally built as concentration camps.

'Concentration camps' were named thus because of the physical 'concentration' of the imprisonment of individuals in one confined facility, although it can be argued that a similar concentration equally applied to the conditions of inhabitants of the ghettos. Ghettos were established as temporary enclosed areas, with restricted access, comprising streets to segregate Jewish people from the rest of the population. They were temporary as the plan was to deport their inhabitants to concentration and death camps. Some ghettos, e.g. the Kovno ghetto in Lithuania which was established in 1941, were converted into a concentration camp (e.g. the Kauen concentration camp in 1943). With reference to Stanton's stages of genocide, segregation in ghettos represents the seventh stage and confinement in concentration, forced labour, or death camps represents the eighth (see p. 17). Many ghetto inhabitants died from disease or starvation.

It is essential that educators explain the meaning of 'ghetto' in the Holocaust context as its contemporary meaning is quite different. The *Oxford Dictionary Online*, n.d.) defines 'ghetto' as 'a part of a city, especially a slum area, occupied by a minority group or groups'. This describes the present-day reality for migrant communities in many European and non-European cities, and inner city areas in the USA where there is a disproportionate percentage of ethnic minorities (usually African Americans and Hispanics). It does not describe the abuses of personal freedom and the forced nature of segregation and poverty that was imposed on the Jews in the Holocaust. The word 'ghetto' was derived from the Venetian *getto*, a segregated area of Venice, enclosed by walls and gates in which Italian Jews, in the early sixteenth century, were compelled to live. It is therefore essential that educators who refer to the above dictionary's definition accompany this with sources that convey information of Nazi policy and the purpose and nature of ghettos in the Holocaust context, to ensure students understand the differences between ghettos in historical and contemporary contexts.

Transit camps were used as a holding place for people before their deportation to the death camps or forced labour camps. They were situated in Nazi-occupied territories, usually in places with good rail connections to the east. These included Drancy in France, Westerbork in the Netherlands (though it also had a permanent camp population), Mechelen in Belgium, and Theresienstadt in the Protectorate of Bohemia and Moravia. These camps were staffed by Germans. Once captured, Anne Frank and her family were taken to Westerbork and stayed there from 8 August until 2 September 1944. There they were assigned to barracks and worked all day breaking up old batteries before they were deported east. Otto Frank wrote:

> Of course, all of us had to work in the camp, but in the evenings we were free and we could be together. For the children especially, there was a certain relief; to no longer be cooped up and to be able to talk to other people. However, we adults feared being deported to the notorious camps in Poland. (Anne Frank Museum, online, n.d.)

The six death camps were Auschwitz-Birkenau, Belzec, Chelmno, Majdanek, Sobibor, and Treblinka. They were initially established to function as concentration camps and all were built in Poland. The most well known of these is Auschwitz-Birkenau, principally because of the scale of the murders that occurred there, but also because that every year visitors to the reconstruction and remains of this camp include tens of thousands of educators and school students from across the world. Where concentration camps served primarily as detention and labour centres, as well as centres for the murder and torture of individuals, death camps served primarily as centres for the mass murder of human beings in an assembly-line style (USHMM, n.d.). Educators should consistently strive to distinguish between these two types of camps as they had two clear and distinctive purposes. Death camps are also called 'killing centres' and 'extermination camps', and we suggest that school educators refer to these as 'death camps' as we consider this to be easier for young people to understand.

While we have demonstrated the challenge of specifying each type of camp, we consider that it is important for educators to avoid, where possible, use of the generic word 'camp'. We consider that students have a better chance of understanding the Holocaust and of understanding survivor testimony if educators have knowledge of the different types of camps and of the appropriate terminology to convey this knowledge.

Educators also need to exercise caution in their use of 'died', 'murdered' and 'killed'. The word 'died' is only accurate if it is used in a suitable context that explains the death. For example, 'people died in Bergen-Belsen from the typhus epidemic' is accurate, but 'millions of people died in the Holocaust' is inaccurate. This is because victims of the Holocaust did not die through natural causes, or an unavoidable accident; those who 'died' in the camps did so through maltreatment or illness inflicted on them by a lack of food and water, hard labour, and poor sanitation, which individuals in power were responsible for. Telling students 'millions of people died in the Holocaust' is therefore meaningless and can lead to students having misconceptions about the Holocaust. The words 'murdered' and 'killed' are accurate words which describe the deaths of the victims of the Holocaust, as these words explicitly convey that these deaths have been *caused* by someone. The Holocaust was not a tsunami, a natural occurrence; it did not either 'have to happen or happen by accident' (Jerichow, 2011: 146). Even though genocides have distinctive features which make each genocide unique, this feature is true of all genocides. It is our professional responsibility that through our use of language, this key message is communicated to every student.

Displaced Person Camps

There were over seven million displaced persons (DPs) who, when peace was declared in 1945, were placed in Displaced Person Camps before their repatriation or return home. These comprised Jewish refugees who were either former inmates of the concentration/forced labour and death camps, or people who had survived by either being in hiding or constantly on the run, prisoners of war, East Europeans who had fled from Communist rule, and Nazi collaborators from Eastern Europe who had murdered Jews. By September 1945, six million DPs had returned to their home countries. More than 250,000 DPs were Jewish, many of whom could or would not return to their home countries. These camps became active Jewish cultural and social centres, with schools, synagogues, theatre and musical groups, sports clubs and their own newspapers.

Set up in the Western occupation zones of Germany, Austria and Italy as temporary facilities, these camps were administered by the Allied Authorities and the United Nations Relief and Rehabilitation Administration (UNRRA). Due to difficulties in repatriating DPs, and the British restriction on Jewish immigration to Palestine, these temporary camps became homes to survivors of the Holocaust for many years. One month before the establishment of the state of Israel in 1948, 165,000 Jewish people were still living in DP camps in Germany; this number reduced to 30,000 five months later (Brenner, 2001).

One can understand why, for these people, the dates indicated in our preferred definition of the Holocaust (see p. 7) do not ring true. The end of the war and the liberation of the concentration and death camps signalled a return to a new life for many DPs, but not necessarily their individual freedom. Many had to wait several years for this. The last DP camp closed in 1957.

Conclusion

Irrespective of what we teach, our use of language is crucial to the achievement of our lesson outcomes. In school-based Holocaust Education, this is arguably even more important as teachers require to avoid students leaving their classrooms with misconceptions about the Holocaust that they have contributed to, due to their lack of clarity and conciseness of language, or their under-representation of women in the Holocaust.

That is not to say that educators should try to do everything. One primary student, for example, at the end of a lesson on the Second World War (and not on the Holocaust), said with a large smirk on his face in front of his class, which included a Jewish student, 'My dad said that Germans killed all the Jews in the war'. His intention was to provoke and upset the Jewish student, and no doubt test the teacher as well. The teacher explained that his dad was mistaken as Jews currently lived in countries all across the world: her priority was to defuse the situation and respond to a potentially racist student, rather than explain in detail the distinction between Germans and Nazis!

We wrote in Chapter 4 of the ways in which language commonly associated with the Holocaust is being used to convey new expressions of antisemitism. The transience of language further justifies this, as some of these words are likely to develop different meanings over a period of time. This is another reason why young people must have a clear and accurate understanding of the key words listed above when they are learning about the Holocaust.

Further Reading

Lower, W. (2014) *Hitler's Furies: German Women in the Nazi Killing Fields*. London: Vintage.

Biography of Shmuel Oswald Rufeisen
Tec, N. (1990) *In the Lion's Den: The Life of Oswald Rufeisen*. London: OUP.

7

PEDAGOGY

Learning Objectives

- To demonstrate the importance of personalisation in examining the Holocaust
- To outline why teaching the Holocaust is a controversial issue, highlighting parents with alternative views/beliefs systems and attitudes to the consensus in society
- To confirm student entitlement to express an alternative/abhorrent opinion from that of the teacher and the link with teacher confidence
- To provide insight into teaching the Holocaust to students with additional support needs
- To outline strategies for teaching the Holocaust to Muslim students, taking into account possible conflicting narratives
- To highlight good practice for interdisciplinary learning in the secondary school

---

The Holocaust as a Controversial Issue

There is little debate about the Holocaust per se or indeed whether it should be taught at some stage to school students. Whilst there are some who think it should not be taught (discussed below), the Holocaust deniers who argue there was no genocide are in reality marginalised within society. However, there are some issues relating to controversy that we need to examine.

Firstly, teaching areas such as the Holocaust, genocide and the abuse of children's rights is upsetting for many students and teachers. It is a matter of debate as to whether these areas can effectively be taught to students without some level of distress. In that sense, teaching the Holocaust is no different from teaching other controversial or difficult topics where there have been hundreds, thousands or millions of victims. There are topics where, because of the scale of the crimes, there can be a lack of engagement with the evidence. Pedagogically, the best way of dealing with this is through personalising the events. By that we mean developing in our students a sense of identification with the particular rather than the abstract. The effect of this was seen in September 2015, when the picture of a refugee child washed up on a Turkish beach engendered a mass worldwide sympathetic activism which made governments reconsider their attitudes towards migrants and refugees. The identification with this victim by millions of people ensured that national politicians could neither ignore nor vilify the refugees. The picture personalised for people what reports of hundreds of people drowning could not. Similarly with teaching the Holocaust, the pedagogical approach of personalisation is a powerful strategy. Student identification with, for example, *The Diary of Anne Frank* or other literature in the field (further developed in Chapters 8 and 9), or the approaches taken by, for example, the United States Holocaust Memorial Museum, elicit a strong sense of empathy and understanding from students. As one History teacher put it:

> 'I think showing photographs of dead bodies or mass graves can only traumatise students and cause disengagement, as students are usually unable to deal with or process images like this and simply switch off. I believe students find it hard to grasp the concept of six million victims. They can however, understand and empathise with one individual and their family.' (*Guardian*, 2012)

Primo Levi (1919–1987), as a witness to the Holocaust and Auschwitz, is so powerful as a writer precisely because his testimony and reflections concentrate on the individual. His power is to transmit the horror and the hope through the experiences of an individual, whether himself or another prisoner, or an (occasional) sympathetic guard, or indeed a collaborator or perpetrator. Through the individual story, whether of Lorenzo, an Italian forced labourer who risked his life on many occasions to help Levi, or Elias, a brutalised individual who had lost all shreds of decency, readers capture the essence of humanity and the barbarism that sought to destroy it. This is the power of personalising the events.

Secondly, and linked to the point above, are teachers' worries about their skills to handle open-ended discussions which they might not be able to control or direct. There are also structural constraints in schools from the lack of tradition in discussion to the physical layout of classrooms. A further issue in primary schools, as we noted in Chapter 2, is a perceived lack of teacher subject knowledge (The Historical Association, 2007). As we mentioned in Chapter 1, the key findings of a study that involved more than 2,000 secondary teachers in England indicated that while teachers perceived themselves to be 'knowledgeable' about the

Holocaust, responses to knowledge-based questions revealed 'important gaps in historical understanding' (HEDP, 2009: 6). This led to the development of a Continued Professional Development Programme in Holocaust Education for secondary teachers in England, which comprises a two-day workshop presented by the Centre for Holocaust Education.

Paradoxically, in secondary schools a study of political consciousness in 28 European countries (Torny-Purta et al., 2001) found that in many countries teachers were afraid to tackle controversial issues because, almost by definition, the discussion becomes multidisciplinary and they are uncomfortable in that zone. However, in analysing how secondary school students understood the place of classroom discussion, Hahn (1998) found that students in the Netherlands did not try to persuade each other, even when discussing highly controversial issues that they felt strongly about, whereas in German and US state schools and English private schools there was strong argument and persuasion. Interestingly, Hahn found that there was virtually no discussion on political issues in the state sector in England, even in Social Science classes where she gathered that the primary purpose of the teaching and learning was to prepare for examinations.

The role of the teacher in this is crucial. As Agostinone-Wilson (2005), Ashton and Watson (1998) and Cowan and Maitles (2012) suggest, a teacher needs to be confident enough and have the honesty to suggest to students that they are not just independent observers but have a point of view, which also can and should be challenged. Whilst this is an area of some discussion in the UK, Wrigley (2003) points out that in Germany teachers are encouraged to allow discussion around controversial issues, present a wide range of views, and be open about their own standpoint whilst allowing for all views to be challenged. Indeed, it is crucial, according to Ashton and Watson (1998), that teachers understand their proactive role where necessary, otherwise backward ideas can dominate the discussion. Students have little problem with this and are not as dogmatic as adults when it comes to changing attitudes and political understanding.

In addition, there are worries about what parents might think about controversial discussions, and the influence of the mass media and politicians as to what might be perceived as influencing students one way or another. For example, in the TEACH report mentioned above there was one school in England whose History department 'avoided selecting the Holocaust as a topic for GCSE coursework for fear of confronting antisemitic sentiment and Holocaust denial among some Muslim students' (The Historical Association, 2007: 15). The BBC reported this online under the title 'Schools "avoid Holocaust lessons": some schools avoid teaching the Holocaust and other controversial history subjects as they do not want to cause offence, research has claimed' (BBC, 2007).

Teachers fear meeting antisemitic sentiment, particularly from Muslim students, related to events in the Middle East. It is our contention that this approach is a mistake and that the lessons of the Holocaust should be learned in all situations. As Yad Vashem (Avraham, 2014) put it 'The value of learning about the Holocaust is based on the assumption that the Holocaust is an historical event of universal ethical significance'. The Holocaust shows how destructive and murderous hatred of the other can really be. And even though Jews were marked as the primary enemy of the Nazi ideology, victims of the Holocaust also included other ethnic 'undesirables' whose right to exist was denied by the Nazis. Consequently, the educational imperative of teaching the Holocaust in countries with people from different ethnic, cultural, religious or national backgrounds can help one arrive at a deeper understanding of the need to establish a society that is open, tolerant, capable of including others on equal terms, and willing to see the strength that diversity can bestow.

In addition, the Holocaust is recognised as one of the chapters in history that has shaped Europe and even the world today, and its study can lead to a better understanding of historical movements and ideas whose activities continue to wield influence. As the Illinois Holocaust Memorial and Education Centre points out 'Students who feel that the suffering of their own people or group has not been addressed may be resistant to learning about the persecution and murder of others' (Illinois, 2010). This suggests that students can become disengaged or offended because they feel their perspective is not being considered. But if teachers capitulate to these students by avoiding any discussion of this controversial subject, contemporary politicisation will have silenced historical truth.

Teachers can encounter serious differences between minority and non-minority students' approaches to lessons on the Holocaust in the multi-ethnic classroom, although we should be clear that not all minority students will share the same perspective. For example, some students with Arabic backgrounds have difficulty separating their perception of Jews in the Holocaust from their perception of Jews in the Israeli-Palestinian conflict. In Denmark, one teacher commented that for 'Danish students the issue is political … [but] for Muslim kids in school, it's religious and personal' (Larsen et al., 2012: 2).

In England, the HEDP study of teachers also asked about teaching the Holocaust in culturally diverse classrooms (Foster et al., 2014). Whilst a majority of those who taught in these classrooms maintained that the cultural diversity in the class did not influence their teaching, there were significant numbers who claimed it did. However, the report also challenged the reports mentioned above on teachers not teaching the Holocaust in classrooms with Muslim students. In this large survey there were no excuses as all teachers taught it. What did happen was that teachers used different methodologies and pedagogies to develop the lessons. Short's (2012) findings in 15 schools in five local authorities in south-east England, where the majority of students were Muslim, were similar. Results were overwhelmingly positive, in that there had been no opposition from parents and students had reacted with horror to the events and generally agreed that the kind of racism towards Jews was completely unacceptable. However, it was less clear whether the horror towards antisemitism then challenged antisemitism now. As Short put it, 'It is thus of concern that a number of them may have completed the course with their anti-Semitic prejudices more or less intact' (Short, 2012: 137). Short summises that the teaching of the Holocaust without discussing Judaism may be the key reason for this.

Classroom Strategies

We believe that how Holocaust Education is developed in ethnic, multi-ethnic and diverse classrooms is fundamentally a pedagogical one, and not something that teachers should shy away from. One strategy is to incorporate learning about genocide and other potentially controversial topics in a human rights perspective. Larsen et al. (2012: 2) maintain that this perspective aims to 'promote the equal treatment of all persons without discrimination'. Human rights-based approaches understand genocide more broadly as an example of rights violations, connecting rather than separating victim and minority groups. For example, the Danish Ministry of Education currently requires Human Rights Education in its high (secondary) school History and Social Science curricula, including elements such as knowledge of the UN Human Rights Declaration and fundamental human rights that must be fulfilled in order to create democracy. Education about the specific genocides mentioned earlier is not mandatory.

National and international school initiatives that strive to integrate human rights as an overlying theme into all subjects, and encourage schools to embed children's rights into their ethos and culture, include Human Rights Friendly Schools, an Amnesty International project under the UN World Programme for Human Rights Education; Anne Frank Schools; and the Unicef UK programme *Rights Respecting Schools*. By putting human rights into practice, one can raise respect, which reduces bullying and discrimination. The environment might also provide a language with which to approach historical subjects that are otherwise shrouded in political connotations for minority students.

A second pedagogical approach, in this case highlighted by the HEDP report, was that some teachers used the cultural diversity positively as a resource to be utilised in the classroom, encouraging students' contributions of personal accounts of racism and prejudice. These teachers argued that relevance to the everyday experiences of the students in the class could give rise to an identification with victims of genocide, including the Holocaust. Interestingly, Heitmeyer (2012) and Zick et al. (2011) found that if someone has antisemitic views they also tend to be islamophobic and anti-immigrant as well. Thus the case for raising the issues becomes more important, particularly in Europe in the light of the June 2016 Brexit referendum result, which triggered a wave of racist incidents, against immigrants, children and grandchildren of immigrants and foreigners in general. The hope is that this is the activity of a small number of bigots, but this clearly needs to be challenged everywhere, and particularly in schools.

A third strategy is to recognise Muslim rescuers of Jews, particularly prevalent during the Second World War in North Africa (Satloff, 2006; Mughal and Rosen, 2010). One elementary school in Berlin included in its study of the Holocaust a visit to Yad Vashem, where students learned about Muslims who saved Jews from the Nazis. They learned about the actions of 17-year-old Refik Veseli from Albania who saved Moshe and Gabriella Mandil and their two children from being captured by the Nazis. Following this visit, staff and pupils voted in 2014 to rename their school the Refik-Veseli-School. This demonstrates how students can look to Muslims as role models who accept and acknowledge diversity and defend human rights.

However, such recognition must not be done at the expense of historical accuracy, and therefore the response of some Muslims, who supported aspects of Nazi policy and practice towards Jews, must also be shown. For example, in the early 1940s, at the same time as Jews were being rescued by Muslims, the Mufti of Jerusalem issued strong support for Nazi policies towards Jews. To highlight these kinds of contradictions is a positive approach, as it suggests that with all historical events there is rarely a unanimous narrative, rather a number of competing narratives.

There is some evidence that within the multi-ethnic classroom developing the Holocaust as a specific case study of genocide can be beneficial. Rutland (2015) found that in Australian schools there was as much resentment from Muslim students towards learning about the Holocaust, but much less so when it was incorporated into a broader study of genocide. One of her interviewees commented that 'learning about genocide as a universal topic that includes the Holocaust is a better way to combat intolerance and anti-Jewish feeling as it draws on the experiences that Muslim students have often personally had and shows the results of targeting a group' (Rutland, 2015: 237).

Concerning the antisemitic views stemming from events in the Middle East, teachers have to patiently explain to students that it is entirely legitimate to be critical of the policies of Israel *and* be vehemently opposed to antisemitism; that antisemitism is an enduring and virulent form of racism which has the same roots and ideas that they too may experience. To conflate the two and oppose Jews as a religious and racial group is to concede to the racists, whereas it is in their best interests to challenge the racism. As one of the respondents to Short (2012: 136) put it, 'I am very conscious to hammer home the distinction between being Jewish and the perception of Israel in the Middle East'.

Classrooms will increasingly contain multi-ethnic students with various political affiliations, and schools must actively address the different needs of this multi-ethnic student body when teaching the history of genocide. If we don't, we will, as Short (2012: 138) points out, 'allow students to struggle silently reconciling fact with fiction, and education with ethnic loyalties, until they come away having learned about nothing but their own uncertainties'.

Finally, a large majority of teachers who responded in the HEDP study (Foster et al., 2014) viewed cultural homogeneity rather than diversity as the problem; that lack of exposure to diversity can lead to misunderstandings and/or prejudices amongst some ethnic majority students. It is not necessarily easier to teach controversial topics such as the Holocaust in ethnically homogeneous classrooms.

Further Pedagogical Issues

It is our contention that it is vital that teachers use the actual word 'antisemitism' when describing events in the Holocaust. There is some evidence that teachers avoid using the word, preferring to describe the actions as racism or persecution. Maitles and Cowan (2006) found that after lessons on the Holocaust a large majority of their sample of primary school students aged 11–12 could define the Holocaust, human rights and racism, but only 5% could define antisemitism. In their discussions with teachers it became clear that they were all committed to Holocaust Education, Human Rights Education and Citizenship Education, but did not use the word 'antisemitism'. On reflection, they said they would do so in the future. Foster et al. (2014), in their study of 80,000 teenagers who had studied the Holocaust in secondary History classes in England, found that only 37% could define antisemitism. Whilst it is true that Nazi policies and actions were clearly racist and full of persecution, we feel it important that young people are able to recognise what antisemitism means if and when they hear it on the news or see the word on the internet.

We have maintained throughout this book that lessons *about* and *from* the Holocaust are linked. In primary school this can be easier, as teachers use more than just History or Religious Studies to develop students' understanding. In secondary school, where subjects are much more discrete and often quite narrow, this can prove more difficult. In terms of teaching strategies it means that in situations where there are limited cross-disciplinary collaborations, RME and History teachers must include a full context for Jewish life in Europe before the Second World War, as well as showing that alongside racists and perpetrators there were a minority of rescuers and a majority of bystanders, and indeed much resistance from both Jewish and non-Jewish partisan and other civilian groups. When this is done, then the explanations of post-Holocaust genocides, atrocities and crimes against humanity can be better developed within their own contexts. This in its turn raises the generalised issues relating to racism, Islamophobia and anti-semitism in the modern world.

Finally, we think it important that teachers include those hidden from history, and in this case we are referring to women who both actively opposed the Nazis and those who rescued Jews. For example, the activities of Sophie Scholl, a young anti-Nazi German student who was one of the founders of the White Rose group and was executed in 1943, aged 22, is an inspiring story. Whilst male rescuers of Jews, such as Oskar Schindler, are well known, it needs to be pointed out that the majority of the 'Righteous' (see Chapter 5, p. 62) recognised by Yad Vashem in Jerusalem (the world-renowned and respected Holocaust remembrance centre) are women. Their stories are outlined on the website in a section entitled 'Women of Valor: Stories of Women Who Rescued Jews During the Holocaust' (Yad Vashem, 2015), listing those who put their lives at risk to rescue Jews. These are not easy issues but these women resisters and rescuers, indeed all resisters and rescuers, are role models to which we and the young people in our charge should aspire.

Teaching the Holocaust to Students with Additional Support Needs (ASN)

We have suggested that the Holocaust has important lessons in all educational establishments and contexts. This includes establishments whose students include students with Additional Support Needs (ASN), particularly because of the well-documented attitudes and practice of the Nazis towards people with disabilities (in England these learners are referred to as learners with Special Educational Needs (SEN) and in the USA and Canada as learners with disabilities). The evidence here is based on feedback from Isobel

Mair School, an all-through special school in Scotland (5–18 years) that participates in the *Rights Respecting School* programme, and whose students have a wide range of challenges. These include profound autism, non-verbal with challenging behaviour, physical and multiple disabilities, and students who study for National Qualifications. The Holocaust is taught to secondary students and the whole-school Holocaust Memorial Day commemorative event is an occasion which staff refer to as a 'shared moment' for the student and staff community.

Holocaust teaching in this school began in response to inappropriate comments or jokes in school made by students who had heard about Hitler from the internet and/or media to their peers who had a Jewish background. While they had an awareness of Hitler as an individual, they did not understand his relevance in history, or understand the emotional impact of the Holocaust.

Although teaching the Holocaust has different challenges for different children there is one challenge that applies to most students. One teacher explains:

> 'Do you tell our children that they would possibly have been sent to the camps had they lived in Germany then? That's very tricky as we spend our whole time building our children up to think you can do anything, you're valued, you're loved, and then say to them, "Well there's some people who would have put you to death just for being you." That's a horrible thing and generally, we don't dwell on it ... although it has been mentioned to the more able children.'

For more able students in an ASN setting, learning about the Holocaust is part of their heritage in a similar way as it is for Jewish and Roma students. Explaining that such a tragedy happened to some children like themselves is important in developing empathy.

In this learning context, all programmes are interdisciplinary. Verbal and non-verbal activities are essential for motivating students and for achieving maximum student participation. This involves engagement in a wide range of Expressive Arts activities. Some of the following guidelines have already been discussed in this chapter and we include them briefly again, to emphasise their importance in this specific teaching context:

1. *Develop links with Holocaust Education providers as they can suggest speakers and provide additional support.* Their resources are often used as the starting point for teachers to adapt and make their bespoke materials. The (UK) Holocaust Memorial Day Trust has a section on SEN Resources on its website. In 2016 this included a 'craftivist' activity sheet (Craftivism is a movement that combines craft and activism), and a comprehensive sensory statement which supported SEN students' engagement with commemorative activities by accessing the meaning of the statement on the Holocaust through sensory stimuli as well as through written text.

2. *Invite people to the school to speak to students.* A person is meaningful to students in a way that a film or documentaries are not. It is easier for students to understand one person's story than to understand history in it broadest sense. For students with verbal communication, make this as concrete as possible, allow them to ask questions and interact with speakers. Consider how students' needs can be addressed, e.g. arrange for someone to sign the speaker's story for students with a hearing impairment.

3. *Avoid using euphemisms with students.* Be concrete with your use of language when explaining the who, where, when and why of the Holocaust. Explanations must be clearly understood by students; failure to do so will lead to them establishing incorrect ideas that will be hard to remove. However, be careful not to frighten students and let them think that this could happen to them. Emphasise that it was in the past, and in another country, separating and distancing it from their lives.

4. *Integrate Holocaust teaching with teaching of Judaism.* In this school, Judaism is taught every year; the Holocaust builds on students' understanding of Jewish people.

5. *Integrate Holocaust teaching with teaching citizenship.* The Holocaust builds on students' understanding of prejudice, human suffering and genocides.

Interdisciplinary Learning in the Secondary/High School Context

Regardless of whichever strategy teachers feel might best suit their individual circumstances, it is our contention (as explained in Chapter 3) that cross-disciplinary or interdisciplinary or multidisciplinary learning approaches, although they differ in certain emphases, offer the best learning opportunities in the area of Holocaust and Genocide studies. This, as we also outlined, can be easier in primary school, where teachers naturally use these kinds of approaches in every topic they develop with their students, but is more problematic in secondary school where subject specialisms are often guarded and topics are much more narrowly defined. As Russell (2006) showed, RME teachers often concentrated on moral or ethical issues without putting the Holocaust into a historical context, whereas History teachers often contextualised but did not explain the significances of the events nor the lessons which should be drawn from it, with the former concentrating on lessons *from* the Holocaust and the latter *about*. It is our contention that both must be done. Nonetheless, in our experience it can be developed in the secondary context, albeit this needs much good will, planning and imagination. We now examine this in a case study (Maitles, 2010b).

Rooted in human rights, the project 'One World' took place in a predominantly white school in an area of the West of Scotland with high unemployment. First-year students were joined by associated primary schools, were taken off their regular timetable for 12 days, and set the following schedule of events:

- Days 1–2: 'What does it mean to be human?' This involved leadership and peer pressure issues, in particular the responsibilities of the individual to challenge racist ideas. Activities were led by both teachers from the school and representatives from external organisations.
- Days 3–6: 'Human Rights workshops' These involved both external organisations and subject departments. For example, Maths teachers developed work around percentages using the 'small earth' project, designed to develop awareness of global sustainability, while English teachers focused on supporting students to research and write about inspirational people.
- Day 7–8: Unicef 'Rights Respecting School' activities
- Days 9–10: trips and workshops outside school relating to Scotland, diversity and racism
- Days 11–12: 'The Holocaust and Genocide' This involved the Anne Frank Trust UK, and workshops on the Holocaust and more recent genocides

A values and attitudes survey was devised to examine student attitudes towards political trust/efficacy; diversity/multi-ethnicity; immigration/racism; equality; general hopes for the future; and responsibility for tackling racism. This survey was issued to students immediately before the initiative started and very soon after it ended. Survey 1 involved 111 students (55 male and 56 female); survey 2, 107 students (53 male and 54 female).

In almost all areas relating to values and attitudes there was improvement, and in the cases of Jews, Muslims, Catholics, English and Women, substantial improvement. In the other two cases, Blacks and Disabled, it was virtually the same. This supported findings from Maitles et al. (2006) who found that students in transition from primary 7 to secondary 1 were more tolerant and understanding after learning about the Holocaust. Interestingly, the attitudes towards English people were lower in both surveys than towards any other group. There are a number of possible reasons for this, highlighted by Maitles et al. (2006). Nonetheless, it seems that as far as diversity is concerned, the students came out of the initiative with a stronger support for diversity.

As regards multi-ethnicity, welcomingly, in most areas the results suggested a positive general outlook. Attitudes towards Jews, Asians and Poles improved over the initiative; attitudes towards Blacks and Chinese stayed constant. Worst overall were the attitudes towards English people. They were the most negative in both surveys and actually less positive after the initiative than before. The research also attempted to gauge the attitudes towards both collective and individual responsibility for dealing with racism. The results here were positive, in particular a large increase in the percentage believing that society as a whole should challenge racism, and a welcomingly high response to individual responsibility in both surveys.

There were clear differences between the attitudes of boys and girls in our sample. In every one of the indices, girls were more progressive in terms of citizenship values than boys. Large-scale comparative attitudes surveys (such as Hahn, 1998, or Torney-Purta et al., 2001, or Schulz et al., 2011) do provide valuable information about values and attitudes but don't provide a gender dimension. Prough and Postic (2008) found that female adolescents in the USA were more intolerant of racists and homophobia and more positive towards social equality than adolescent males. Soule and Nairne (2006) found that girls were slightly more interested in politics, more participative, and more politically tolerant than boys. Similarly Badger et al. (1998), who measured gender preferences in terms of caring and personal values, found girls to be more positive. Contrastingly, Flanagan and Tucker (1999) found no consistent gender pattern in adolescents' political attributions, and drawing on interviews and observations with high school students in the USA, Morimoto (2007) argued that boys' and girls' explanations for participating were strikingly similar.

However, there is little of this type of evidence from the UK and this was one of the areas we wished to examine. British studies, for example Archer (2003) and Archer and Francis (2007), examined the values of Muslim boys in the former and British-Chinese in the latter. Whilst most of the evidence is ethnic in nature and shows a generalised racism in schools, a key finding is of a generalised male sexism and a macho 'laddish' outlook that impinge negatively on their values. Cowan and Maitles (2010) found that their adolescents (aged 15–16 years) showed significant gender differences in terms of values and attitudes. The study reported here shows similarity with the research discussed above that girls are much more understanding and tolerant in general than boys. We find clear evidence to support this.

There can be issues when examining this kind of evidence as to whether one sees the glass as half full or half empty. For example, should one be pleased that over three-quarters of the students felt that they had personal responsibility for challenging racism or worried that 25% think that racism has nothing to do with them? Overall, there was evidence of a general improvement in values and attitudes after the students undertook the initiative, although in most issues (excepting attitudes towards gay and English people) there was a high(ish) level before the citizenship initiative. Nonetheless, the fact that in the vast majority of categories students were more positive after than before suggests that the initiative was worthwhile. The caveat to this is that we can only see the improvements as short term; a longitudinal study would be necessary to determine longer-term effects, and it is extremely difficult to eliminate variables over time in this kind of research.

However, the research can be of value as we evaluate the best ways to develop citizenship in young people. There are two particular points to consider: firstly, the involvement of every subject in the school can take Citizenship Education, and in this case Holocaust Education, out of a potential isolation and place its understanding at the heart of the school. The fact that this happened is important for developing one of the aims of the Scottish curriculum and a central plank in most school curriculums, i.e. that there should be opportunities for the development of values and attitudes associated with citizenship. Secondly, the 12 days spent on out-of-class activities, involving outside speakers and trips, gave the students some interesting learning experiences. For example, in their genocide awareness days, the impact of a Rwandan school student outlining aspects of the Rwandan genocide, and the workshop by two senior students at the school outlining their experiences of Auschwitz as part of the Lessons from Auschwitz Project, was powerful for the students and helped their understanding of some of the issues through cross-curricular active learning experiences for deeper learning.

From this small-scale piece of research, the two areas that may need some examination in terms of overall strategy are attitudes towards English and gay people. Negative attitudes towards both are problematic and may not be challenged anywhere in a way that other aspects of discrimination are. Welcomingly, girls are much more relaxed towards the issue of gays, suggesting that boys' sexuality is far less well developed; it would be very difficult for any boy to 'come out' as gay in a situation where only some 40% of boys think there should be equality for gay people. However, it is our contention that this is a pedagogical issue; it is the responsibility of the class teacher to ensure that the homophobic attitudes do not dominate in a classroom where the vast majority of the girls and half the boys do not agree with it. In this sense lessons about the Holocaust, which would also include the murderous intent of the Nazis towards gay people, can be powerful.

Conclusion

It may be tempting for some schools and teachers to avoid issues which will be hard to control in the classroom, and/or may touch upon the sensitivities of students in the class, or particularly in the secondary school, may prove problematic for timetabling reasons – that it is impossible to do justice to the topic in a very short timescale. We think that to avoid lessons *about* and *from* the Holocaust whatever the reasoning is a mistake. Even in the most difficult circumstances, the lessons which can be drawn from the Holocaust if the right pedagogy is used can be powerful and lasting. And such lessons are not just about the past but weigh on our understanding of the modern world. It may be that in individual circumstances the teaching strategies will alter; as we have explained, we believe that in many cases the lessons from the Holocaust are best developed in a human rights and citizenship perspective, and developing where possible a personalisation of the events. The BBC called their programmes on this period *The Nazis – A Warning from History* and *Auschwitz – A Warning from History*, and that is how teachers should see it. As a survivor, making the case for Holocaust Education in the USA, put it (see Chapter 2, p. 16), 'Reading, writing, and arithmetic are important only if they serve to make our children more humane'.

8

TEACHING THE HOLOCAUST IN PRIMARY SCHOOLS

> **Learning Objectives**
>
> - To explore the debate about teaching the Holocaust to primary students
> - To justify teaching the Holocaust to primary students
> - To discuss key pedagogical principles in teaching this age group
> - To identify suitable themes for primary students

Introduction

The Holocaust is taught in many European primary schools and is mandatory in primary and secondary schools in France (where it is called 'the Shoah'). Yet, teaching the Holocaust in primary school is a contentious issue as there is no consensus as to the 'best age' at which to teach it (Supple, 1998: 18), or which aspects of the Holocaust are appropriate for primary students. Totten (1999) and Landau (2008) claim that the history of the Holocaust is too complex and inappropriate for this age group; Kochan (1989) argues that such teaching can be harmful to students. Empirical findings from primary schools in Scotland (Maitles and Cowan, 1999; Cowan and Maitles, 2002) and England (Burtonwood, 2002) challenge this and demonstrate that with age-appropriate resources and suitable methodologies, the Holocaust can be taught effectively to primary students from 10 years of age.

Some Holocaust educational organisations encourage the involvement of younger students. For example, in the UK the Holocaust Memorial Day Trust designs activities for HMD for students from 4-years-old. These age-appropriate activities focus on broad concepts such as the importance or the purpose of remembering, and do not directly refer to the Holocaust. Totten (1999) argues that Holocaust Education comprises the events leading up to the Holocaust *and* the genocide itself. We argue that an event leading up to the Holocaust (on its own), such as *Kristallnacht*, is school-based Holocaust Education. However, we do not consider the generic remembrance activities above, or school-based activities for students of this age on anti-bullying or diversity which do not directly refer to the Holocaust, to be Holocaust Education. Although these activities engage younger students in this commemorative Day they are NOT lessons *about* the Holocaust, and given that these students have not yet learned anything *about* the Holocaust, they are not lessons *from* the Holocaust either. Teaching the Holocaust to this younger age group may be justified in Israel where 'its presence and the importance to national identity cannot be underestimated' (Stevick and Gross, 2014: 69), as its citizens comprise a large number of survivor families, and young children hear the siren on *Yom HaShoah* (see p. 63). It may also be justified elsewhere in Jewish primary schools as these students may have family members who suffered in the Holocaust.

Established in 1995, the central aim of Yad LaYeled, the children's Holocaust museum in Israel, whose visitors are aged 10 years and over, is to ensure that students' first encounters with the Holocaust are stimulating, meaningful, and age appropriate. This is of universal importance for primary educators as this first encounter can significantly impact on students' subsequent attitudes to learning about the Holocaust. Narratives used have a clear beginning (life before the war), middle (life during the war), and end (after the war). The museum's principles of presenting information about real people who lived during the Holocaust in a narrative form through authentic materials, such as diaries, audio and video testimonies, artefacts, documents and photographs, and presenting simple structured stories that focus on life rather than death, can be easily transferrable to the primary classroom. As we stated in Chapter 7 (p. 87) personalisation can be very powerful and aid understanding of the complex events.

The museum's main exhibition, *The Story of the Jewish Child during the Holocaust*, focuses on the lives of Jewish children in Europe during the Holocaust. The museum additionally contains other permanent and temporary exhibitions that complement the main exhibition. One of these, *Korczak of the Children*, focuses on author, educator and paediatrician Dr Janusz Korkzak (1878–1942), the principal of a Jewish orphanage in the Warsaw ghetto. This variety of programmes, that are suited for different ages, acknowledges the personal interests of the learner and demonstrates that there is not a sole definitive way to engage young learners in Holocaust Education.

Provision of choice can also be transferred to the primary classroom school by teachers supporting their students in researching an (appropriate) aspect of the Holocaust that is of interest to them.

Our experience as tutors on school experience in primary schools in Scotland is that as with Citizenship Education, good quality Holocaust Education involves a commitment to ethos as well as its teaching in the classroom and/or assemblies on an aspect of the Holocaust. One example of this is a primary school where a large framed and printed copy of the survivor's letter we previously mentioned in Chapter 2 (see p. 16), requesting teachers to help their students become responsible citizens, is prominently displayed in the reception area. This conveys a strong message to visitors on their arrival of the core values of the school.

Justifying Holocaust Education in Primary School

There are many reasons why school-based Holocaust Education should begin at primary school:

1. Teaching the Holocaust in the primary schools widens learning opportunities for the Spiral Curriculum, a curriculum that is based on Bruner's cognitive learning theory (1960), which asserts that young people can be taught anything as long as the material is organised appropriately. This curriculum encourages students to revisit a topic, theme or subject several times throughout their school career. With this approach, primary teachers would introduce the Holocaust to their students, and secondary teachers would then build on students' previous knowledge. This requires dialogue and collaboration between primary and secondary teachers, as it is necessary to reintroduce previously taught content with more complexity and in a different way. This will build on students' prior learning and develop their knowledge and understanding of the Holocaust. It does, however, run the risk of over-exposing students to Holocaust Education, and places the onus on teachers to ensure that this 'reintroduction' is not 'repetition' and that a range of themes is explored in stimulating and different ways. Failure to do this can lead to Holocaust fatigue, which arises from students becoming tired of the Holocaust.

2. The following empirical evidence demonstrates additional benefits to teaching the Holocaust in the primary school:

   i) Claire's (2005) findings that demonstrate that primary students' learning the story of Anne Frank contributed to their responses in discussions on wider moral dilemmas

ii) The TEACH report that cites the Holocaust as an example of good practice in teaching primary students emotive and controversial history (The Historical Association, 2007)

iii) Our findings on primary students' values and attitudes (Cowan and Maitles, 2006) that demonstrated learning about the Holocaust was a contributing factor to students' improving attitudes towards minority groups and aspects of citizenship. This improvement was both short and long term. Students who had studied the Holocaust at primary school tended to have more positive values than their peers who had not previously learned about it.

3. There is research evidence that students express and receive racial and ethnic prejudice in the primary school. Devine et al. (2008: 369) demonstrated that children from Travelling communities in Ireland were consistently subjected to racist stereotyping at primary school, and that 'racist name-calling in particular, was shown to be an important tool used by some children in the assertion of their status with one another'. Short and Carrington (1995,1996) showed that primary students express negative stereotypes of Jewish people and bring antisemitic stereotypes of Jews to the classroom. Further, findings from an Australian case study in state schools in Sydney and Melbourne demonstrated that antisemitism extended to the playground, with the researchers commenting

> To our amazement, both primary and high-school Jewish students in state schools spontaneously told us that they loved to attend Special Religious Education classes because they found them to be a 'safe place' in the face of the antisemitism that they were experiencing in the playground. (Gross and Rutland, 2014: 315)

This justifies the need for primary schools to adopt a systematic programme that discusses issues relating to racism and antisemitism in its Citizenship Education programmes. Though not an antidote for racism, xenophobia, antisemitism, sectarianism or antiziganism, Holocaust Education can contribute to this and play an important role in countering and dispelling negative attitudes towards minority groups. Our findings of primary students' attitudes (Cowan and Maitles, 2006) were that after learning about the Holocaust, there were improvements in attitudes towards Jews, yet a small number of students had negative attitudes. Three students (n = 99) agreed with the statement *I think it is ok for children to make racist comments about Jews*, and where despite a declining population of Scottish Jewry which at the time of this research was approximately 5,000, 10% of the cohort agreed with the statement *I think there are too many Jews in Scotland.*

Also, students discussing the Holocaust and prejudice at home with their families can extend the impact of Holocaust Education. Our conversations with primary teachers suggested that this led to improved attitudes towards refugees by family members:

1. Many primary students acquire knowledge of Hitler, Nazis and Jews through the vast material that is easily accessible on the internet. Depending on the nature of this content, this can lead to student misconceptions of the Holocaust, and similar to the students with ASN in the previous chapter (see pp. 93–95), their making inappropriate comments about it. Engaging in a study of the Holocaust is beneficial for students' understanding of diversity and to their personal development.
2. Holocaust Education can help primary students reflect on their own identities as well as their perceptions of others. In one of our earlier studies, an investigation of Anne Frank's ancestry prompted primary students to examine their own backgrounds. The teacher recalled that one student '... saw himself as a Pakistani Muslim, but found out that his grandfather had fought in the Indian army. He hadn't known that his family had originally come from India. His parents and grandparents appreciated that this was being taught in schools' (Cowan and Maitles, 2000: 85).
3. Primary school offers easier opportunities for interdisciplinary learning and less time restrictions than the secondary timetable. Primary teachers also have the flexibility to respond to their students and where necessary can follow up on a specific teaching point the next day, or indeed later on in the same day. Additionally, the close relationship between a primary teacher and their class can be beneficial in predicting, eliciting, and responding to students' emotional responses.
4. The Holocaust can make a positive contribution to students' understanding of the Second World War which is a popular topic at primary school. In the UK, this is frequently taught with a focus on the Home Front, which includes lessons on child evacuees. Comparing the experiences of child evacuees with *kinder*, the children who came over to the UK on the *Kindertransport programme*, or with the rights of children in the Holocaust, can enhance students' understanding of the war, as well as develop their understanding of how war, persecution and/or governments that will not or cannot protect individuals from serious human rights abuses, lead people to flee their country and become refugees.

Pedagogical Principles

We agree with Totten that the horrors of the Holocaust should not be included in Holocaust teaching programmes in the primary school. One common approach is to end such programmes *at the gates of the camp* rather than metaphorically take primary students inside. Teaching the Holocaust to primary students is not about scaring or traumatising students, playing on their emotions, or causing them psychological distress. Primary students may well be out of their comfort zones when engaging in Holocaust Education, and the safe school environment provided by a class teacher is important to ensure that the emotional impact on students is not harmful or gets out of control. For this reason, class teachers are advised to get to know their students before teaching them the Holocaust, and unless they have taught these students at a previous stage in the school, to avoid teaching it at the beginning of the first school term. Zembylas and McGlynn (2012: 56–7) advocate an ethic of empathy where teachers ensure that students know that they are emotionally and intellectually supported by their teachers, and where students are empowered to confront racist behaviour with confidence.

The accessibility of information on the internet can empower students in a different way. For example, teachers may well conclude their topic on Anne Frank with a brief acknowledgement that Anne was sent to Bergen-Belsen where she died from typhus, but interested students can easily search the internet at home for more information. One click on 'Bergen-Belsen' on YouTube provides a range of archival footage, most of which will contain the horrors that primary teachers will have carefully avoided. Students may then want to share their findings with their school peers. Teachers must strive to direct these students appropriately by listening to them and checking that their information and understanding are correct; directing them to an age-appropriate source that will allow them to find out more about Anne Frank, e.g. *Anne's Amsterdam* app from the Anne Frank House, Amsterdam, and explaining that learning about the concentration camps is for another day, possibly at secondary school.

Further, it is not always feasible to leave students *at the gates of the camp* as there are several excellent resources for primary-aged students that do not stick to this rule. One example is the United States Holocaust Memorial Museum's exhibition *Remember the Children: Daniel's Story*. Designed for ages 8 and above (and their families), this exhibition tells of the experiences of a fictional Jewish boy called Daniel who survives the Holocaust. Based on historical imagery gathered from family photo albums, documentary sources, and pictorial diaries of the period, Daniel's experiences include life in a ghetto and a concentration camp. This interactive exhibition allows visitors to touch, listen, and see Daniel's world as it changes during the Holocaust.

Another example is the children's book *Hana's Suitcase* (Levine, 2003). This true story of Hana Brady, who was born in 1931, takes readers into the Theresienstadt ghetto and concentration camp. It also tells how a group of Japanese children with the curator from the Tokyo Holocaust

Education Resource Centre investigated what happened to Hana. The book juxtaposes the experiences of the Japanese children and Hana, with the text switching from contemporary Japan to Czechoslovakia in the 1930s and twenty-first century Canada as the story unfolds. Even with an introduction that provides the context to the story and explains the concentration camps and the murders, this book is easy to read and appropriate for students from 10 years of age.

One can argue that *Hana's Suitcase* takes primary students *beyond the gates* in a safe and appropriate way. The text of *Hana's Suitcase* is interspersed with family photographs and Hana's drawings that personalise the story, support the text, and add poignancy. While these are entirely appropriate for primary students, some books marketed for this age group contain images that students will find very upsetting. We agree with Shawn's (1999) view that books with graphic imagery and details of these horrors are to be avoided in the primary classroom. Yet an image that one teacher considers to be unsuitable for their students may be deemed suitable by another teacher who considers it no worse than a news item or documentary on television that their students frequently watch. Hence primary teachers need to look carefully at images in informational books on the Holocaust to check their suitability for students.

Rose Blanche (Innocenti and McEwan, 1985) is a beautifully illustrated picture book that teachers can choose for its illustrations rather than or as well as the text. It tells a fictional story of the Holocaust from a child's perspective, and like *Hana's Suitcase* introduces readers to the concentration camp, albeit an illustrated and not an actual one.

Also worthy of consideration is whether primary students who have no contact with, or experience of Jews, understand what being Jewish means. This is justified by Short's (2003) findings that 8- to 9-year-olds had either an inaccurate conception or no conception of Jews, and that 10- to 11-year-olds held a range of negative stereotypes of Jews. As the 'notion of Jewishness as a racial category is central to Nazi ideology' (Short, 2003: 124), and the children in the above-named resources were Jewish, teaching students about aspects of the Jewish way of life before they begin their study of the Holocaust is advised. In this way they can bring their prior learning to the study, and acquire learning of a new dimension of Jewish life, as well as engage in interdisciplinary learning in the curricular areas of History and Religious and Moral Education.

The Jewish festival of *Purim* (pr. Poor-eem) can be connected to the Holocaust as its story is about the attempted genocide of the Jews in the ancient Persian Empire. Like Hitler, Haman, one of the King's advisers, wanted to kill all the Jews. The festival celebrates the intervention of Queen Esther which led to the Jews being saved. The book (or scroll) of Esther is read in the synagogue on *Purim*. *Purim* is an entertaining and rowdy occasion and the custom is to dress up in colourful costumes and masks. Another practice is to give at least one person *Mishlo'ach Manot,* a basket of two items of food and/or drink and some token gifts. This is meant to ensure that everyone has enough food for the *Purim* feast held later in the day, and to encourage love and appreciation of others and friendship.

In addition to developing knowledge of the Jewish way of life or Judaism that is, excepting Jewish students, important for all primary students in their understanding of the Holocaust, so too is learning about human rights, as regardless of age these belong to everyone. As we showed in Chapter 3 (pp. 32–33), Holocaust Education can contribute to students' awareness of basic human rights which can then assist them in recognising and protecting their individual rights, and remind them of the way in which they should behave to one another. A study of the Holocaust can also facilitate learning of children whose rights are currently being denied, e.g. child soldiers and child labourers. Integrating Human Rights Education into Holocaust Education is supported by the following announcement by the UN Secretary General on International Holocaust Remembrance Day 2008:

> But it is not enough to remember, honour and grieve for the dead. As we do, we must also educate, nurture and care for the living. We must foster in our children a sense of responsibility, so that they can build societies that protect and promote the rights of all citizens. (Ban Ki-moon, 17 January 2008)

Another example of interdisciplinary learning is where students use the Holocaust in the Expressive Arts to develop their drawing and painting skills. As a classroom displaying 25 children's drawings of *Kristallnacht,* or paintings of Anne Frank in hiding, may not promote a happy learning environment and might upset younger students coming into the classroom, careful consideration is required as to how to display students' artwork. Possible ways of addressing this are being very selective as to what artwork is displayed in the classroom and ensuring that only a small amount is displayed, collecting Holocaust artwork in individual student portfolios, using digital cameras to record artwork and compile electronic (e) folders of individual students' work, or for students to make a collection of Holocaust artwork from their class. One innovative primary teacher displayed her students' artwork of Anne Frank in a private area, in a storeroom in the attic of her school, and students were only allowed to see this a group at a time. This effectively added an element of drama and set the topic apart from others.

Music can also be incorporated into Holocaust Education as the cultural life at Theresienstadt included a range of musical activities. One primary teacher used the Holocaust as a stimulus to provide students with opportunities to listen to and respond to music, as well as developing their skills in musical notation, playing musical instruments and performance direction, and developing their knowledge of the Phrygian Dominant Scale (also called the Freygish Scale) which is prevalent in Middle Eastern and Klezmer music.

Using *Hana's Suitcase* with his class, this teacher focused on the life of Czech composer and pianist Raphael Schächter (1905–1945), one of the many Jewish musicians who was sent to Theresienstadt. When delegates of the Danish Red Cross and the International Red Cross inspected this camp in 1944, inmates performed Verdi's *Requiem* and the children's opera *Brundibar* for the delegation. Shächter organised male and female choirs for this performance as well as for other performances for fellow inmates and guards. The short story and picture book, *The Mozart Question* (Morpurgo, 2008), tells of the experiences of Jewish musicians in the Holocaust.

As we pointed out in the previous chapter, conveying the enormity of the scale of the Holocaust is difficult for anyone to understand (p. 87), and for younger students 'six million' can be just another number. One famous way of visualising this was the Paper Clip project undertaken by Whitwell Middle School in Tennessee, USA (for students aged 11- to 13-years-old), in 1998. Students brought in paper clips, wrote letters to famous people requesting that they send a paper clip, and to share their reasons for doing so. To date over 30 million paperclips have been counted by students and these are housed permanently in an authentic German transport car as a memorial to those murdered in the Holocaust. In addition, a collection of letters, documents, books and artefacts about the Holocaust that have been catalogued by students are on display in the Children's Holocaust Memorial Research Room in the school. In 2015 Carmyle Primary School in Scotland, UK, established links with Whitwell Middle School, and adapted the idea by asking students to collect bottle tops which they used to make a permanent mural as they studied the Holocaust (TES, 2015).

The city of Lublin in Poland adopted an alternative approach. Since 2005, every Holocaust Remembrance Day (in Poland, 19 April) young people are encouraged to 'remember' Henio Zytomirski, a Jewish boy from Lublin who was born in 1933 and died in 1942. Henio would have started school on 1 September 1939, the day that the Nazis invaded Poland. Henio survived the Lublin ghetto but was murdered at Majdanek death camp. Schoolchildren in Lublin and the surrounding towns are encouraged to write letters to Henio and send them to his last known address in Lublin. A special postbox is placed outside the bank, where Henio stood for what was to be his last photograph. Letters are returned to their senders' homes stamped 'address non-existent, recipient unknown' to encourage discussion at home about what happened to Polish Jews during the Holocaust (Yad Vashem/ODIHR, 2006). Tours of places in Lublin related to Henio's life are also organised.

We mention parents in the primary teaching context elsewhere in this book (see Chapter 9, pp. 123 and 126), and here we want to emphasise the benefits of sharing with parents the content and activities involved in teaching the Holocaust to primary students. This is more important in countries where Holocaust Education is not mandatory in primary school as these parents may perceive such teaching as highly controversial, unnecessary, and such teachers as being on a mission. The purposes of sharing information with parents are to:

• reassure them that all lessons and materials used will be age-appropriate
• obtain any information from parents that can impact on the planned lessons, e.g. if a pupil has Jewish or Roma heritage, or if their great grandfather was a soldier who liberated one of the concentration camps
• challenge any misconceptions that parents have about the Holocaust
• explain the importance of parental controls on the internet, and where relevant show parents how to access this and adjust the settings on their computer

Appointing a member of staff with responsibility for Holocaust Education in the school can be beneficial to achieving a consistency and continuity in teaching the Holocaust. This may be the person who leads Citizenship Education in the school, or involve collaboration with this person or a teacher with responsibility for teaching History. A consultative team approach can be beneficial in identifying suitable resources as teachers who lead one specific curricular area will have a good knowledge of the resources in the school.

Many primary schools organise a Holocaust Memorial Day assembly at which (upper) primary students who have studied the Holocaust perform a presentation for their younger peers. These younger students are not *remembering* the Holocaust because they have not yet acquired knowledge of it. As this will be these students' first encounters with the Holocaust, making this commemorative event inclusive may not be entirely appropriate. Our preferred alternative is a joint school assembly between primary students in local primary schools who have studied the Holocaust, or with students who have studied the Holocaust in an associated secondary school, or with their parents. In addition to achieving 'remembrance', this can make the Day more meaningful.

Themes for Primary Students

The remainder of this chapter focuses on four suitable Holocaust themes for primary students: Anne Frank, the SS *St Louis*, the *Kindertransport programme* and the Rescue of the Danish Jews. The purpose of identifying these is to support primary teachers who are newly engaging in school-based Holocaust Education. It is, by no means, a definitive list, and experienced primary teachers who teach alternative suitable themes or resources, such as *Hana's Suitcase,* should continue to use these. This does, however, not apply to *The Boy in the Striped Pyjamas* (Boyne, 2006), which is discussed in detail in the following chapter and not recommended for the primary classroom (see pp. 118–20).

Anne Frank (1929–1945)
The Diary of Anne Frank tells of discrimination and persecution towards Jewish people from the perspective of a German-Dutch Jewish girl who was given a diary as a present for her thirteenth birthday. This personalises the Holocaust by introducing readers to the Frank family and their familial relationships, and provides insight into the experiences of those who were forced to go into hiding in the Netherlands. As the diary is lengthy and challenging, with some content, particularly in its more recent publication (Frank, 2007), that may not be considered appropriate for primary students, primary teachers tend to select passages of the diary they think will work most effectively with their class, rather than read or encourage students to read the whole book. That said, students may well wish to rise to the challenge and read the whole book because they find it so interesting. Student responses are not always predictable. One primary teacher told us that one of her students applied and developed his skills in the videogame *Minecraft* (2009) to recreate Anne's attic.

Human rights' issues include Anne's experiences of the restrictions and conditions that were imposed on Jews living in occupied Holland from 1940, such as having to wear a yellow star and go to a segregated Jewish school, as well as those during her experience in hiding in the annexe at 263 Prinsengracht, and those after her capture. While the Frank family did not arrive in Amsterdam as refugees, they had emigrated to Holland from Germany because of increasing antisemitism and fear for their safety as Jews.

Anne's entry in the diary (7/12/42) referring to the eight day Jewish festival of *Chanukah* and Christmas or 'St Nicholas Day' falling closely together is an opportunity for students to learn about these festivals. Both festivals involve exchanging presents and lights. The only religious observance of

Chanukah is the lighting of the candles and reciting the accompanying blessings. Anne's diary entry refers to a wooden candlestick that Mr Van Daan made and how the candles which should have been kept alight to burn were lit for ten minutes only.

It is easy to focus on the story of Anne Frank without recognising the extraordinary courage of the Austrian born and Dutch citizen Miep Gies (1909–2010), the young woman who helped Anne Frank, her family and four other Jewish people who were also hiding in the Secret Annexe at 263 Prinsengracht. Buying food for those living in the Annexe required careful planning as they had to do so on the 'black market', sometimes with illegal ration cards. This meant buying from a number of greengrocers and making several trips to the factory every day, as carrying more than one shopping bag, and buying from one seller, would arouse suspicion. These daily risks demonstrated bravery and responsibility that often go unnoticed. Gies modestly pointed out in her memoir (Gold, 1987) that more than 20,000 Dutch people hid Jewish people and others in need of somewhere to hide during the Holocaust and wrote,

> There is nothing special about me. I have never wanted special attention. I was only willing to do what was asked of me and what seemed necessary at the time ... My story is a story of very ordinary people during extraordinarily terrible times. Times the like of which I hope with all my heart will never, never come again. It is for all of us ordinary people all over the world to see to it that they do not. (Gold, 1987: 11–12)

It was Miep, Otto Frank's secretary, who provided an income by keeping his business going, returned to the Secret Annexe and collected Anne's diaries, and gave these to Otto Frank after the war. Were it not for her actions, the world would never have known about Anne Frank.

SS *St Louis*

The experiences of the 937 German Jewish passengers on board the luxury cruise liner, the SS *St Louis* (1939), whose destination was Cuba, demonstrate the reality of a world in which countries did not welcome refugees. This had been demonstrated one year earlier at the Evian Conference where delegates from 32 countries met to discuss the growing number of Jewish refugees fleeing Europe. While the delegates expressed sympathy most countries, including the USA and UK, did not increase their immigration quotas and take in more Jews.

Although the Nazi flag flew above the ship, its captain, Gustav Schröder (1885–1959), instructed his crew to treat Jewish passengers like any others, which meant helping them with their luggage, a service that was not

common practice at that time in Nazi Germany. The captain also converted one of the rooms into a temporary synagogue so that passengers
did not have to pray in secret. Passengers of the SS *St Louis* had purchased
what they had assumed were the required visas to seek asylum in Cuba
and then travel on to the USA. Yet faced with new legislation their visas
were not accepted. After being held in Cuban waters for several days, they
were turned away and forced to return to Europe. Schröder decided to
assist the passengers by not returning to Germany without first seeking
safety for his passengers. Through negotiations, passengers disembarked
in Belgium, France, the Netherlands and the UK. Hence this story brings
opportunities to discuss aspects of citizenship relating to individual
responsibility and the moral obligation of others.

It also encourages students to consider the plight of modern-day refugees, as well as reflect on countries' current quotas of refugees and on
whether today's world community is more welcoming. The principle laid
out in Article 33 of the 1951 Convention relating to the Status of Refugees
states that no state

> ... shall expel or return ('refouler' in French) a refugee in any manner whatsoever
> to the frontiers of territories where his life or freedom would be threatened on
> account of his race, religion, nationality, membership of a particular social group
> or political opinion. (United Nations, 1951)

We consider that an appreciation of one's personal responsibility in the
wider global arena should begin in the primary classroom and be taught as
part of global citizenship.

The *Kindertransport programme* (1938–1939)
(pr. keender-transport)

The *Kindertransport programme* was a British scheme in which 10,000 predominantly Jewish children, from Germany, Austria, Poland and
Czechoslovakia, were brought to the UK for safety. Most were aged
between 5 and 17 although there were also some babies. Parents were not
allowed to enter the UK or accompany their children on the trains.
Chaperones who accompanied the children on the trains were required to
return to Europe immediately after delivering their charges. The *kinder*
(children) were allowed to enter the UK on temporary travel visas and
their care, education and eventual emigration from the UK were covered
by private citizens or organisations. The biggest transport was due to leave
Prague on 3 September 1939, the day the UK entered the war. Although
250 families waited at Liverpool Street Station, London, that day, sadly
the train never left the station in Prague, and none of the 250 children on
board survived the Holocaust.

This story is often taught alongside the experiences of children who were evacuated from cities in the UK during the Second World War. Both groups of children suffered hardships in being separated from their families and experienced cultural change. The *kinder* additionally had a new language to learn and very little contact with their families; many Jewish children were denied their religion as they were taken to non-Jewish homes (for example those in the Barbican Mission) who were devoted to converting Jews to Christianity. This may seem unimportant as these children were spared the experiences of the ghettos and the camps, but is relevant in terms of developing an understanding of human rights. The right to practise one's religion is clearly explained in Articles 14 and 30 of the *UN Convention of the Rights of the Child*. While child evacuees returned to their homes and were reunited with their parents and families, few *kinder* returned to mainland Europe, and many of their parents and family members did not survive the Holocaust.

The *Journey exhibition*, at the (UK) National Holocaust Centre near Nottingham in England, tells the story of a fictional 10-year-old German Jewish boy called Leo Stein who came to England on the *Kindertransport programme*. This exhibition is designed for students of primary age and is text free. Visitors enter Leo's home, sit in his classroom at school, visit his father's tailoring shop, and can view a selection of artefacts which relate to the *Kindertransport programme*. Visitors can also explore a hiding place as the narrative explains that Leo's sister had to go into hiding as she was too young for the *Kindertransport programme*.

One key figure in the *Kindertransport programme* was Sir Nicholas Winton (1909–2015). Appointing himself Honorary Secretary of the British Council for Refugees from Czechoslovakia, Sir Nicholas organised the rescue of more than 600 children from Czechoslovakia, lobbied western governments to accept them, and when the UK and Sweden agreed to take in children in small numbers, he found the required funds and foster parents. His statement that 'It was only nine months out of my 92 years' (Emanuel and Gissing, 2001) demonstrates that like Miep Gies one person can make a difference.

The Rescue of the Danish Jews

The Rescue of the Danish Jews, also referred to as the 'Escape' or 'Flight' of the Jews in Denmark, is the only example where an occupied country actively resisted the Nazis' attempts to deport its Jewish citizens. Levine claims that one of the many reasons for this operation's success was that in Denmark, Jews were 'not defined as "the other" … People respected one another's differences and seemed to care more about ordinary decency than abstract ideals' (2000: viii). This explains why Jews maintained their rights to Danish citizenship under Nazi occupation. They did not wear a yellow star, were not segregated from society, and their property was not confiscated (Rittner et al., 2000).

German diplomat Georg Ferdinand Duckwitz (1904–1973) secretly informed the Danish resistance of the Nazi plan to round up the Jews of Denmark and deport them to Theresienstadt concentration camp. This led to a nationwide operation in which more than 7,000 Jews were smuggled onto boats and ferried by Danish fisherman to neutral Sweden. Like *The Diary of Anne Frank*, this story provides an opportunity for students to learn about the Jewish way of life. The planned round-up of the Danish Jews was scheduled for a Friday night (the beginning of the Jewish Sabbath), and the second day of the Jewish New Year, *Rosh Hashanah*, when most Jews would be at home with their families. Jews were informed of the Nazis' intentions at synagogue in the morning. They quickly left their homes and were hidden and looked after by their fellow Danish across the country, until the fishermen were ready to take them to Sweden.

The operation was not, however, totally successful: 500 Danish Jews *were* deported to the Theresienstadt ghetto, and 51 of these were murdered. The Danish Jews who survived the Holocaust did so largely due to the pressure that Danish officials placed on the Germans. They, together with all the other prisoners who had been deported, returned to Denmark from Theresienstadt on The White Buses (also known as the Bernadotte Operation) arranged by the Danish Aid Corps. This is another reason why Denmark has become the model of citizenship amongst the occupied countries of Europe. The story of the Rescue of the Danish Jews is fictionalised in the children's novel *Hitler's Canary* (Toksvig, 2005).

Conclusion

In this chapter we have discussed why Holocaust Education should begin in the upper stages of primary school. The mainstreaming of school-based Holocaust Education has led to an increasing number of resources in this area, which has impacted on resources for primary students. We have identified a few such resources in this chapter. We have also emphasised the importance of knowledge about Jewish people prior to a study of the Holocaust, and how aspects of citizenship, in particular human rights, permeate this study. We do not underestimate teachers' responsibility in this and recommend that they have opportunities to develop their expertise in teaching the Holocaust by participating in Continued Professional Development (CPD, or inservice, inset) courses. These will not only lead to enhancement of teachers' skills and knowledge, but also encourage the development of Holocaust teaching in primary schools.

Further Reading

Leapman, M. (2000) *Witnesses to War: Eight True-Life Stories of Nazi Persecution.* London: Puffin.

Matas, C. (1993) *Daniel's Story.* New York: Scholastic.

Paper Clips (2004) Directed by E. Berlin and J. Fab, Miramax.

Petit, J. (1993) *A Place to Hide: True Stories of Holocaust Rescues.* London: Scholastic.

9

CLASSROOM TEACHING APPROACHES

Learning Objectives

- To explore issues around the use of literature and role play and simulations in Holocaust Education
- To discuss the benefits and challenges of using survivor testimony on the internet
- To provide support on using survivor testimony

Introduction

We have discussed in Chapter 7 some pedagogical approaches and areas of difficulty in developing lessons *about* and *from* the Holocaust in the classroom. In this chapter we want to raise in greater detail some specific areas that in our experience and opinion raise complex and difficult questions for primary and secondary teachers. We are concerning ourselves here with examining specific learning methods and resources, i.e. literature, testimony (both in person and online) and role play/simulations that can be very powerful in the class, but have to be well developed and thought through or can lead to unintended consequences.

Using Literature

Holocaust literature covers a wide range of genres that includes memoirs, diaries, biographies, testimonies, fictionalised autobiographies and novels. In exploring issues that accompany the use of literature in school-based Holocaust Education, this section will focus on the use of the novel as it is our experience that whereas in the past a novel was used as a stimulus to gain student interest in the Holocaust or to accompany historical sources, in today's classrooms it is used as a principal teaching resource to teach the Holocaust. It is therefore our intention to raise issues about this use of fiction.

Before doing so, it is firstly worth considering the difficulty in classifying novels as fiction in the context of the Holocaust. For example, the graphic novel *Maus*, a two-volume biography of the author's father who survived the Holocaust (Spiegelman, 1987, 1992), was moved in 1991 from the *Times* bestseller fiction category to non-fiction, and the Pulitzer Prize committee was equally uncertain as to which genre this text belonged (Banner, 2000). Secondly, there are authors who are Holocaust survivors: for example, Elie Wiesel (1928–2016) is an author of Holocaust testimony, and while his writing is real in that it is based on his Holocaust experiences, it is also a personal response that employs fictional modes and narrative techniques (Vice, 2000).

Drawing on the writing of children's author Geoffrey Trease (1909–1998), Gamble (2013: 183–4) offers a specific approach in classifying fiction. He distinguishes *period fiction*, a fictional text 'about the past that is set in an identifiable period but does not refer to historical events', from the *historical novel*, a text that 'seeks authenticity of fact – but so far as it is humanly discoverable – a faithful recreation of minds and motives'. Lathey (2001) makes another distinction by identifying two types of fictional writers: those who passionately want to make a historical period come alive to the reader, and those who use history as a stimulus for the reader's imagination. These distinctions suggest that teachers must give serious consideration to the type of fiction they use when they plan to use it as a medium for teaching History. In the context of the Holocaust, there are two reasons why it is essential that students' knowledge and understanding *about* the Holocaust are developed through teachers' delivery of accurate information. Firstly, because of the importance of historical accuracy in the Holocaust context due to the presence and growth of Holocaust denial (see Chapter 4); and secondly, because inaccurate or mis-information leads to difficulties in students learning *from* the Holocaust. This is supported by the assertion that teachers 'must get the facts right' when teaching about genocide (Davies, 2012: 112).

We have already expressed our concern that students may acquire misconceptions of the Holocaust through teachers' use of language (see Chapter 6); in this chapter we argue that this can equally apply to teachers' use of fiction. Previous research by Totten (2000a) and Short et al. (1998) provided evidence of student misconceptions of the origins of the Holocaust and of Jews. Unlike the priority of fictional authors to write texts that readers *enjoy* reading, teachers and educators have a professional responsibility to convey an interpretation of the past based on facts. That is not to say that we do not recognise the benefits of using different forms of fiction in the classroom. We understand that a novel can appeal to students who are not instantly, or especially, interested in History, or indeed in this specific area of history; help students identify and use the language of discrimination and racism; personalise and humanise the Holocaust experience; provide a rich shared experience for learners; and that it has the potential to be informative and contribute effectively to interdisciplinary learning. Additionally, the illustrations in picture books (e.g. Innocenti and McEwan, 1985) provide young readers with age-appropriate visual images that can support their learning.

The Boy in the Striped Pyjamas

One recommendation that is commonly agreed in using fiction in school-based Holocaust Education is that teachers need to be judicious in their text selections. Such judgement relies upon their views as to what constitutes the 'best' novels. For some, the criteria will be texts that achieve the greatest participation and/or enjoyment of students; for others, the extent to which a text informs students of this historical event will be more important. Either way, teachers require to support students in their understanding of the Holocaust. If a fictional text contains incorrect information, then the teacher's role is crucial in ensuring that students are not misinformed and that they understand key facts of the Holocaust. Some authors (e.g. Gleitzman, 2006; Morpurgo, 2008) assist in this by inserting a note or letter at the end of their novel that clarifies the elements of truth in their story.

The Boy in the Striped Pyjamas is a bestselling novel and DVD (2009) and these are popular resources in primary and secondary classrooms. The popularity of this novel amongst secondary students in England is supported firstly by Gray's findings (2014a: 114) that 75.8% of 298 secondary students had either read this book or watched its subsequent film (this percentage was considerably higher than those who had engaged with Anne Frank: Diary of a Young Girl (2007) or Schindler's List (1993)), and the Centre for Holocaust Education's findings that from its nearly 8,000 student participants, this was the 'most-read book and the most watched film about the Holocaust' (2014: 71). In a piece of unpublished research involving 44 primary teachers in Scotland's largest local authority in 2013, we found that more of them were using The Boy in the Striped Pyjamas and that The Diary of Anne Frank was less widely used. This offers some explanation as to why when one primary 7 class were told by their teacher that they were going to be learning about the Holocaust and would be reading *Hana's Suitcase* (see Chapter 8), one pupil asked the teacher, 'Why are we not reading *The Boy in the Striped Pyjamas*?'. Furthermore, conversations with teachers of secondary students, whose needs are better met in specialist settings rather than in mainstream schools, report their use of this novel to teach the Holocaust.

We consider that *The Boy in the Striped Pyjamas* can be categorised according to Trease above as *period fiction*, and struggle with Lathey's categories, as Boyne's character development and setting do indeed bring this period of history alive for readers, *and* it can be argued that Boyne uses history to stimulate readers' imagination. We consider this book to be an original, well-crafted book that can be an effective resource to teach English. However, because of its historical inaccuracies, we do not consider that it is a novel that primary teachers should be using in their students' study of the Holocaust, as it involves too much work on the part of the teacher to – as Davies writes above – 'get right'. Further, we consider that secondary teachers need to exercise caution when using this novel with their students, and consult or work with History colleagues to seriously facilitate students' engagement with a range of informational texts and historical enquiry alongside their fictional reading.

This book has received a great deal of criticism from academics in the literary and historical worlds. Indeed Gray (2014b: 133) concludes that it is a 'curse' for Holocaust Education. Ruth Gilbert describes the book's climactic sequence of events as 'contrived' and 'implausible', and reports that Boyne 'admitted that he changed many facts [of the Holocaust] to suit the story' (2010: 361). Eaglestone claims that this novel conveys 'Auschwitz as "real" as a fantasy context such as Harry Potter's Hogwarts School' (2007: 52). Cesarani (2008: 4) accuses Boyne of a lack of knowledge of the Holocaust and of Auschwitz-Birkenau in particular, of distorting history, and writes that it is 'fiction in the worst sense of the word'. In addition to this, there are concerns over the theme and messages of this book.

Rather than inform the reader of something new about the Holocaust, Boyne uses the Holocaust as a setting to explore the friendship between two 9-year-old boys, one the son of the Camp Commandant and the other a Jewish prisoner in the camp. As Auschwitz-Birkenau had guarded electric fences and 9-year-old Jewish children were usually murdered on arrival at this camp, the novel misinforms readers about the Holocaust. One of the messages of this book is that Camp Commandants were respectable individuals and loving fathers who had to do their job. The actual Commandant of Auschwitz-Birkenau, Rudolf Hoess (1900–1947), was found guilty of manslaughter and sentenced to ten years in prison in 1924 for his part in the killing of Walter Kadow, a Party member who was suspected of betraying another member. Kadow had been beaten with clubs before his throat had been cut (Harding, 2013). Hoess (voluntarily) joined the SS in 1933, trained as a supervisor in Dachau concentration camp in 1934, and was appointed adjutant of Saschenhausen concentration camp in 1938 where he was responsible for camp discipline and executions; he was not in any sense, a model citizen. Hence this too is misleading.

Perhaps the most controversial point about this novel, however, is the emotional journey on which the author takes the reader. At the end of the book, the reader feels sympathy for the son of the Camp Commandant who is mistakenly murdered in the camp, and his grieving family, and *not* for the primary victims of the Holocaust. This empathy for the perpetrators does not sit easily with Holocaust survivors or ourselves. One's first lessons of the Holocaust should focus on an understanding of what the Holocaust was, and this cannot be achieved unless students have a clear understanding of who the victims and perpetrators were. This is another reason why we recommend that this novel is not used in the primary classroom, and treated with caution in the secondary.

Our worry is that this book is currently leading to distorted perceptions of the Holocaust which present serious challenges to History teachers. This is supported by evidence from interviews with secondary students in England that the book reinforced an 'inaccurate perception of German ignorance of the Holocaust' (Centre for Holocaust Education, 2014: 71), and feedback from History teachers that students' inaccurate perceptions of the camps after studying or reading this book, are 'difficult to dispel' (HET, n.d.). Such perceptions are no doubt welcomed by those who would deny or trivialise the Holocaust. Boyne's assertion that this book is 'a fable' is also concerning, as setting such a genre in Auschwitz-Birkenau, the iconic symbol of the Holocaust, arguably diminishes the reality of this terrible place. We agree with the advice of US educators who comprise the Holocaust Educators' Consortium in urging teachers to 'Avoid this book' (Holocaust Educators' Consortium, 2014: 127).

We suggest that teachers choose informational texts such as true-life stories that are written by real children (e.g. Holliday,1996; Leapman, 2000; Zapruder, 2002), and non-fiction books that are written in a narrative, 'fictional' style (e.g. Levine, 2003) for the experiences of child victims of the Holocaust. With the inevitability that more novels will be published that teachers and students will enjoy and adore, that contest the reality of the experiences and events of the Holocaust, and the lessening of living evidence of the Holocaust, there is an urgent need for teachers and educators to give this greater consideration. One approach is to use (non-fictional) informational texts in conjunction with fictional texts. This is demonstrated in the following case study.

Bracey et al. (2006) investigated the use of historical fiction with 11- to 12-year-old students in teaching the Second World War and controversial issues such as the treatment of refugees and displaced children. This study unit approach focused on two novels: *Safe Harbour* (Conlon-McKenna, 1995), which tells of the experiences of the London Blitz; and *Faraway Home* (Taylor, 1999), which focuses on the experiences of two *kinder* who fled Vienna for Northern Ireland, and a range of informational texts. This approach is based on the rationale that students should read historical fiction alongside researching its context, thereby relating informational context from fiction to actual evidence and contributing to historical enquiry. This responds to the concern that students who do not have a firm grounding of the historical context of the Holocaust will be unable to distinguish between fantasy and reality (Brabham, 1997).

Informational sources included newspaper reports, personal testimonies and court records. These enabled students to make comparisons and engage in historical enquiry. For example, students compared the treatment of one character in *Faraway Home* with the actual treatment of Austrian and German refugees during the Holocaust, and discussed how the fictional author could have selected sources for their text. This study concluded that this use of historical fiction motivated students not only in their learning of the Holocaust, evacuation and refugees, but also in their reading of fiction and in their writing historical fiction (Bracey et al., 2006: 107).

Testimony

Survivor and eye-witness testimonies can, therefore, also make a significant contribution to addressing the difficulties arising from fictional texts. Whether in the form of a diary, a memoir, audiovisual or live (in-person) testimony, the version of events as told by witnesses adds a new dimension to the learning process. Survivor and eye-witness testimonies can dispel popular understandings, such as Holocaust survivors 'living' in one camp during their incarceration; the reality was that survivors were moved to and from a number of camps. It can also provide insight into incidents that students have read about or studied in their lessons, such as that of Gena Turgel (b. 1923) that verifies Anne Frank's illness at Bergen-Belsen.

The following extracts are from two audiovisual testimonies that were made available to schools in Scotland to accompany the introduction of Holocaust Memorial Day in the UK. Each of these demonstrates the insight that testimony can provide in commonly studied aspects of the

Holocaust. Both of the survivors were inmates of several concentration camps. The first testimony was recorded for students in the upper stages at primary school; the second for secondary school. In the first, Holocaust survivor Rev. Ernest Levy (1925–2009) tells about his experience as he lay on the dust at Bergen-Belsen when the British soldiers came to liberate the camp (LTS, 2000). In the second, artist Marianne Grant (1921–2007) speaks about her arrival at Auschwitz-Birkenau:

> By the time the British army came to liberate Bergen-Belsen I was more dead than alive. I weighed three or four stone. I was a skeleton. I could not stand on my feet. I could just, and no more, raise my head and wave a hand to welcome the soldiers ... There was no water in Bergen-Belsen. The British soldiers had to bring hundreds of hoses from the town of Bergen to provide water. (LTS, 2000: 20)

> Floodlight, shouting, SS, tall, black boots. Doberman dogs definitely doberman dogs. Large doberman dogs barking, jumping up at you. Of course there were bodies in each cattle wagon, people had died during the journey so they had these 'kapos' there who had to clear the dead bodies out of the cattle wagon. And also the luggage, we were under orders to drop the luggage and leave it. There were these grey and blue striped figures of men, which I had never seen in my life, grey and blue striped pyjama clad men running around lifting the luggage and putting it onto carts and collecting the dead. (LTS, 2002b: 17)

These demonstrate that survivor and eye-witness testimonies contribute to the following:

- *Personalising the Holocaust experience.* As we discussed in an earlier chapter (see p. 87), engaging with personal stories helps students understand the unbelievable and inconceivable reality of the Holocaust.
- *Addressing the gender imbalance in history.* Bauer states that the experiences of women in the Holocaust are 'barely touched upon in Holocaust literature' (2002: 167). Testimonies by women provide insight into the female perspective.
- *Rehumanising the victims.* The process of the Holocaust with its camps system successfully dehumanised millions of people. Testimony allows survivors the opportunity to reclaim their identity and this helps students develop empathy for their fellow men.
- *Challenging Holocaust denial.* Hearing the testimony face-to-face, or on film, from a person who lived through this event, supports well-documented evidence of the Holocaust, and can provide new evidence that initiates further research on the Holocaust.

That said, there may be discrepancies and/or inconsistencies with the dates between survivors' or eye-witnesses' memories and actual events. Teachers have to be aware of this and understand that survivors and eye-witnesses are not historians. Most are recollecting their experiences many years after they occurred. Teachers also need to recognise the subjective nature of testimony (Moisan et al., 2012), and make time for students to reflect on this at the end of the lesson.

Teachers who are fortunate to have a survivor or eyewitness speaking at their school should, if possible, check with their speaker beforehand that the content of their talk is suitable for students, and ensure that those students have the required contextual and historical knowledge. Teachers should also inform their students of the background of a speaker beforehand to prevent student misunderstandings. One primary teacher in Scotland, who invited a *kinder* refugee who lived nearby to come and speak to her primary 7 class, invited parents to come along and share the experience with their children. At the event, parents sat with their children in the classroom, and at the end of the talk, parents and children took turns to ask questions.

Allocating time for questions from students is beneficial as this allows the speaker to directly engage with students, and can reveal student misunderstandings that were unknown to the teacher. Questions can also reveal a sophisticated depth of reflection by students. At the end of his talk to primary 7 students, Rev. Levy was asked two such questions. The first was, *What was your prized possession in the camps?* He replied, *A friend.* The second was, *After all this, what is your motto in life?* He replied *When God sends a warning, like Noah, you get ready. You build your ark. We did not build our ark.*

At an event to commemorate fifty years of the end of the war, a former British soldier who had liberated the Bergen-Belsen camp spoke of his experience. This burly, middle-aged man walked confidently up to the stage. As he delivered his prepared speech, describing what he had witnessed, he broke down in tears and was unable to regain his composure. The power of listening to live oral testimony cannot be overestimated.

Yet it is important to remember that the era in which there will be no one with a living memory of the Holocaust is fast approaching. Today the youngest survivors are 80-years-old and were children in the Holocaust who were either hidden or sent by their parents to safety on the *Kindertransport programme.* They cannot provide information about the ghettos or camps. Such information is now provided by second or third generation survivors who speak about the experiences of their parent(s) or grandparent(s), or through the digitisation of large collections of testimonies by organisations such as the USC Shoah Foundation Institute for Visual History and Education. These ensure the availability of a rich oral history collection for future students.

Online testimony cannot be compared to seeing and hearing a survivor or eyewitness face to face. It does not contain the element of uniqueness or privilege, does not give students the opportunity to ask questions in response to what the speaker has said. Yet online testimony is more accessible in that students can view this in their own time at home, or on the transport they use to get to these places, as well as at school, and can bring the survivor's or eyewitness's voice into the classroom at a time of the teacher's choosing. As with face-to-face testimony, online audio-visual testimony displays a speaker's body language and emotions. One of the benefits of online testimony is that it can be repeatedly viewed and listened to, and some testimonies are accompanied with transcripts or subtitles. This can facilitate deeper criticality, and is particularly useful for students with short concentration spans, or those who would have difficulty in understanding what a speaker was saying. These students can 'catch' what they have missed on first viewing by watching or 'playing' it again. Further, many online testimony sites contain links to relevant sources and contextual information which enhances student understanding.

The USC Shoah Foundation is the leader in online video testimony of the Holocaust and other genocides. Testimonies from its *Visual History Archive* (VHA) collection, a selection of which can be found on YouTube, and are between one and two and a half hours in length, are valuable resources for teachers. Its *IWitness* online programme is an educational platform with more than 50,000 first-person stories from survivors and witnesses of genocides available to students from age 13 to 18, via multimedia-learning activities that are accessible on Macs, PCs, and tablet devices connected to the internet (USC, n.d.). It aims to develop students' knowledge of the subject matter and their skills in digital literacy, research and critical thinking. This platform supports teachers with planning by providing the estimated completion time and age-appropriate information for each activity. Activities contribute to a number of subject areas that include Social Studies, History, English Language, Modern Foreign Languages, and Citizenship (Civic or Character) Education.

Another innovative approach that *IWitness* adopts is the use of introductory films that focus on how to use its collection in a responsible and educational manner. This emphasis on the importance of ethical editing in creating films, and of respecting each testimony before students engage with that testimony, is both diligent and timely. While students assume a responsibility in their engagement of online testimonies, teachers have to exercise their responsibility in ensuring that all content is age-appropriate for their students.

The wide range of websites that contain Holocaust survivor testimony that is suitable for students from 11-years-old onwards includes audio testimony from The British Library which can be accessed through *Learning Voices of the Holocaust: Survivor Testimonies* and *Sounds: Jewish Survivors of the Holocaust*, and video testimonies on the *Survivor Profiles* section on the *Facing History and Ourselves* website, *The Voices of Survivors* section on the Yad Vashem website, and *The Holocaust Explained* website. Some of these testimonies are structured talks, some are interviews. As these are not suitable for younger students, primary teachers will need to adapt the above to their use, which while time consuming is still worthwhile. It is necessary to remember that while testimony effectively personalises the Holocaust, each testimony is unique and not representative of other survivors' experiences.

The development of virtual memorials, i.e. memorials on the internet, raises new issues. One example of this is the Facebook page set up to remember Henio Zytomirski (see Chapter 8, pp. 108–109). This page remembers Henio by posting photographs and 'testimony' although he never wrote or provided any testimony. The 'testimony' is provided through his imagined voice with his imagined words. The advantage of this virtual approach is that it encourages today's young people to remember people who may otherwise be forgotten. However, its principal sources are neither survivor or eyewitness testimony. Supporters of this approach consider anything that keeps the memory of the Holocaust alive to be worthwhile. We do not subscribe to this view. This approach raises serious ethical questions about whether one should create testimony from a dead person. We consider that the conflation of fact and fiction in virtual memorials can lead to misconceptions about the Holocaust, and confusion between the reality (historical accuracy) and fiction or hearsay.

Role Play and Simulation

Role-play and simulation strategies can be tremendously powerful classroom teaching strategies, but need to be used with caution, forethought and reflection. Whilst aimed at developing pupil empathy for the victims of Holocaust experience they can lead to students becoming distressed. For example, in an attempt to show the dangers of prejudice, discrimination and isolation, one class teacher in Scotland was reported to have told her primary 7 (age 11) students that she had received a letter from the Scottish Government saying that nine children were to be separated from their classmates because they were born in January, February and March, and had lower IQs as a result of a lack of sunlight in their mother's womb.

These students were told that they had to wear yellow hats and would need to go to the library (*Mail Online*, 2010). Lasting about 15 minutes, several students were in tears while one boy demanded to speak to someone in charge (*East Kilbride News*, 2010). As well as the disruption this caused in the classroom, one parent called for the teacher to be suspended and the local council issued an apology, advising parents that this activity would not be repeated in the school (*Telegraph Online*, 2010). While one may applaud the efforts of this student to exert his rights, this example raises issues concerning the ethical use of classroom simulations in this context, teachers' skills in using this approach in the classroom, and parental communication.

In another case Maitles (2010a) found that a simulation, this time with students aged 12, led to distress, with some students very upset and feeling that 'the school has turned against us'. Interestingly, Maitles found that many students (15 of the 120 students involved) complained about the treatment of their peers, although most felt they could do nothing about it. Should teachers deliberately seek such an emotional response from students? Perhaps students would benefit from learning when taken from their comfort zone? Yet we would argue that it is inappropriate and/or unethical for teachers to be quite so deceptive. Quite apart from the hysterical responses it may yield from students, it can cause serious damage to teacher–student relationships and the school–parental partnership.

However, teaching controversial areas such as the Holocaust, genocide and the abuse of children's rights *is* upsetting for many students. It is, indeed, a matter of debate as to whether these areas can effectively be taught to students without some level of distress. Role play can be used to develop empathy by, for example, giving students a choice of scenarios or allowing them to devise their own scenario where they can apply what they have learned about racist Nazi policy. One common example used in primary schools is when students role play a scenario where an employer interviews an applicant with the required skills and experience but does not give them the job because they are Jewish. This example arouses emotions in students and can develop their empathy for victims of prejudice in an appropriate way.

Teaching about the Holocaust and genocide can thus be tremendously valuable but it is also tremendously difficult. Nowhere is this clearer than in using simulations. The most famous simulation is that of Jane Elliott (Peters, 1987). Known as *Blue Eyes/Brown Eyes*, the experiment was designed to show the impact of discrimination on both victims and bystanders. In response to the assassination of Martin Luther King Jr over forty years ago, Jane Elliott devised this controversial exercise which labels participants as inferior or superior based solely upon the colour of their eyes and exposes them to the experience of being a minority. It is still in use and has been the subject of much debate which is discussed below. Similarly, the Gestapo Holocaust simulation, devised by Raymond Zwerin and Audrey Friedman Marcus in 1976, has been the subject of controversy (Fallace, 2007). And the controversy surrounding using simulations has continued since (Narvaez, 1987) and indeed is still a live issue in the present day (Short News, 2006; Elliott, 2009).

The critique is that simulation debases the memory of the Holocaust and does not reflect what really went on. As one example, an 8th grade teacher in the USA called upon his colleagues to be involved in the experiment on discrimination as 'a day of sheer pleasure for the staff being themselves as Nazi officers and becoming Adolfs ... because staff need the stress relief and entertainment' (Elliott, 2009). Critiques come from individuals and organisations heavily committed to Holocaust Education. Dawidowicz (1990) and Totten (2000b), for example, argue that simulations reflect poor pedagogy and oversimplify Holocaust history. Totten is particularly critical. He argues that:

> For students to walk away thinking that they have either experienced what a victim went through or have a greater understanding of what the victims suffered is shocking in its naivety. Even more galling is for teachers to think that they have provided their students with a true sense of what the victims lived through – and/or to think they have at least approximated the horror and terror the victims experienced. (Totten, 2002: 122)

The US Anti-Defamation League claims that simulations can trivialise the experience, stereotype group behaviour, distort historical reality, reinforce negative views, impede critical analysis, and disconnect the Holocaust from its historical context. It cites one simulation (in Florida) where children were very distressed and crying, and one child reported that 'The only thing I found out today is that I don't want to be Jewish' (ADL, 2006). In other words, this approach can have the exact opposite impact from the one teachers intended. Further, there is a fear of psychological scarring shown by the blue eyes/brown eyes children experiencing stress and disengagement for a period afterwards (Smetana, 2006; Power et al., 2007). One parent in the primary school mentioned earlier in Scotland thought the simulation activity was 'cruel' and 'traumatic' (*Mail Online*, 2010). Nonetheless, there are those who argue that using simulation is an issue of pedagogy, and if done well, can encourage students to consider the Holocaust from the perspectives of bystanders, victims and perpetrators (Narvaez, 1987; Pederson, 1995; Ruben, 1999; Schweber, 2003; Ben-Peretz, 2004; Drake, 2008; Maitles, 2010a).

Jane Elliott, an advocate of such simulations, expresses caution. She argues that these require experienced teachers, extensive debriefing, experienced facilitators and a strong rapport between students and teachers for them to work (Drake, 2008). Maitles (2010a) also found the debriefing to be crucial. In this case, the students were much more empowered to speak out when it became clear that the adults in the room were both encouraging them to do so and were themselves reflecting on and sometimes disagreeing about some of the issues. The discussion, for example, on organising to challenge the discrimination involved a large number of students, encouraged by the teachers themselves disagreeing on how to interpret that 25 students had approached members of staff unhappy about the discrimination but had not had the confidence to go beyond the complaint. This was a confident, questioning debrief; it was what was required to draw some lessons from the day. However, a caveat must be made here: this pedagogy does not challenge the wider issues relating to institutional discrimination within a school. The parameters were set tightly in that discrimination was seen in a narrower focus with the emphasis on personal responsibility rather than challenging an overall ethos.

Whilst being critical of simulations, the United States Holocaust Memorial Museum does point out that simulations and role play can develop thinking around areas such as fear, scapegoating and conflict. It states that complex events and actions can be over-simplified and students can be left with a skewed view of the Holocaust (USHMM, 2009). In addition, the simulation strategy can be used without giving students either the historical understanding of the rise to power of the Nazis or an understanding of antisemitism (Hammond, 2001) and where Jews are seen solely as victims, leading to patronising feelings of pity (Illingworth, 2000). Alternative strategies to simulations tend to involve survivor and eyewitness testimony, primary source material, reflective writing experiences, in-class discussions, and incorporating the Holocaust into a wider study of the Second World War for example, or contemporary world problems (ADL, 2006; USHMM, 2009).

The key point here is that while the school and its local authority may value Holocaust Education and the teachers are undertaking the simulation for the best of reasons, the pedagogical issues need to be fully explored beforehand. This is not to suggest that simulation and role play should not be used. Exercising caution, and putting the simulation explicitly and appropriately into its historical context, can work very well. This raises issues of teacher confidence and development of skills which are relevant to teachers' Continuing Professional Development (CPD). If done well, the simulation approach can contribute in a meaningful way to a better understanding of the Holocaust and citizenship.

Conclusion

We have discussed in this chapter three potentially powerful but problematic areas of learning in Holocaust and Genocide Education. The issues we have raised are both specific to Holocaust Education and reflect general issues in dealing with controversial citizenship issues in the classroom. We, along with many educators, believe that learning techniques and indeed content around the Holocaust do raise potentially disturbing issues for students, and it is important that we understand such issues may (indeed perhaps should) take students outside their comfort zone. When using literature, testimony and role play it is crucial that aims and objectives and reflection are clearly understood. Teachers also need to be cognisant that not all resources – even if powerful – should necessarily be used. We have argued in this chapter, for example, that not all simulation is valuable, and indeed that a novel and film like *The Boy in the Striped Pyjamas* raises such problematic issues that teachers should be reconsidering their use as major resources in Holocaust Education.

Further Reading

On *The Boy in the Striped Pyjamas*:

The Holocaust Educational Trust (HET) (online n.d.), *Teaching the Holocaust in English*, www.het.org.uk/media/english%20guide.pdf

Cowan, P. (2015) A selected, annotated guide to Holocaust websites, *Prism: An Interdisciplinary Journal for Holocaust Educators*, pp. 96–100. New York: Yeshiva University.

Maitles, H. (2010) Why does wearing a yellow bib make us different'? A case study of explaining discrimination in a West of Scotland secondary (high) school, *Journal for Critical Education Policy Studies*, 8 (1): 246–61. www.jceps.com/index.php?pageID=article&articleID=183

10

LEARNING FROM AUSCHWITZ

Learning Objectives

- To explore the rationale for visits to Auschwitz-Birkenau, concentrating on the Lessons from Auschwitz Project
- To examine the Lessons from Auschwitz Project, alternative models of school/ group visits to Auschwitz-Birkenau, and alternative perspectives
- To analyse the educational experience provided at the Auschwitz-Birkenau Memorial and Museum, with reference to academic research and other texts
- To discuss the contribution of visits to community relations, by breaking down barriers

Auschwitz remains the byword for the epitome of inhumanity and barbarism. Designed and implemented following the Wannsee Conference of December 1941, the concentration and death camps at Auschwitz-Birkenau, situated in the Polish town of Oświęcim (named in German, *Auschwitz*), constituted a vast work and killing arena, with the deeply ironic *Arbeit Macht Frei* [Work Sets You Free] on the gates. Its purpose was explained by Rudolf Hoess (see p. 119), the longest serving Camp Commandant there, in 1946 as 'the largest human slaughterhouse that history had ever known' (Hoess, 2000: 207), consisting of the 'assembly line style murder of human beings' (USHMM, 2016), as the most modern techniques of industrialisation at the time were used to kill the maximum numbers feasible. As Primo Levi (1988: 9–10) put it, '… never were so many human lives extinguished in so short a time, and with so lucid a combination of technological ingenuity, fanaticism and cruelty'.

That the events took place in the centre of Europe seventy years ago is a warning from history that is relevant today. Designated a UNESCO world heritage site in 1979, educational school visits to the Auschwitz-Birkenau Memorial and Museum (ABMM) have been primarily organised in a number of different ways. The first are targeted visits, such as those in the UK that since 1999 have been organised and subsidised by the Holocaust Educational Trust (HET) and integrated into the Lessons from Auschwitz Project (LFAP) (Holocaust Educational Trust, 2006) for students aged 16- to 18-years-old. The second type is one organised by a school, group of schools or an agency such as a church or scouts' association to take a number of young people to the site. However, whilst we will concentrate on the experiences of participants on the LFAP and their impact, we must note that there is a range of organised visits. For example, in Israel, the Ministry for Education subsidises such visits for school students every year, as part of the *Journey to Poland* Project. Introduced in 1988, this involves students visiting Jewish sites of interest as well as concentration and death camps. Nitzan Horowitz's (2016) claim in the Israeli newspaper *Ha'aretz*, that Dachau in Germany (which he sees as a precursor for the camps in Poland) would better explain to students why the Holocaust occurred, demonstrates that there is a debate in Israel as to the value of visiting the ABMM.

Another example is that exemplified by some Norwegian schools which takes parents, school students and teachers on the visit (Henderson, 2015). This is of particular interest in that the emotional experiences and often isolation reported by students can be overcome as this shared experience provides young participants with additional support. Some schools which have organised their visits have disseminated their participants' experiences online. Interestingly, these visits often include younger students, for example the website of one school contains reports from years 9 and 10 students (14- to-15-years-old) (Wolfreton School, 2014). One of the worries of individual school visits is the lack of knowledge with regard to how the young people have been prepared. We know that in England, students currently engage in a (relatively short) study of the Holocaust as part of the National Curriculum, although this will change under current government plans for all schools to be academies or free schools, as these schools will no longer have to follow the National Curriculum. In Wales, some students who chose History will have examined Nazi policies towards the Jews prior to the visit, but this is no guarantee that students will have received the required input that will prepare and orientate them for their visit to the ABMM.

There are specific Jewish visits to Auschwitz-Birkenau, such as those organised as the *March of the Living* (MoTL, 2016) which is an educational programme that brings Jewish people from all over the world to Poland on *Yom HaShoah* (see p. 64) to collectively march from Auschwitz to Birkenau. Its significance is to show how the Nazi attempt to destroy all Jews has so patently failed and to remember the victims. This tends to be an uplifting experience as survivors, relatives of survivors, and new generations of Jewish youth, celebrate their survival, mourn the victims, and commemorate this Day.

As we show below, the students on organised visits tend to be senior students from secondary schools, often lacking in ethnic diversity. We would make two points about this. Whilst we are of the opinion, expressed in other chapters in the book, that younger children can learn about the Holocaust, it seems to us that 16 and above are the best ages for young people to visit and accept the emotional challenges of a visit to Auschwitz. Interestingly, The Council of Europe (2006) suggested that young people from 14- to 15-years-old can cope with the emotional impact of Auschwitz-Birkenau if (and only if) preparations are thorough and there is significant background learning. Secondly, as regards participation, Cowan and Maitles (2009) and Chapman et al. (2010) wondered if greater diversity, in terms of ethnicity, ability and social disadvantage, was worth considering. Interestingly, albeit with an older age range, the Unite Against Fascism visit to Auschwitz (UAF, 2015) includes a wider range of ethnicity and socially disadvantaged participants. Its November 2015 visit included a number of young Muslim women, although these participants are more likely to share an ideological anti-fascist position than the school students on the LFAP. The experiences of young Muslims on the visit, outlined on the site, suggest that visiting the ABMM can both enhance their understanding and their social activism to challenge racism, whether in its Islamophobic or antisemitic manifestations.

As the title of the LFAP suggests, its aim is for participants across the UK to learn universal and contemporary lessons *from* the Holocaust and Auschwitz in addition to learning *about* it. To ensure participation from the maximum number of schools, two students between 16 and 18 years and an accompanying teacher from each school are allowed to participate annually. This has been seen as a strong model, with the Prime Minister's Holocaust Commission Report (2015: 11) commending the LFAP as an 'example of excellent practice'.

The LFAP comprises four components: an orientation seminar the week before the visit at which a Holocaust survivor speaks to the group (four hours) and students are given readings and prepared for their visit; the visit to the ABMM which includes visiting the concentration camp Auschwitz 1 and Auschwitz-Birkenau death camp (one day); a follow-up seminar which takes place one week after the visit at which students are debriefed, given an opportunity to reflect on the visit, and discuss practical approaches to passing on their learning (four hours); and the Next Steps component where students are required to organise a school and/or community activity as a means of passing on their learning.

Auschwitz in Context

Adorno's statement that 'it is impossible to write poetry after Auschwitz' (in Klaus, 2005), and Hilberg's reference to the expression 'planet Auschwitz' used by Holocaust survivors (Hilberg, 1992), convey the idea that the constraints of conventional language hinder one's expression of the Holocaust and sets Auschwitz apart from everything else. In the school context, Dudek similarly claims that Auschwitz cannot be taught, like other subjects, within the curriculum (in Holden and Clough, 1998). Although neither Auschwitz nor the Holocaust are school subjects as such, it follows that alternative educational tools, museums and memorial sites have an important contribution to make. For Marcus (2007: 106), museums provide 'more hands-on ways than an average classroom setting' to learn about the past. This interactive approach sits well with curriculums which promote active learning methods and recognise the value of educational experiences that take place beyond the classroom. Visits to museums and historical sites are included in its wide range of outdoor learning experiences (House of Commons Education and Skills Committee, 2005), while visits to countries are included in government international education agenda. For school students, a visit to the ABMM will provide insight into European history and further their understanding of the Second World War.

Oleksy claims that the young visitor's place of origin is a key factor in determining their meaning of Auschwitz (in Davies, 2000). Miller suggests that Auschwitz is important to anti-racist education in recognising the Nazi persecution of people of different backgrounds and those who colluded in the genocide that occurred (Copley, 2005). Garside considers that a visit to Auschwitz links the genocide of Jews and the murder of other European citizens to more recent genocides (Garside, 2008). Wollaston (2005: 79) challenges the broader impact of the ABMM by stating that this memorial museum has avoided addressing the relationship between the Holocaust and previous and subsequent genocides, 'preferring to focus solely on the history of the camp, and more recently, Polish-Jewish relations'. This suggests that young people's understanding of contemporary racism and genocides may not automatically be increased by a visit to the ABMM, but that these broader contemporary lessons may require additional input. This is supported by findings from two studies of Israeli youth. Lazar et al. (2004) compared the impact of Holocaust Education, which included a visit to the ABMM, on young people who were related to Holocaust survivors to those who were unrelated. Their findings were that unrelated participants were more aware of the universal, humanistic lessons of the Holocaust than their related peers. Schechter and Salomon

(2005) examined whether a visit to the ABMM increased empathy for contemporary groups portrayed as victims – in this case Palestinians. They found that the visit increased empathy among youth participants with initially more positive attitudes towards the Palestinians, but it also decreased empathy among those with initially more negative ones. It cannot therefore be assumed that a visit to the ABMM per se will challenge assumptions. Fuchs (2007) found similar from his research into German youth visits to Auschwitz (albeit his students were in their late teens and early 20s). He concluded (2007: 192) that 'the excursion had had no significant impact on the positions they had occupied before the beginning of the memorial visits'. Nonetheless, he also found that many of the participants both wanted to do something and wanted to further research the events. His point (2007: 193) about the visit being '(almost) a waste of time' seems unnecessarily negative to us, as we try to show below by looking at events organised by many students on their return. Romi and Lev (2007), examining the Israeli 'Journey to Poland' programme (outlined above), which is an entitlement to all Israeli young people, found that there was little difference in emotional engagement between those who went on the programme and those who didn't. Feldman (2002) and Schechter and Salomon (2005) argue that a potential (and real) problem with the visits to the museum can be that the students are engaged in a sensory, emotional experience rather than an educational one; they become 'dark tourists'. Nonetheless, as Henderson (2015) points out, it may be that the attempt to differentiate between emotional experiences and cognitive experiences may not be relevant, that they are indeed linked. Indeed, in Israeli visits there are exceptionally strong emotional responses and sensitivities. The ABMM needs to address this, although on occasions it has been heavy-handed when dealing with Israeli groups (*Israel National News*, 2014). These sensitivity needs also extend to Jewish and Roma visitors in general for whom Auschwitz evokes very strong emotions.

Learning from Auschwitz

While a visit to the ABMM cannot replicate the reality of this death site, in that for example its gas chambers have since been blown up, and the visitors' experience does not include the presence of victims' bodies, seeing and walking round the ABMM can provide young visitors with a greater understanding of the scale of the inhumanity and tragedy that occurred there. This can assist them in addressing denier rhetoric, which is particularly important for the time when Holocaust survivors will no longer be able to provide direct oral testimony and when a further development of denial strategies is inevitable. In contrast, memorial sites in Rwanda or Cambodia often include the presence of victims' bodies (see Kushner, in Vice, 2003).

There are two principal reasons as to why young visitors need to apply analysis when visiting museums rather than adopt a passive receptive stance. Firstly, despite the educational nature of this visit, visits to the ABMM, as we pointed out above, are often referred to as the 'dark side of tourism' or simply 'dark tourism'. Visitors pose in front of the *Arbeit Macht Frei* sign in Auschwitz 1 taking photographs of each other, school parties sit 'on the ruins of the crematorium eating sandwiches' (Lennon and Foley, 2000: 61), and thus this visit is perceived by many as a 'commercial, political and religious exploitation of the site' (Wollaston, 2005: 66). Indeed, there can be concerns that some young people today regard their visit to the ABMM as a kind of pilgrimage; it is something they should do at some stage in their life, something that can be ticked off a 'bucket list'.

Whether a visit to Auschwitz-Birkenau is included as a tourist attraction of Krakow, part of an educational day visit that accommodates plane schedules, or part of a larger visit to Holocaust sites in Poland, its quick, organised pace can be criticised in that its visitors may require considerably more time to absorb its contents than is allocated to them. Further, there is evidence (Henderson, 2015) that it is precisely in moments of reflection – what are called pedagogical hinges – that students find time to reflect on their learning of the Holocaust in peer-to-peer discussions. Indeed, Henderson argues that some of the best reflections on Auschwitz *will* take place over the sandwiches and other less structured activities. In an interesting insight, Henderson observed that a delay in the transport of school students from Auschwitz to Birkenau led to positive reflective discourse amongst the students. Unfortunately, it is exactly these opportunities that are often squeezed out in the fast-paced tours and visits.

Further, museums are becoming more sophisticated in how they present the past (Marcus, 2007), that they tend to 'promote a moral framework to the narration of historical events', and have a 'missionary' quality (Williams, 2007: 8). This can be due to the respective people and/or guides being more dedicated and committed to their work than professional in their applying a critical detachment to the respective historical issues and/or to the museum's designers or the respective government's own agenda. It can also be due to museum designers who construct a particular message to be conveyed to their audience (Gross, 2009). Indeed, as we pointed out on page 60, as late as 1989 there was a lack of recognition in the museum of the distinctive issue of destruction of European Jews and Roma/Gypsies, which by 2003 had been rectified. Blum's earlier experience of the ABMM supports the claim that the interpretation of the Holocaust as a Polish tragedy was an approach used by the former Communist authorities (Lennon and Foley, 2000).

Nonetheless, we have previously pointed out that there is a wide range of research that supports the positive contribution of Holocaust Education to developing students' understanding aspects of citizenship (Cowan and Maitles, 2007). Awareness of racism, antisemitism and genocides is an example of the contemporary lessons that can be taken *from* visits to Auschwitz. However, understanding is only one side to citizenship; behaviour and action are another (Kratsborn et al., 2008). One of the lessons of the Holocaust, Bauman (1989) claims, is that evil can be resisted as human beings have a choice, and during the Holocaust some people exerted that choice by choosing moral duty over self-preservation.

Although a visit to a memorial or death site is not a recent phenomenon (Seaton, 1996), there is little known about the value that such visits have on participants in general (Lennon and Foley, 2000), and even less about the educational impact this has on school students and their teachers specifically. However, later studies by Cowan and Maitles (2009) and Chapman et al. (2010) have investigated the impact of the LFAP on Scottish school students and English students respectively. These found that firstly, the most academic students in the school studying Social Subjects made up the student cohort and that most were chosen by the school; secondly, that there was clear evidence of personal development and that students were deeply moved by the visit, in contrast to Fuchs (2007) and Romi and Lev (2007) outlined above; thirdly, that the highest perceived gains in knowledge were in the areas of genocide and human rights; and finally, that students took their responsibilities on their return very seriously and organised a wide range of events, both in their schools and in their communities. Maitles and Cowan's Scottish students' school-based activities are summarised as follows:

- 64% spoke at a school assembly
- 40% wrote an article for their school magazine
- 20% produced a video for a school presentation
- 59% spoke to one year group or more
- 44% made a display of photos for the school
- Two pupils gave multimedia presentations to each year group in the school, culminating in a Holocaust Memorial Day service for senior pupils and invited members from the community
- Two pupils talked to all year groups at assemblies using PowerPoints on the theme of Hate – 'So you think you can hate?' The following quotes highlight the innovativeness of some students' Next Steps:

We made up an eight-week lesson plan in the subjects History, English and Religious and Moral Education for a second year class based on ideas we got from the Holocaust; discrimination, racism etc. Before the lesson plan began we organised a visit from a Holocaust survivor to our school who spoke to the second year class as an introduction to the Holocaust.

Met with social education teachers and helped to draw up a lesson plan to be implemented in younger classes discussing the Holocaust and the lessons that can be learned from it today.

Interview data showed that some students engaged in further school-based activities and provided further insight into the nature of student involvement. They included presentations and lessons to various year groups, school assembly presentations, discussions with teachers as to improving and developing lessons on the Holocaust, and visits to local primary schools to talk to final year students there about Auschwitz-Birkenau and what they had seen.

The students' Next Steps activities suggest that the LFAP led to a range of activities in their wider communities throughout Scotland. Students spoke to a variety of groups that included Rotary Clubs, church groups, parent council meetings, college students, and primary school teachers. Community activities are summarised as follows:

- 48% featured in the local newspaper
- 10% produced a video community presentation
- 15% helped organise a community event
- Two students gave presentations to their local MPs and MSPs
- Students attended an event at the Scottish Parliament, at which they highlighted their experiences; present at the event was the First Minister and other cabinet ministers and MSPs

The findings of Chapman et al. (2010) were strikingly similar to those of Cowan and Maitles above. They reported that students were deeply moved by the visit. One commented that 'It definitely does change the way you view certain, some priorities in life'; another that 'I think it forces you to think about it a bit more … you can't detach yourself from it because it's all around you'. These students found the orientation seminar talk by the Holocaust survivor, the visit itself, and the service of remembrance at the end as particularly memorable. It must be noted that Chapman et al. had pointed out that all their students had some prior knowledge of the Holocaust through its inclusion in the National Curriculum. This may not be the case in the future (see p. 131) and LFAP will have to take this into account in the future

Although Chapman et al. found that only 5.8% of their sample viewed the next steps as the element they valued most (not particularly surprising as it would have had to be chosen over the camp itself and the survivor testimony), the respondents were very positive about what they had done. As with the Scottish students, they organised assemblies, contributed to a school publication, made a visual display in the school, undertook some teaching, gave an outside talk, wrote for a local newspaper, worked with local primary schools, produced a short film, and gave a talk at the local Rotary Club. One student commented:

> I have taught several year 8 classes and have drawn up a PowerPoint using pictures. I am completing assemblies to all year groups and to school governors. I am also writing an article for the local newspaper and have sent a letter to the Prime Minister.

Maitles and Cowan (2010) and Chapman et al. (2010) also examined the impact of the visit on those teachers who accompanied their students. The former involved 43 teachers and the latter 116. It is important that we do not over-generalise from this. Nonetheless, there are a number of points which can be drawn from it. Firstly, in terms of their own personal development, this group of teachers were deeply moved by their visit to Poland. Those who perceived they already had a sound knowledge of the issues recognised that they had additionally learned about these from the LFAP and that it had contributed to their Continued Professional Development. Secondly, they appreciated all aspects of the LFAP. They valued the orientation seminar and thought the Holocaust survivor talk was particularly effective. The follow-up seminar was valued as a reflective experience, although a number of the Scottish teachers felt that it was too controlled by the LFAP educators, limiting student involvement and interaction. This is clearly an important point and any programme involving students and teachers has to ensure the student voice is heard in the feedback. Thirdly, in terms of the impact on the schools, whilst the claim cannot be made for every secondary school, the LFAP led to significant extra teaching of the Holocaust in those Scottish secondary schools whose teachers took part in this survey, and also gave rise to an increased informal awareness about the Holocaust as LFAP participants talked to their peers informally about their experiences on their return to school. Finally, teacher support with Next Steps varied from discussing ideas and helping students to implement these, to not providing any support at all; it cannot be assumed that all schools that participate in the LFAP will provide teaching staff who will effectively assist their students with their Next Steps. There is no doubt however that those teachers interviewed felt there was a significant impact in their schools and communities. However, whilst there was much varied activity, the quality of the Next Steps activities in the schools remains to be evaluated in further research on future visits.

As well as teachers accompanying their students on the LFAP visit, the HET also organises groups of teachers – usually about 150 per visit – to visit the ABMM. As well as showing the teachers what their two student representatives per school go through, the visit is also designed to help teachers prepare better learning experiences in the classroom. Participants said that they hoped it would help them in the classroom by both highlighting what happened there and feeding into projects on conflict resolution and diversity (Morrison, 2009). In that sense it is both developing lessons *about* and *from* Auschwitz.

Some schools organise visits themselves, and hence are in a position to take a wider range of students than the two per year who go on the LFAP. The experiences of those schools and students needs a full evaluation, particularly if Fuchs and Schechter and Salomon (see above) are correct that a visit to the ABMM reinforces rather than challenges outlooks. This section will concentrate on the experiences of one Scottish school visiting outwith the LFAP.

This school was a large Catholic comprehensive (aged 12- to 18-years-old), with all ranges of abilities, in the West of Scotland. The Archdiocese of Glasgow organised the four-day visit, involving four senior students from several Catholic schools in the area. This included a visit to the ABMM, the saltmines in Krakow, and the Divine Mercy Chapel. This case study encapsulates a group interview with four students after their return but before their formal follow-up reflection meeting.

The students had all learned about the Holocaust in primary and/or secondary school. They thought they were as prepared as they could be, but highlighted that there were things at the ABMM for which one cannot be prepared, such as the size.

One described it as '... *never ending. It kept going on and on'*.

Their key memories were of the gas chamber area: *'it was quiet ... something I'll remember until I die'* (student 2).

Another, that it was the children's clothes *'because I have a wee sister ... it really sticks with me'* (student 4).

Interestingly, and related to discussion we have had in other chapters, they did not understand what antisemitism meant as a word. They used the phrase *'discrimination against the Jews'* (student 1). They were reflective on their experiences of Auschwitz-Birkenau relating to discrimination against Jews.

One put it that:

> *'It wasn't really about the Jews, it was about anyone who was murdered there ... we know that Hitler hated the Jews. They were the target to eliminate ... it was about the amount of people.'* (student 3)

The teacher who accompanied the students highlighted the importance of the guide in this area, noting that their guide did not mention antisemitism. We regard this as problematic and unacceptable. The word and the ideas behind 'antisemitism' need to be linked. Students should not come back from Auschwitz not having heard the word. Indeed, the orientation before the visit – whether formal classes or discussions – needs to ensure that students understand and recognise this word.

Conclusion

We believe that the evidence outlined above suggests that there are many positive benefits from visiting the Auschwitz-Birkenau site. Whilst we can agree with some of the comments about visits not perhaps being universally life-changing, we would not agree that the visits are worthless. In terms of personal growth, as regards reflecting the experience back into the school and in terms of wider community action, there is much increased activity around Holocaust learning. One point that might have to be examined is the timescale. Chapman et al. (2010: 11) argue that 'fitting everything into one day proved exhausting for some students and teachers and there is scope for reviewing the content, structure and time allocation for the visit to Poland in the light of this finding'.

A final point about the actual make-up of the groups is worth considering. Cowan and Maitles (2009), Maitles and Cowan (2010) and Chapman et al. (2010) found that the students chosen tended to be sympathetic to the importance of learning from the Holocaust, generally liberal in outlook, and academically able. Both the schools and the HET could see the importance of these students representing the school as they would be able to come back and translate what they saw and experienced into the Next Steps phase of the programme. Nonetheless, both sets of researchers wondered whether the group could be more diverse in terms of its ethnicity, ability, social disadvantage, and even subject specialisms.

As schools in England convert to academy status, there is a possibility that, like Scotland, students who participate in the LFAP may not have learned about the Holocaust prior to their visit to the ABMM. The worst scenario is that schools do not teach the Holocaust and use the HET through the LFAP as the core providers of Holocaust Education, rather than nurture and encourage their staff to develop Holocaust Education in their schools. Future contributions of the LFAP in enhancing Holocaust Education in schools might well involve stronger partnerships between the HET and participating schools than before.

Further Reading

Bauman, Z. (1989) *Modernity and the Holocaust.* Cambridge: Polity Press.

Cowan, P. (2008) 'Seeing, hearing and feeling: how can a visit to Auschwitz encourage young people to practise citizenship?' In A. Ross and P. Cunningham (eds), *Reflecting on Identities: Research, Practice and Innovation.* London: London Metropolitan University. pp. 511–20.

Levi, P. (1947) *If this is a Man/The Truce.* London: Abacus.

11

EPILOGUE

> **Learning Objectives**
>
> - To summarise the development of Holocaust Education
> - To identify the challenges to Holocaust Education
> - To provide insight into student teachers' responses to learning about the Holocaust
> - To discuss the legacy of the Holocaust

We have provided examples throughout this book that support the development of Holocaust Education in Europe, Israel, and other English-speaking countries. We have shown the opportunities that Citizenship or Civics Education, and the establishment of an international Holocaust Memorial Day, can bring to this development. While we have focused strongly on school-based Holocaust Education, we are well aware that such development extends to universities, young offenders' institutions, prisons and museums, and that across the globe many organisations that provide Holocaust Education have emerged and are now well established. It is ironic that when Inge Auerbacher, a survivor of Theresienstadt concentration camp, spoke to the inmates at Polmont Young Offenders Institution in Falkirk, Scotland, in 2016, she began by commenting that while walking down the corridor from the entrance of the building to the hall, one of the boys had asked her if she had ever been in a prison before!

As the title of this book suggests, the aim of this book is to broaden and develop teachers' and educators' understanding of the key issues in Holocaust Education. Because this book is not a practical guide for teaching the Holocaust, we have not addressed online issues such as which websites and apps are particularly helpful for primary or secondary teachers, or provided information on websites that offer Holocaust survivor testimony in English (see Cowan, 2015, for further information on this), or discussed the value of MOOCs (Massive Open Online Courses) to Holocaust Education. We have however (from Chapter 6 onwards) focused on broad practical issues, such as the use of language and fiction, to support teachers and educators.

At the very beginning of this book, we justified one's suspicion of education (see Chapter 2, p. 16) in the context of the Holocaust, and it is worth returning to this point as education is often perceived as something that is unquestioningly beneficial and worthwhile. Of the 15 officials who attended the Wannsee Conference in 1942 to discuss the implementation of the 'Final Solution of the Jewish Question', eight held PhDs. Education is therefore not a panacea for racism or something that automatically instils or creates responsible and democratic citizenship. We would go so far as to argue that education without humanity can lead to the railway tracks into Auschwitz. The *content* of education, whether based on history, citizenship, human rights and/or values, and the quality of education, i.e. *how* the content is taught, have a significant impact on learners' education. For teachers and other educators, this means that it is not simply a matter of allocating time for teaching the Holocaust, or having sufficient commitment and enthusiasm for the task; it is about developing knowledge of the Holocaust, genocide, antisemitism and citizenship, and also developing the skills to ensure that students are actively engaged in their learning. In this we are convinced that the evidence suggests that studying the Holocaust can be transformational, particularly where teachers specifically examine both lessons *about* and lessons *from* the Holocaust. However, teachers and educators should also be aware of the challenges of Holocaust Education, and identifying those challenges is a key step to effectively teaching the Holocaust.

The Challenges

De-Judaisation of the Holocaust

We consider that the use of contradictory definitions of the Holocaust, as we presented in Chapter 1, is a serious challenge to Holocaust Education. That the Nazis wanted to kill every Jewish person living in Europe, and indeed extended this policy to North Africa, is a fundamental feature of the Holocaust, that according to Bauer (2002) makes it an unprecedented historical phenomenon. Teachers and educators who neither recognise this, nor the distinctive treatment of the Jews as victims of Nazism, in their understanding of the Holocaust, are marginalising the Jewish experience in the Holocaust. The impact of this understanding of the Holocaust will impact on their pedagogy and practice and has the potential to distort students' understanding of the Holocaust. It is concerning to consider that teachers and educators who *think* they are teaching the Holocaust are in effect doing the opposite of what they have intended, i.e. teaching the Holocaust effectively.

We remarked in Chapter 10 that one guide at the ABMM did not mention the Jewish experience. When Cowan accompanied a schools' visit to the ABMM, she overheard a conversation between two girls when returning to the bus, in which one commented that the guide had been talking a lot about the Jews, and asked her friend why should he be doing this as it wasn't *only* the Jews who were murdered during the Holocaust. Her friend agreed with her that the guide should not be talking so much about the Jews. These students knew that many groups of people were murdered at Auschwitz. Yet even after visiting this camp, they were unaware that eleven million Jews were deported to Auschwitz, and that the overwhelming number of people who were murdered at this camp were Jews; 960,000 Jews compared to 74,000 Poles and 21,000 Roma. Hence the first challenge to Holocaust Education is the tendency to marginalise the Jewish aspect from the Holocaust, or as Gray (2014a: 74) writes 'marginalising the Jewish specificity of the phenomenon'. Gerstenfeld (2009) and Gray (2014a) refer to this as the 'de-Judaisation' of the Holocaust.

Using *The Boy in the Striped Pyjamas* as a core Holocaust teaching resource can be regarded as encouraging de-Judaisation of the Holocaust. While teachers and educators may not be deliberately engaging in this strategy, they should consider the misconceptions and distortions that it develops in students. The popularity of this book in primary and secondary schools across the globe raises the following questions:

- Is it easier to teach the Holocaust when Jews are not the principal victims?
- Is there a possibility that teachers and educators *prefer* to use this text in primary and secondary (high) schools because it marginalises the Jewish experience of the Holocaust?
- Has de-Judaisation of the Holocaust contributed to the popularity of Holocaust Education, or has the mainstreaming of Holocaust Education contributed to the de-Judaisation of the Holocaust?

It is possible that student and teacher attitudes and ideologies about Israel and the Middle East, and the desire to be inclusive, impact on marginalising Jews in Holocaust Education. Teachers may well consider de-Judaisation of the Holocaust as less contentious or controversial for students from a diverse range of faiths and cultures. While young people's learning of history is influenced by their assumptions and cultural background (Seixas, 1997), teachers need to find new ways of engaging students of all faiths and cultures in learning about the Holocaust, and they should take care to ensure that the Jewish experience of the Holocaust is accurately presented in their lessons.

Popularisation of Holocaust Education

One consequence of the success of international and national Holocaust Remembrance Days, and the increasing amount of literature, films, documentaries and artwork on the Holocaust, is that the Holocaust has become a popular topic for school students and the wider public to engage with. Such popularity is accompanied by challenges, and one of these is ensuring that the specificity of the Holocaust which includes the racist and antisemitic Nazi ideology is recognised and understood. Framing a discussion of contemporary antisemitism in the general context of racism or intolerance does not always achieve this. In this book, we have consistently focused on the complexities and distinctive features of the Holocaust to support teachers. Yet paying more attention to the Holocaust than other genocides can convey to young people that the genocidal crimes against the Jews are more important than for example the genocidal crimes against the Tutsis in 1994, or since 2003, to the Darfuri. This perception of double standards is another challenge to Holocaust Education.

We have pointed out that the Holocaust can be and is being taught without making reference to the word 'antisemitism', and that the distinctive treatment of the Jews is absorbed into 'racism' rather than developing students' understanding of antisemitism. Similarly, absorbing the distinctive treatment of the Roma and Sinti in 'racism' does not develop students' understanding of anti-Gypsyism or antizyganism. The continuing hostility, prejudice and discrimination towards Jews, Roma and Sinti justify teachers adopting greater specificity that links the traditional/historical expressions of antisemitism and anti-Gypsyism with more contemporary forms.

Teacher and Student Teacher Attitudes

Teachers
Teacher confidence and attitudes towards teaching controversial issues and the Holocaust in particular can present further challenges. We highlighted

that teachers can be afraid of teaching the Holocaust in primary school (see Chapter 2, pp. 25–27) and in particular of addressing dissenting parental views. The following British primary teacher's view emphasises the dilemma that teachers can face:

> 'I'd like to teach the Holocaust in my multicultural, multi-ethnic class, but I would worry what to do if one of the white pupils said to me, "Miss, maybe Hitler's ideas weren't SO bad, maybe he had the right idea".'

Our response is that if the teacher perceives that they are unable to appropriately address the above situation, then they should not teach the Holocaust. Yet clearly if this teacher knows or suspects that such students' attitudes exist, they should proactively be engaging in a planned programme of anti-racist education, and creating opportunities for celebrating diversity, rather than reacting to incidents or racist comments as these arise. Our advice to this teacher was, firstly, develop your confidence in teaching controversial issues, and secondly, consider how Holocaust Education can contribute to achieving a positive ethos in your classroom and across the school.

In the secondary teaching context in Scotland it is evident that not all teachers who teach or want to teach the Holocaust receive support from their colleagues. One Religious and Moral Education teacher who had taught the Holocaust for many years, and encouraged its interdisciplinary teaching across several subjects in his school, reported that his colleagues had nicknamed him 'Schindler' after Oskar Schindler (see Chapter 6, pp. 74–75), because of this teacher's long-term commitment to Holocaust Education.

Another teacher in Scotland organised a lunch-time film club and showed films on the Holocaust as it was not taught in her school and she wanted her students to learn about it. While the club was a great success with a high attendance of students, after showing *Escape from Sobibor* (1987) over a few weeks, she experienced disapproval from her colleague on the Senior Management Team who told her to stop the club. These two examples demonstrate that teachers who are committed to teaching the Holocaust are not always welcomed by their peers or their line managers, and are sometimes regarded as 'zealots'.

Further, at the multi-ethnic primary school in London (see Chapter 4, pp. 50–51), as the drama educator was checking students' understanding of the word 'ghetto', the class teacher intervened and said 'For those of you who don't understand what a ghetto is, it's very similar to the Gaza strip in Israel'. The Gaza strip has, since 2005, been a self-governing Palestinian area which after elections has been under the control of Hamas (see Chapter 5, pp. 66 and 68) who refuse to recognise Israel as a country. Israel is holding

Gaza under a blockade; rockets are regularly fired from Gaza into Israel. The teacher's comparison above is disrespectful to those who suffered and died from malnutrition and disease in the ghettos during the Holocaust, to the people who were killed in those ghettos, and to those who were deported from there to concentration and/or death camps. Nothing like this, has, or is, happening in Gaza. The airing of such disrespectful and politically charged statements in the classroom demonstrates that teachers' attitudes bring challenges to effective Holocaust Education.

Teachers' attitudes to tolerating the intolerant are also important as students have the 'right to freely express an opinion in all matters affecting him/her and to have that opinion taken into account' and the 'right of young people to form associations' (UN, 1989, Articles 12 and 15). These entitlements can be difficult to put into practice with students who are Holocaust deniers, Neo-Nazis or antisemites, as teachers need to be skilful in handling class disagreements. Yet young people also have the 'right to be educated for tolerance' (UN, 1989, Article 29). Hence the parents of the primary student who was a Holocaust denier (see Chapter 4, pp. 50–51) could feasibly blame the school for not educating their child in this. Students have the right to express their opinions, even those which most people would find wrong and abhorrent. However, they do not have the right to do so if these opinions transgress other individuals' civil liberties.

Student Teachers

The Swedish study of student teachers' attitudes towards teachers and students with Nazi sympathies provides further insight (Orlenius, 2008). This was based on a real-life case when Sven (not his real name), a secondary student, and member of an established Nazi group, was suspended from school for expressing his sympathies towards Nazism at school by writing Nazi slogans on a test in class, and organising meetings after school and in between lessons at school with friends. Orlenius asked 120 student teachers two questions:

- Should a person with Nazi sympathies be allowed to work as a teacher if he does not consciously influence his students?
- Should students with Nazi sympathies be suspended from school?

Findings were that 50% of the student teachers agreed and disagreed that a teacher with Nazi sympathies should be allowed to work as a teacher if they did not consciously influence students, and that 4 out 10 of student teachers more or less agreed with Sven's suspension. The others' responses support UNESCO's view (1995: Article 4.2) that education is the most effective means of preventing intolerance. It is assumed that with more knowledge, students like Sven will change their attitudes and behaviour; of course the PhD graduates at the Wannsee conference seriously challenged this assumption.

The data presented in this section come from eight undergraduate primary student teachers, who during their third year on the Bachelor of Education programme in 2011 at the University of the West of Scotland (UWS) completed an optional module entitled Holocaust Studies and Citizenship. These students were interviewed in groups and asked questions on the module and its contribution to their personal and professional development. The following comments show that they had shared some of their learning experiences with their family and friends, and had engaged with their grandparents who were born during the Second World War; seven students discussed this module outwith classes. This suggests that the impact of Holocaust Education extends beyond its direct learners:

'I spoke to my dad because he was in the army ... I mean sometimes I'd come home and he'd be like, "No that's not what happened!", and we'd disagree, but he was so interested. After I'd written my essay, he said, "Well I've learned something".' (Student 1)

'Every week I spoke with my gran and papa, I mean he was ten when WW2 broke out. He was there. He knew. I was just telling him what I was learning. I mean he was so interested, he kept asking me questions.' (Student 2)

'I went home after every "Holocaust" day, and I would sit and just spill out everything to my mum, it was so interesting. And my dad had a good knowledge, he was glad I was taking an interest, and it was so interesting that you just wanted to tell people. And because not many people in uni' do this sort of thing, because it is new, then you wanted to tell people about it.' (Student 3)

'I wanted to tell my friends about it, if you are sitting round talking on a Friday night with your friends, you know you talk about it, and they are studying different things at uni' y'know it's interesting, it's new to talk about.' (Student 4)

'I did discuss it at home with my mum, she teaches History and it's one of the subjects she teaches. She already knows what I'm talking about. I also spoke to my gran and grandpa about what they knew, but they didn't really know a lot. They knew more about the home front and stuff, I was surprised, I thought they would know about the Holocaust.' (Student 5)

Students reported that their study of the Holocaust had made them more 'passionate' about their teaching in general, and about teaching about genocide and the Holocaust in particular. Similar to previous research findings, students did not specify antisemitism in this. They also voiced their difficulty in engaging with the required reading which included *The Holocaust: The Jewish Tragedy* by Martin Gilbert (1986).

'I mean I started reading Gilbert and I was like, I don't want to read that!

I remember getting to bits and putting it down and thinking that's enough.

I wanted to learn about the Holocaust and citizenship but not that ... more from the citizenship angle. I mean there were some horrible things in that book.' (Student 2)

'It was a good book, but sometimes you almost wanted to run away from it.' (Student 6)

Students conveyed their appreciation for planned times for discussion and reflection on the lectured inputs, and for the opportunity for them to raise questions that clarified their understanding. As evidenced below, learning about the Holocaust contributed to their personal and professional development in a range of ways. It developed their understanding of how Scottish society has evolved in the wider British, European and global contexts, the plight of refugees who are currently coming to Scotland, and the importance of respecting people's religious, ethnic, cultural and multi identities.

'And it was strange to think that there are people in Scotland who have such big stories behind them. It was fascinating to see that there are people in our midst who have gone through all of this, you know it's not just old people – everyone has a past.' (Student 7)

'You know when we were learning about the Kindertransport I went home and said to my mum, I don't know if I know anyone who – if a group of Afghan kids came to [Name] Town Hall, and they were looking for people to look after them and take them home – I don't know anyone who would help ... People in society now want money for looking after children, it's like nobody will just take a child who is in the opposing side of the war we are fighting. And it's just quite sad.' (Student 2)

'It's brought me closer to my stepmother, seems a strange thing to say and she was a "squaddie" [a private soldier] and involved a lot with Kosovo and the things she experienced link with this module. Like when she had to deal with different camps and experience things, that made me go "wow". And I now know what she must have gone through. I mean she is still quite cagey about it.' (Student 4)

'It gave me a better understanding of people's faith. It's made me more aware of stereotyping, and persecution ... I mean in your classroom you might have different faiths and cultures, and encounter bullying and racism and I think learning about the Holocaust can help you deal with that better. If you understand that people have different opinions then you are more equipped to deal with them.' (Student 8)

In 2013, four of these students demonstrated their commitment to learning more about the Holocaust by participating in a week-long seminar in Jerusalem, organised and subsidised by the University and the International School for Holocaust Studies at Yad Vashem. The many benefits that they reported from this 'life-changing experience' are best summed up by the following comment from one participant:

'I felt connected to the subject in a new way and being immersed in the culture has helped broaden my appreciation for not only the religious aspect, but the historical element and current politics too. Yad Vashem's philosophy on teaching the Holocaust is something that has really struck a chord with me and (being the eternal optimist!) I really appreciate the positive and hopeful outlook and the desire to safely teach such a harrowing subject in that way.'

Other School Issues

As Holocaust Education is developing across the world, the commitment and development of Continued Professional Development (CPD, or inservice, inset) courses and opportunities for teachers are struggling, and in many cases not keeping up with this development. Many teachers are self-taught and the knowledge and skills of some fall short of the requirements. Findings amongst secondary teachers in England were that even teachers who perceive themselves to be knowledgeable about the Holocaust have gaps in their historical understanding (HEDP, 2009). This could explain why some teachers focus heavily on moral education. It also strengthens the case for ongoing CPD. In addition, the common practice for teachers to work in isolation is not always conducive to developing Holocaust Education; more peer learning and collaborative teaching opportunities would be beneficial. Such opportunities facilitate teachers to learn from each other as well as from their own practice.

Irrespective of whether the Holocaust is mandatory in their curriculum, secondary (high) school teachers in particular often complain about the lack of time they have available to teach the Holocaust. Rushed teaching can lead to all sorts of student misconceptions and misunderstandings which can only be addressed if students have opportunities at a later stage in their schooling to develop their learning. This is why we advocate a spiral approach to Holocaust Education (see Chapter 8, p. 102), where the Holocaust is taught at various stages in one's school experience. We also consider that the emotional responses and complexities of the Holocaust often require time for reflection during lessons, and that this should be included in lesson plans.

Assessment is a further factor as students, teachers and schools are driven by assessment. While teacher feedback demonstrates that they tend to regard the Holocaust as a 'special' subject or topic to teach, including it in school or class assessments would raise its students' standing. Assessment would also determine their actual knowledge of the Holocaust and facilitate teachers to follow up on students' misconceptions and gaps in knowledge.

Parent Attitudes

Parents have an important contribution to make in Holocaust Education and we have indicated this at various points in this book (see Chapters 8 and 9). Recognition of their rights and their duties is equally important. However, parents whose belief systems differ to the general consensus in society may not want their child to learn *about* or *from* the Holocaust. In this context, one can understand a teacher's cautious approach to teaching the Holocaust. Discussing this programme of work with parents, asking for their participation, informing them of how Holocaust Education fits into the School Development Plan, and explaining the reasons behind this programme, can assist in allaying many parental fears and anxieties, but it may confirm others. Our previous research in Scotland (Maitles and Cowan, 1999) concluded that data from primary teachers showed that parents from a range of diverse backgrounds were very positive about their children learning about the Holocaust, although our experience of presenting Continued Professional Development courses to primary teachers is that they were committed to avoiding a possible confrontation with parents who may not approve.

No Living Memory of the Holocaust

The contribution of Holocaust survivors and eye witnesses cannot be underestimated. Holocaust Education owes a lot to those now elderly individuals who freely give their time to tell their story repeatedly to young people. This is exhausting and for most very painful, but because *they* survived the Holocaust, and many of their peers and family members did not, they have a remarkable inner strength to inform others of their experiences, a determination to remember those people they met during these experiences (some of whom they were unable to trace after the war, because they did not know their full names!), and extraordinary resilience. The interest in the Holocaust which has accompanied the establishment of national and international Holocaust Remembrance or Memorial Days has led to survivors and eyewitnesses of the Holocaust being in great demand. In addition to contributing to one's understanding of the Holocaust, they have been models for survivors and eyewitnesses of more recent genocides and have inspired many to speak out.

Soon there will be no living memory of the Holocaust. From this time on, young people will be reliant on publications, audiotapes and films of Holocaust survivors and eye witnesses, and the contributions of second and third generation survivors, i.e. the children and grandchildren of people who survived the Holocaust. No doubt in our ever-changing tech-nological world, these will be sophisticated, and engage new generations, but exactly how effective these will be in the long term, and how effectively these will address the increasing amount of Holocaust denial and distor-tion, is uncertain. In this area, how we use the technology and indeed technologies in the future that we cannot even imagine, is very much a pedagogical question that will depend on teacher direction and advice. That, in turn, places a responsibility on teacher education and on CPD.

Similar to 'equalisation', referred to earlier in this book (see Chapter 5, pp. 67–68), is Holocaust relativism. Relativists present the Holocaust as simply another tragic event in European or in their nation-state's national history. So, for example, Holocaust relativists from the territories occupied by the former Soviet Union consider the Holocaust to be no more unique or tragic than the crimes of Stalinism. Moreover, the Holocaust in several countries in Europe, such as Lithuania and Estonia, is considered to be overshadowed by the repression carried out on their citizens by the Soviets. This explains why many Lithuanians and Estonians consider the Holocaust to be over-emphasised, with too little attention being given to the suffering of their non-Jewish citizens since the Holocaust.

In Eastern Europe, where there was some support for the Nazi agenda towards both the Soviet Union and the Jews as well as the post-war expe-rience of Stalinist and post-Stalinist Soviet control, there is an over-concentration on the latter and a neglect, bordering on what we would argue is a denial, of the former. In the Museum of Political History in Riga, Latvia, for example, the Holocaust is explained by a plaque which outlines that the Second World War was 'not a happy time for Riga's Jews'! Further, in the Museum of History of Bucharest in Romania, the Second World War is explained in a small room, where visitors are told that while Romania was indeed in the war, Bucharest continued to be known as 'Little Paris', and that the military uniforms added to the colour of the city! There is nothing about the pro-fascist government, the adoption in 1940 of Romania's equivalent of the Nuremberg Laws depriving Jews of most citizenship rights, the units of Romanians fighting on the Eastern Front with the Nazis, nor the pogroms which led to tens of thousands of Jewish deaths across Romania. In contrast, half of the building is dedi-cated to opposition to Ceauşescu and his crimes against culture, politics, society and the city.

Thus Holocaust Education requires many countries to face up to their involvement, and in some cases their complicity, in the Holocaust. At the time of writing, not all are ready to accept this, and developing Holocaust Education in these countries especially in a world with no living memory of the Holocaust will be a particular challenge.

Legacy

If one phrase for humanity summed up the Holocaust it would be 'Never Again'. Yet, there is a problem here for humanity, Holocaust and genocide scholars, and politicians. There had been terrible massacres and genocides prior to the Holocaust – the mass deaths during the slave trade, the extermination of the South and North American natives, the Turkish genocide of the Armenians – but there have been genocides that have occurred since the Holocaust across the globe. Rwanda, for example, is a country still reeling from a genocide in which conservative estimates would indicate that some 800,000 native Tutsis and Hutus were murdered. Even more horrifically, this took place in a 100-day period. Or there is Bosnia-Herzegovina: in 1995, Bosnian Serb forces conquered the UN-protected safe area of Srebrenica. Bosnian Muslim men and boys were separated from the rest of the population, under the eyes of Dutch UN peacekeepers. They were then taken to a nearby football stadium where between 10,000 and 15,000 were executed and buried in mass graves. Massacres in Cambodia and Darfur in the 1970s were also recognised as genocide. And as we write, the crimes of ISIS are being interpreted by academics and politicians as genocidal. While the legacy of Auschwitz and the Holocaust are still to the fore, atrocities continue with very little intervention from organisations like the United Nations.

Even as the last generation of survivors begin to draw their final breaths, humanity is committing similar atrocities to those seen in Nazi Germany before and during the Second World War. As we are dangerously entering a phase in world history where we are beginning to prematurely judge others based upon their faith, we need to ensure that the legacies of the Holocaust are not forgotten. To ensure that humanity going forward does not contain the horrific atrocities of the twentieth century, a renewed emphasis must be placed on the atrocities committed and how to learn from these.

In the words of Auschwitz survivor Primo Levi, 'it happened therefore it can happen again ... it can happen and everywhere' (Levi, 1988: 167). Thus, while we understand fully the questioning by philosophers such as Adorno (1983:17) that 'to write poetry after Auschwitz is barbaric', or Primo Levi's statement that 'There is Auschwitz, so there cannot be God' (Levi, in Camon, 1989: 68), we are adamant that this does not mean we should not learn about both Auschwitz and the Holocaust. The legacy of the Holocaust means that it is both conceptually difficult to comprehend and so urgent that we do try to comprehend it.

There are some clear guidelines that come from our understanding of the Holocaust. The United Nations, for example, passed the *Convention on the Prevention and Punishment of Genocide* directly as a result of the Holocaust. Article 2 states that genocide means 'any of the following acts committed with intent to destroy, in whole or in part, a national, ethnical, racial or religious group'. Acts of genocide include:

1. Killing members of the group
2. Causing serious bodily or mental harm to members of the group
3. Deliberately inflicting on the group conditions of life calculated to bring about its physical destruction in whole or in part
4. Imposing measures intended to prevent births within the group
5. Forcibly transferring children of the group to another group

Stanton (2013) argued that the prevention of genocide requires a structural understanding of the ten stages of the genocidal process (see Chapter 2, p. 17). The problem facing us though is how to avoid the economic, social and political upheavals that give rise to these stages. It is hard to do something about the genocidal murders once the process has got underway. Yet to tackle the precursers of genocide would need intervention at an early stage of financial and social rupture. No country is willing to either accept or carry out that type of intervention. Nonetheless, the warnings from the Holocaust, the memorials, the survivor testimony, Auschwitz, the education processes that have learning about the Holocaust and human rights as central, can be powerful mechanisms for alerting us to genocide. This is part of the legacy of the Holocaust.

One further aspect of the legacy of the Holocaust is understanding the ordinariness of the perpetrators. We like to imagine our devils as monstrous and vicious sadists, and whilst of course there were vicious sadists, the Holocaust suggests that ordinary people engaged in crimes. In his poem, 'All there is to know about Adolf Eichmann', Leonard Cohen (1964) argues how normal Eichmann (the architect of the Final Solution) was. Others, such as Hannah Arendt (1963), point this out too – what she called 'the banality of evil' (see Chapter 2, p. 15). It is important that we understand this lesson – that when we take humanity out of our understanding then people can be persuaded to become genocidal murderers.

In the UK, initiatives such as the Anne Frank Schools and Ambassador Programme, and the Beacon Schools Programme, encourage schools to engage in Holocaust Education and teachers to develop their skills and knowledge in this area. One example of a school that places Holocaust Education at the centre of its education is Watford Grammar School for Girls. Awarded Beacon status for Holocaust Education in 2011, every teacher in this multiculturally diverse school in Hertfordshire, England, receives CPD in Holocaust Education from staff at the Centre of Holocaust

Education at University College London (UCL). This means that all form teachers and Heads of Year have an understanding as to how the Holocaust can contribute to the school's values and ethos. Additionally, the Holocaust is taught to years 9 and 10 in a multidisciplinary approach, in Religious and Moral Education and History, with an optional study opportunity in the Netherlands that involves a visit to either Vught, Westerbork or Amersfoort concentration camp. This school also includes Holocaust Education in its sixth form programme for its 1,300 students. This involves a study conference on the Holocaust and Holocaust-related issues, with Holocaust survivors talking in groups to students. There are also further opportunities for senior students to participate in study trips in Europe, e.g. in Prague, Budapest and Berlin. Hence teachers, and particularly head teachers, have the potential to contribute to the legacy of the Holocaust.

There are other positive initiatives that can encourage good learning and teaching about the Holocaust. The USHMM in Washington, for example, recognises excellence through its *Exemplary Lessons* initiative. Teachers from across the USA submit Holocaust Education-based lesson plans which are then evaluated by a panel of eight master educators from the museum's education division, and two consultants from Project Zero at Harvard University's Graduate School of Education. Winning educators receive a certificate of achievement and a cash award. Some of the lessons are filmed in the classroom for subsequent presentation on the museum's website.

There are many facets to the educational legacy of the Holocaust. One of these is the *Aladdin Project* which was launched under the patronage of UNESCO in 2009. This organisation aims to facilitate mutual knowledge between Jews and Muslims by producing and translating books, films, documentaries and websites on history, religion and the culture of people from different cultures in their mother tongue. With a special arrangement with the publishers that allows internet users to download books free of charge, this project has successfully made available Arabic and Persian translations of *The Diary of Anne Frank, If This Is a Man* (Levi, 1947) *and Shoah* (Lanzmann, 1985).

Finally, we want to conclude this section on the legacy of the Holocaust by linking attitudes towards refugees in the 1930s and 1940s to that of the greatest humanitarian crisis facing us so far in the twenty-first century – the refugees fleeing war and hopelessness, primarily from Africa and the Middle East. In this, the legacy of the Holocaust becomes clear. Not only do the events at the Evian conference in 1938 and attitudes in the 1930s towards Jewish refugees bear striking similarities to present policy towards refugees, in that the attitudes of the world's powers in the 1930s were to ensure that

Central European Jewry was not welcome in the west, but also the sending back of migrants who do not have the right papers today mirrors the attitudes towards fleeing German Jews in the 1930s. Indeed, to its shame, the British Government sent back hundreds of Jews without correct papers to Germany every year from 1934 to 1939.

The events during the Holocaust remind us that antisemitism, anti-Roma and the treatment of fleeing refugees today, need to be viewed through the prism of human rights, humanity and citizenship. We may collectively group people and talk about numbers, but each group is comprised of individuals, and each number is a human being. Studying the Holocaust can aid the development of this humanity.

REFERENCES

ADL (2006) 'Teaching about the Holocaust: why simulation activities should not be used'. Available at www.adl.org/education/simulationsinteachinghol.pdf (last accessed 15 November 2015).

Adorno, T. (1983) *Cultural Criteria and Society*. Cambridge, MA: MIT Press.

Advisory Group on Citizenship (1998) *Education for Citizenship and the Teaching of Democracy in Schools*. London: DfEE.

Agostinone-Wilson, F. (2005) Fair and balanced to death: confronting the cult of neutrality in the teacher education classroom, *Journal for Critical Education Policy Studies*, 3 (1). Available at www.jceps.com/?pageID=article&articleID=37 (last accessed 28 April 2016).

Aktives Museum Fashismus und Widerstand in Berlin (2012) Konzentrationslager 'Gutschow-Keller'. Available at http://www.gedenktafeln-in-berlin.de/nc/gedenk tafeln/gedenktafel-anzeige/tid/konzentrationslager/(last accessed 31 October 2016).

All-Party Parliamentary Group Against Antisemitism (APPGAA) (2006) *Report of the All-Party Parliamentary Inquiry into Antisemitism*. London: The Stationery Office Limited. Available at www.antisemitism.org.uk/wp-content/uploads/All-Party-Parliamentary-Inquiry-into-Antisemitism-REPORT.pdf (last accessed 29 April 2016).

All-Party Parliamentary Group Against Antisemitism (APPGAA) (2015) *All-Party Inquiry into Antisemitism*. London: PPCA. Available at www.antisemitism.org.uk/ (last accessed 12 February 2015).

Ambrosewicz-Jacobs, J. (2011) 'Świadomość Holokaustu wśród młodzieży polskiej po zmianachsystemowych 1989 roku [Holocaust Consciousness among Polish Youth after the 1989 Collapse of Communism]'. In F. Tycha and M. Adamczyk-Garbowskiej (eds), *Następstwa zagłady Żydów: Polska 1944–2010* [Jewish Presence in Absence: The Aftermath of the Holocaust in Poland, 1944–2010]. Lublin: Wydawnictwo UMCS, Jewish Historical Institute. pp. 625–58.

Ambrosewicz-Jacobs, J. and Szuchta, R. (2014) The intricacies of education about the Holocaust in Poland: ten years after the Jedwabne debate, what can Polish school students learn about the Holocaust in history classes?, *Intercultural Education*, 25 (4): 283–99.

Angvik, M. and von Borries, B. (1997) *A Comparative European Survey on Historical Consciousness and Political Attitudes Among Adolescents*. Hamburg: Korber-Stiftung.

Anne Frank Museum (online, n.d.) 'Deported to the camps'. Available at www. annefrank.org/en/Anne-Frank/Discovery-and-arrest/Deported-to-the-camps/ (last accessed 28 September 2015).

Archer, L. (2003) *Race, Masculinity and Schooling: Muslim Boys and Education*. Maidenhead: Open University Press.

Archer, L. and Francis, B. (2007) *Understanding Minority Ethnic Achievement: Race, Gender, Class and 'Success'*. London: Routledge.

Arendt, H. (1951) *The Origins of Totalitarianism*. New York: Harcourt, Brace and Company.

Arendt, H. (1963) *Eichmann in Jerusalem: A Report on the Banality of Evil*. New York: Viking.

Arnstine, D. (1995) *Democracy and the Arts of Schooling*. Albany: State University of New York Press.

Ashton, E. and Watson, B. (1998) Values education: a fresh look at procedural neutrality, *Educational Studies*, 24 (2): 183–93.

Avraham, D. (2014) *The Challenge of Teaching the Holocaust in a Multicultural Classroom*. Jerusalem: Yad Vashem.

Badger, K., Craft, R. and Jensen, L. (1998) Age and gender differences in value orientation among American adolescents, *Adolescence*, 33: 27–52.

Bage, G. (2000) *Thinking History 4–14: Teaching Learning Curricula and Communities*. London: Routledge-Falmer.

Balodimas-Bartolomei, A. (2012) Political and pedagogical dimensions in Holocaust education: a comparative analysis among task force member countries, *Journal of Multiculturalism in Education*, 8 (1): 1–35.

Ban Ki-moon (2008) Available at www.un.org/press/en/2008/sgsm11379.doc.htm (last accessed 28 April 2016).

Banner, G. (2000) *Holocaust Literature: Schulz, Levi, Spiegelman and the Memory of the Offence*. London: Vallentine-Mitchell.

Bauer, Y. (2002) *Rethinking the Holocaust*. New Haven and London: Yale University Press.

Bauman, Z. (1989) *Modernity and the Holocaust*. Cambridge: Polity Press.

Baumel, J.T. (2001) 'Concentration camps'. In W. Laqueur (ed.), *The Holocaust Encyclopedia*. New Haven, CT: Yale University Press. pp.133–35.

BBC (2006) 'Major wins appeal over Nazi jibe'. Available at http://news.bbc.co.uk/1/hi/england/london/6065124.stm (last accessed 1 June 2016).

BBC (2007) BBC%20NEWS%20%7C%20Education%20%7C%20Schools%20'avoid%20Holocaust%20lessons' (last accessed 8 January 2016).

BBC (2011) 'St Andrews student guilty of Israel flag racism'. Available at www.bbc.co.uk/news/uk-scotland-edinburgh-east-fife-14638515 (last accessed 3 May 2016).

BDS (online, n.d.) 'What is BDS?'. Available at https://bdsmovement.net/what-is-bds (last accessed 31 October 2016).

Ben-Peretz, M. (2004) Identifying with horror: teaching about the Holocaust, *Curriculum Inquiry*, 33 (2): 189–98.

Bergmann, W. (2013) 'Antisemitism in Europe today: the phenomena, the conflicts'. Berlin: Jewish Museum. Available at www.jmberlin.de/antisemitism-today/Bergmann.pdf (last accessed 29 April 2016).

Berkeley, A. (n.d.) 'The matter of war crimes committed by Japanese nationals and in the matter of the ill-treatment of prisoners of war (civilian internees) at Fukuoka'. Available at www.mansell.com/pow_resources/camplists/fukuoka/moji_hospital/berkeley_affidavit.htm (last accessed 28 September 2015).

Blum, L. (2004) The Poles, the Jews and the Holocaust: reflections on an AME trip to Auschwitz, *Journal of Moral Education*, 33 (2): 131–48.

Blumberg, R.L. (2007) 'Gender bias in textbooks: a hidden obstacle on the road to gender equality in education'. Background paper prepared for the Global Monitoring Report 2008, *Education for All by 2015: Will We Make It?*, UNESCO.

Boyne, J. (2006) *The Boy in the Striped Pyjamas*. London: Puffin.

Brabham, E.G. (1997) Holocaust education: legislation, practices and literature for middle school students, *The Social Studies*, 88 (3): 139–42.

Bracey, P., Gove-Humphries, A. and Jackson, D. (2006) Refugees and evacuees: enhancing historical understanding through Irish historical fiction with Key Stage 2 and early Key Stage 3 pupils, *Education 3–13: International Journal of Primary, Elementary and Early Years*, 34 (2):103–112.

Brenner, M. (2001) 'Displaced persons'. In W. Laqueur (ed.), *The Holocaust Encyclopedia*. New Haven, CT: Yale University Press. pp.150–9.

Brown, M. and Davies, I. (1998) The Holocaust and education for citizenship: the teaching of history, religion and human rights in England, *Educational Review*, 50 (1): 75–83.

Browning, C. (1993) *Ordinary Men: Reserve Police Battalion 101 and the Final Solution in Poland*. New York: Harper Perennial.

Bruner, J.S. (1960) *The Process of Education*. New York: Vintage.

Burke, C. and Grosvenor, I. (2003) *The School I'd Like: Children and Young People's Reflections on An Education For The 21st Century*. London: RoutledgeFalmer.

Burtonwood, N. (2002) Holocaust Memorial Day in schools-context, process and content: a review of research into Holocaust education, *Educational Research*, 44 (1): 69–82.

Cabinet Office (2015) *Britain's Promise to Remember: The Prime Minister's Holocaust Commission Report*. Available at www.gov.uk/government/uploads/system/uploads/attachment_data/file/398645/Holocaust_Commission_Report_Britains_promise_to_remember.pdf (last accessed 13 June 2016).

Cajani, L. (2007) 'Citizenship on the verge of the 21st century: the burden of the past, the challenges of the present'. In L. Cajani and A. Ross (eds), *History Teaching, Identities and Citizenship*. Stoke-on-Trent: Trentham. pp.1–2.

Camon, F. (1989) *Conversations with Primo Levi*. Marlboro, Vermont: Marlboro Press.

Campaign Against Antisemitism (CAA) (2015) *Annual Antisemitism Barometer 2015 Full Report*. Available at http://antisemitism.uk/wp-content/uploads/2015/01/Annual-Antisemitism-Barometer-Report.pdf (last accessed 12 February 2015).

Carrington, B. and Short, G. (1997) Holocaust education, anti-racism and citizenship, *Educational Review*, 49 (3): 271–82.

Cassidy, C., Brunner, R. and Webster, E. (2014) Teaching human rights? 'All hell will break loose!', *Education, Citizenship and Social Justice*, 9 (1): 19–33.

Central Bureau of Statistics (Israel) (2015) *Society and Population*. Available at www1. cbs.gov.il/reader/ (last accessed 28 September 2015).

Centre for Holocaust Education (2014) *What Do Students Know and Understand About the Holocaust?* London: University College London. Available at www.holocausteducation. org.uk/wp-content/uploads/What-do-students-know-and-understand-about-the-Holocaust2.pdf

Cesarani, D. (2008) Review of *The Boy in the Striped Pyjamas, Literary Review*, October, p. 4. (Reproduced by the Holocaust Educational Trust at www.het.org.uk/media/english%20guide.pdf (last accessed 22 October 2015).)

Chapman, A., Edwards, C. and Goldsmith, E. (2010) *Evaluation of the Holocaust Education Trust's Lessons from Auschwitz Project*. London: Holocaust Education Trust.

Chettiparamb, A. (2007) 'Interdisciplinarity: a literature review', The Higher Education Academy. Available at www.heacademy.ac.uk/resource/interdisciplinarity-literature-review (last accessed 14 June 2016).

Claire, H. (2005) '"You did the best you can": history, citizenship and moral dilemmas'. In A. Osler (ed.), *Teachers, Human Rights and Diversity*. Stoke on Trent: Trentham. pp. 99–113.

Cohen, L. (1964) *Flowers for Hitler.* Toronto/Montreal Canada: McClelland and Stewart.

College of Policing (2014) *Hate Crime Operational Guidance*. Available at www.college. police.uk/What-we-do/Support/Equality/Documents/Hate-Crime-Operational-Guidance. pdf (last accessed 29 April 2016).

Conlon-McKenna, M. (1995) *Safe Harbour.* Dublin: O'Brien.

Copley, T. (2005) 'Silent pilgrimage', *Times Educational Supplement*, 2 December.

Council of Europe (2006) *European Pack for Visiting Auschwitz-Birkenau Memorial and Museum*. Strasbourg: Council of Europe.

Cowan, P. (1994) 'The Holocaust that Reading Lists Neglect', *Times Education Supplement* (Scotland), 24 June, p.19.

Cowan, P. (2008a) 'Seeing, hearing and feeling: how can a visit to Auschwitz encourage young people to practise citizenship?'. In A. Ross and P. Cunningham (eds), *Reflecting on Identities: Research, Practice and Innovation*. Available at http://archive. londonmet.ac.uk/cice-docs/docs/2008_511.pdf (last accessed 21 July 2015). London: CiCe. pp. 511–20.

Cowan, P. (2008b) Learning about the Holocaust and responsible citizenship in Scotland, *Race Equality Teaching*, 26 (2): 36–9.

Cowan, P. (2012) 'Anti-Semitism'. In P. Cowan and H. Maitles (eds), *Teaching Controversial Issues in the Classroom*. London: Continuum. pp. 188–99.

Cowan, P. (2015) A selected, annotated guide to Holocaust websites, *Prism: An Interdisciplinary Journal for Holocaust Educators*, 7: 96–100.

Cowan, P. and Maitles, H. (2000) Feature or footnote? Teachers' attitudes towards teaching of the Holocaust in primary schools in Scotland, *Scottish Educational Review*, 32 (1): 78–87.

Cowan, P. and Maitles, H. (2002) Developing positive values: a case study of Holocaust Memorial Day in the primary schools of one local authority in Scotland, *Educational Review*, 54 (3): 219–29.

Cowan, P. and Maitles, H. (2005) Values and attitudes – positive and negative: a study of the impact of teaching the Holocaust on citizenship among Scottish 11–12 year olds, *Scottish Education Review*, 37 (2): 104–15.

Cowan, P. and Maitles, H. (2007) Does addressing prejudice and discrimination through Holocaust education produce better citizens?, *Educational Review*, 59 (2): 115–30.

Cowan, P. and Maitles, H. (2009) 'Never Again: How the lessons from Auschwitz (LFA) project impact on schools in Scotland'. Report prepared for Holocaust Education Trust/ Pears Foundation. Available at www.co-lab.org/downloads/ScotlandLFAReport.pdf (last accessed 13 April 2016).

Cowan, P. and Maitles, H. (2010) 'Positive values and gender: an investigation of the longer term impact of Holocaust education on Scottish adolescents', *Prospects,* 40: 257–72.

Cowan, P. and Maitles, H. (2011) 'We saw inhumanity close up': what is gained by school students from Scotland visiting Auschwitz?, *Journal of Curriculum Studies*, 43 (2): 163–84.

Cowan, P. and Maitles, H. (eds) (2012) *Teaching Controversial Issues in the Classroom: Key Issues and Debates*. London/New York: Continuum.

Cowan, P., Kenig, N. and Mycock, A. (2014) *The Complexities of Citizenship Education and Remembrance*. London: CiCe.

Crick, B. (2000) 'A Subject At Last', *Tomorrow's Citizen*, Summer.

Crick, B. and Porter, A. (eds) (1978) *Political Education and Political Literacy*. London: Longman.

Davies, I. (ed.) (2000) *Teaching the Holocaust*. London: Continuum.

Davies, I. and Hogarth, S. (2004) 'Political literacy: issues for teachers and learners'. In J. Dermaine (ed.), *Citizenship and Political Education Today.* Basingstoke: Palgrave Macmillan. pp. 181–99.

Davies, I. (2012) 'Teaching about Genocide'. In P. Cowan and H. Maitles (eds), *Teaching Controversial Issues in the Classroom: Key Issues and Debates*. London: Continuum. pp.108–119.

Davis, R.W. (1996) Disraeli, the Rothschilds and Anti-Semitism, *Jewish History*, 10 (2): 9–19.

Dawidowicz, L. (1990) 'How they teach the Holocaust', *Commentary*, 90 (6): 25–32.

Deutscher, I. (1968) *The Non-Jewish Jew*. New York: OUP.

Devine, D., Kenny, M. and Macneela, E. (2008) Naming the 'other': children's construction and experience of racisms in Irish primary schools, *Race Ethnicity and Education*, 11 (4): 369–85.

Dewey, J. (1915) *The school and society*. Chicago: University of Chicago Press.

DfEE (Department for Education and Employment) (2000) *Remembering Genocides: Lessons for the Future*. London: DfEE.

Drake, I. (2008) 'Classroom Simulations: Proceed with Caution', *Teaching Tolerance Magazine*, 33: 1–3.

Dumitru, D. (2008) The use and abuse of the Holocaust: historiography and politics in Moldova, *Holocaust and Genocide Studies*, 22 (1): 49–73.

Eaglestone, R. (2007) 'Boyne's Dangerous Tale', *Jewish Chronicle*, 23 March, p. 53.

East Kilbride News (2010) 'St Hilary's Primary Kids Traumatised by Teacher's Holocaust Game', 10 March. Available at www/eastkilbridenews.co.uk/lanarkshire-news-lanarkshire/local-news-east-kilbride/2010/03/20/st-hilary-s-primary-kids-traumatised-by-teachers-Holocaust-game-68653-25996610/ (last accessed 16 November 2015).

Eckmann, M. (2015) 'Is teaching and learning about the Holocaust relevant for human rights education?' In Z. Gross and D. Stevick (eds), *As the Witnesses Fall Silent: 21st Century Holocaust Education in Curriculum, Policy and Practice*. New York: Springer. pp. 53–66.

Elliott, E. (2009) 'Teacher's Holocaust E-Mail Raises Concerns', *Baltimore Jewish Times*, 25 June.

Emanuel, M. and Gissing, V. (2001) *Nicholas Winton and the Rescued Generation: Save One Life, Save the World* (Library of Holocaust Testimonies). London: Vallentine Mitchell & Co Ltd.

Encyclopaedia Judaica (1971a) 'Ghetto', Vol 7. Jerusalem: Keter.

Encyclopaedia Judaica (1971b) 'Jewish Quarter', Vol 10. Jerusalem: Keter.

Encyclopaedia Judaica (1971c) 'Pogrom', Vol 13. Jerusalem: Keter.

Erll, A. (2011) Locating family in cultural memory studies, *Journal of Comparative and Family Studies*, 42 (3): 303–18.

European Union Agency for Humans Rights (FRA) (2015) *Antisemitism Overview of Data Available in the European Union 2004–2014*. Vienna: FRA. Available at http://fra.europa.eu/sites/default/files/fra_uploads/fra-2015-antisemitism-update_en.pdf (last accessed 10 June 2016).

Evans, K. (1995) Competence and citizenship: towards a complementary model, *Journal of Education and Work*, 11 (2): 1–11.

Fallace, T. (2007) 'Playing Holocaust: the origins of the Gestapo Simulation Game', *Teachers College Record*. Available at www.tcrecord.org/Content.asp?ContentID=14489> (last accessed 20 November 2015).

Fardon, J. and Schoeman, S. (2010) A feminist post-structuralist analysis of an exemplar South African school History text, *South African Journal of Education*, 30: 307–23.

Faulks, K. (1998) *Citizenship in Modern Britain*. Edinburgh: Edinburgh University Press.

Faulks, K. (2000) *Citizenship.* London: Routledge.

Fein, H. (2009) 'Alternative definitions'. In S.Totten and P.K. Bartrop (eds), *The Genocide Studies Reader.* Oxford: Routledge. pp. 34–56.

Feldman, J. (2002) Marking the boundaries of the enclave: defining the Israeli collective through the Poland experience', *Israel Studies,* 7 (2): 84–114.

Fife Regional Council (2007) *Anne Frank (+you): The Festival.* Cardenden: Fife Regional Council.

Finkelstein, N. and Birn, R. (1998) *A Nation on Trial: The Goldhagen Thesis and Historical Truth.* London: Verso.

Firsht, N. (2016) 'Students Terrified as Violent Thugs Attempt to Halt Israel Meeting', *Jewish Chronicle,* 22 January. pp. 8–9.

Flanagan, C. and Tucker C. (1999) Adolescents' explanations for political issues: concordance with their views of self and society, *Developmental Psychology,* 35 (5): 1198–209.

Foster, S., Pettigrew, A., Pearce, A., Hale, R., Burgess, A., Salmons, P. and Lenga, R.A. (2014) *What do Students Know and Understand about the Holocaust? Evidence from English Secondary Schools.* London: UCL Centre for Holocaust Education.

Frank, A. (2007) *The Diary of a Young Girl* (Definitive Edition). London: Puffin.

Fuchs, J. (2007) 'Visiting memorials: a worthwhile cathartic experience or a "waste of time and money"?' In M. Davies and C. Szzejmann (eds), *How the Holocaust Looks Now.* London: Palgrave Macmillan. pp. 185–96.

Gamble, N. (2013) *Exploring Children's Fiction* (3rd edn). London: Sage.

Gardner, J.P. (1994) *Hallmarks of Citizenship.* London: The British Institute of International and Comparative Law.

Garside, R. (2008) News and comment, *Race Equality Teaching,* 26 (2): 5.

Gathering the Voices (2012) Available at www.gatheringthevoices.com

General Teaching Council Scotland (GTCS) (2012) *The Standards for Registration: Mandatory Requirements for Registration with the General Teaching Council for Scotland.* Available at www.gtcs.org.uk/web/files/the-standards/standards-for-registration-1212. pdf (last accessed 21 October 2016).

Gerstenfeld, M. (2009) *The Abuse of Holocaust Memory: Distortions and Responses.* Jerusalem: Jerusalem Centre for Public Affairs.

Ghosh, S. (2012) Activating Citizenship – the nation's use of education to create notions of identity and citizenship in south Asia, *International Journal of Progressive Education,* 8 (1): 128–39.

Gilbert, M. (1986) *The Holocaust: The Jewish Tragedy.* London: Fontana.

Gilbert, R. (2010) Grasping the unimaginable: recent Holocaust novels for children by Morris Gleitzman and John Boyne, *Children's Literature in Education,* 41 (4): 355–66.

Ginott, H. (1972) *Teacher and Child: A Book for Parents and Teachers.* New York: Macmillan.

Gleitzman, M. (2006) *Once.* London: Puffin.

Gold, J. (1987) *Escape from Sobibor*, Zenith Productions.

Goldhagen, D. (1997) *Hitler's Willing Executioners: Ordinary Germans and the Holocaust*. New York: Abacus.

Graham, C., Williams, G. and Bryce, S. (2014) Pillars and lintels: the what's, why's and how's of interdisciplinary learning in stem education. Available at www.royalsoced.org. uk/cms/files/education/Learned%20Societies%20Science%20Education/pillars_and_ lintels.pdf

Gray, M. (2014a) *Contemporary Debates in Holocaust Education*. Basingstoke: Palgrave Macmillan.

Gray, M. (2014b) *The Boy in the Striped Pyjamas*: a blessing or curse for Holocaust education?, *Holocaust Studies*, 20 (3):109–36.

Gross, M. (2013) To teach the Holocaust in Poland: understanding teachers' motivations to engage the painful past, *Intercultural Education*, 24 (1–2): 103–20.

Gross, Z. (2009) Analysis of Holocaust discourse while visiting the Auschwitz-Birkenau Museum, *Canadian Diversity*, 7 (2): 97–100.

Gross, Z. and Rutland, S.D. (2014) Combating antisemitism in the school playground: an Australian case study, *Patterns of Prejudice*, 48 (3): 309–30.

Guardian (2012) 'Teaching the Holocaust: The Power of Personal Stories'. Available at www.theguardian.com/teacher-network/teacher-blog/2012/oct/15/teaching-holocaust-stories-second-world-war (last accessed 4 February 2016).

Guardian (2016a) 'Asylum Seekers Made To Wear Coloured Wristbands in Cardiff'. Available at www.theguardian.com.uk/uk-news/2016/jan/24/asylum-seekers-made-to-wear-coloured-wristbands-cardiff (last accessed 29 April 2016).

Guardian (2016b) 'NUS President Must Address Concerns Over Antisemitism, Say Jewish Students'. Available at www.theguardian.com/education/2016/apr/21/nus-president-malia-bouattia-must-redress-concerns-over-antisemitism-say-jewish-students (last accessed 3 May 2016).

Gundare, I. and Batelaan, P. (2003) Learning about and from the Holocaust: the development and implementation of a Complex Instruction Unit in Latvia, *Intercultural Education*, 14 (2): 151–66.

Hahn, C. (1998) *Becoming Political*. Albany: State University of New York Press.

Hammond, K. (2001) From horror to history: teaching pupils to reflect on significance, *Teaching History*, 104: 15–23.

Hannam, D. (1998) 'Democratic education and education for democracy through pupil/student participation in decision making in schools'. In D. Christie, H. Maitles and J. Halliday (eds), *Values Education for Democracy and Citizenship*. Glasgow: Gordon Cook Foundation/University of Strathclyde.

Harding, T. (2013) *Hanns and Rudolf: The German Jew and the Hunt for the Kommandant of Auschwitz*. London: Random House.

Harvie, J. (2012) Interdisciplinary education and co-operative learning: perfect shipmates to sail against the rising tide of 'learnification', *Stirling International Journal of Postgraduate Research*, 1(1).

HEDP (Holocaust Education Development Programme) (2009) *Teaching About the Holocaust in English Secondary Schools: An Empirical Study of National Trends, Perspectives and Practice*. London: Institute of Education.

Heitmeyer, W. (ed.) (2012) *Deutsche Zustande*. Frankfurt: Suhrkamp.

Henderson, S. (2015) 'A Trip to the Dark Side? A sociomaterial analysis of the spaces of Holocaust pedagogies at Auschwitz-Birkenau State Museum', PhD thesis, University of the West of Scotland.

Hilberg, R. (1985) *The Destruction of the European Jews* (revised and definitive edition). New York: Holes and Meir.

Hilberg, R. (1992) *Perpetrators, Victims, Bystanders: The Jewish Catastrophe 1933–45*. London: Harper Perennial.

The Historical Association (2007) *T.E.A.C.H. Teaching Emotive and Controversial London: The Historical Association, History 3–19*. Available at https://www.history.org.uk/files/download/784/1204732013 (last accessed 4 November 2016).

Hoess, R. (2000) *Commandant of Auschwitz*. London: Orion.

Holden, C. and Clough, N. (ed.) (1998) *Children as Citizens*. London: Jessica Kingsley.

Holliday, L. (1996) *Children in the Holocaust and WW11: Their Secret Diaries*. New York: Washington Square.

Holocaust Educational Trust (2006) *Lessons from Auschwitz Project*. Available at https://en.wikipedia.org/wiki/Holocaust_Educational_Trust#Lessons_from_Auschwitz_Project > (last accessed 15 April 2016).

Holocaust Educational Trust (n.d.) *Teaching the Holocaust in England*. Available at www.het.org.uk/media/english%20guide.pdf (last accessed 3 June 2016).

Holocaust Educators' Consortium (2014) What books shall we choose for our children? A selective guide to 30 years of Holocaust narratives for students in grades 4 Through 8, *Prism*, 9: 120–7.

Holocaust Memorial Day Trust (n.d.) Why mark 27 January Holocaust Memorial Day? Available at http://hmd.org.uk/page/why-mark-27-january-holocaust-memorial-day (last accessed 19 July 2015).

Horowitz, N. (2016) 'Students should go to where the Holocaust really began', *Ha'aretz*, 26 January. Available at www.haaretz.com/opinion/.premium-1.699419 (last accessed 20 March 2016).

House of Commons Education and Skills Committee (2005) *Education Outside the Classroom*. London: HMSO.

IHRA (International Holocaust Remembrance Alliance) (n.d.) *What to Teach About the Holocaust*. Available at www.holocaustremembrance.com/node/318 (last accessed 20 February 2015).

IHRA (2013) *Working Definition of Holocaust Denial and Distortion*.Available at www.holocaustremembrance.com/working-definition-holocaust-denial-and-distortion (last accessed 13 June 2016).

Illingworth, S. (2000) Hearts, minds and souls: exploring values through history, *Teaching History*, 100: 20–4.

Illinois (2010) *Teaching the Holocaust.* Available at www.ilholocaustmuseum.org/wpcontent/uploads/2013/12/Teachingguidelines_Grades7-12_2010-05-06.pdf (last accessed 6 February 2016).

Independent (2016a) 'NUS Delegates Criticised By MPs After Arguing Against Holocaust Memorial Day Commemoration'. Available at www.independent.co.uk/student/news/nus-delegates-criticised-by-mps-after-arguing-against-holocaust-memorial-day-commemoration-a6994356.html (last accessed 3 May 2016).

Independent (2016b) 'Oxford University Labour Club Co-Chair, Alex Chalmers, Resigns Amid Anti-Semitism Row'. Available at www.independent.co.uk/student/news/oxford-university-labour-club-co-chair-alex-chalmers-resigns-amid-anti-semitism-row-a6878826.html (last accessed 29 April 2016).

Innocenti, R. and McEwan, I. (1985) *Rose Blanche.* London: Jonathan Cape.

Institute of Education (2010) *Evaluation of the Holocaust Educational Trust's Lessons from Auschwitz Project.* London: Institute of Education

Isaac, B. (2004) *The Invention of Racism in Classical Antiquity.* Princeton and Oxford: Princeton University Press.

Israel National News (2014) 'Jews Fined for Singing "Ani Maamin" at Auschwitz', 8 March. Available at <http: Jewish World - News - Arutz Sheva.html#.VxYCxCR2vx4> (last accessed 15 April 2016).

Jennings, L. (2015) 'Holocaust education and critical citizenship in an American 5th grade: expanding repertoires of meanings, language and action'. In Z. Gross and D. Stevick (eds), *As the Witnesses Fall Silent: 21st Century Holocaust Education in Curriculum, Policy and Practice.* New York: Springer. pp. 185–208.

Jerichow, A. (2011) 'The educational imperative'. In J. Zarankin (ed.), *Reflections of the Holocaust.* New York: Humanity in Action. pp.145–55.

Jordan, S., Jordan, A., Robinson, S. and Taylor, P. (2012) The potential of history within the school curriculum in England for developing and enhancing the understanding of being a citizen in the twenty-first century, with an emphasis on the later primary experience and the start of secondary education, *Citizenship, Social and Economics Education,* 11 (1): 57–68.

Katz, D. (2010) 'Halting Holocaust Obfuscation', *Guardian,* 8 January. Available at www.theguardian.com (last accessed 3 June 2016).

Keneally, T. (1982) *Schindler's Ark.* London: Hodder & Stoughton.

Kerr, D. (2003) 'Citizenship: Local, national and international'. In L. Gearon (ed.), *Learning to Teach Citizenship in the Secondary School.* London: RoutledgeFalmer. pp. 5–27.

Kerr, D., Lines, A., Blenkinsop, S. and Schagen, I. (2001) *Citizenship and Education at Age 14: A Summary of the International Findings and Preliminary Results for England.* Slough: NFER.

Kinloch, N. (1998) Learning about the Holocaust: moral or historical question?, *Teaching History,* 93.

Kiwan, D. (2008) *Education for Inclusive Citizenship.* Abingdon: Routledge.

Klaus, H. (2005) Poetry after Auschwitz – Adorno's Dictum, *German Life and Letters*, 58 (2): 182–94.

Kochan, L. (1989) 'Life Over Death', *Jewish Chronicle*, 22 December.

Kor, E. (2015) 'We Can Heal with Forgiveness', *The Jewish Chronicle*, 1 May: 42–43.

Kratsborn, W., Jacott, L. and Öcel, N.P. (2008) Identity and citizenship: the impact of borders and shifts in boundaries, *Children's Identity & Citizenship in Europe*. London.

Kushner, T. (2003) The Holocaust and the museum world in Britain: a study of ethnography. In S. Vice (ed.), *Representing the Holocaust*. London: Vallentine Mitchell.

Kushner, T. (2006) From 'This Belsen Business' to 'Shoah Business': history, memory and heritage, 1945–2005, *Holocaust Studies*, 12 (1–2): 189–216.

LaCapra, D. (1994) *Representing the Holocaust: History, Theory, Trauma*. London: Cornell University Press.

LaCapra, D. (1998) *History and Memory After Auschwitz*. New York: Cornell University Press.

Landau, R. (1998) *Studying the Holocaust*. London: Routledge.

Landau, R. (2008) 'Teaching the Shoah', *Jewish Chronicle*, 12 September.

Lanzmann, C. (1985) *Shoah*. New York: Da Capo.

Larsen, A., Salinovic, S. and Sender, C. (2012) *Whose Story is History? History Education and Minority Students*. Available at www.humanityinaction.org/knowledgebase/321-whose-story-is-history-history-education-and-minority-students (last accessed 21 December 2015).

Lathey, G. (2001) 'A havey-cavey business: language in historical fiction with particular reference to novels of Joan Aiken and Leon Garfield'. In F.M. Collins and J. Graham (eds), *Historical Fiction for Children: Capturing the Past*. London: David Fulton. pp. 32–42.

Lazar, A., Chatlin, J., Gross, T. and Bar-On, D. (2004) Jewish Israeli teenagers, national identity and the lessons of the Holocaust, *Holocaust and Genocide Studies*, 18 (2): 188–204.

Leapman, M. (2000) *Witnesses to War*. London: Penguin.

Lennon, J. and Foley, M. (2000) *Dark Tourism: The Attraction of Death and Disaster*. London: Continuum.

Leon, A. (1971) *The Jewish Question*. London: Pathfinder Books.

Levene, M. (2006) Britain's Holocaust Memorial Day: a case of post-Cold War wish-fulfilment. Or brazen hypocrisy?, *Human Rights Review*, April–June: 26–59.

Levi, P. (1947) *If This Is A Man/The Truce*. London: Orion.

Levi, P. (1988) *The Drowned and the Saved*. London: Abacus.

Levi, P. (1989) in F. Camon (ed.), *Conversations with Primo Levi*. Marlboro, VT: Marlboro Press.

Levi, P. (1993) *Survival in Auschwitz*. New York: Collier.

Levin, B. (1998) 'The educational requirement for democracy', *Curriculum Inquiry*, 28(1): 57–79.

Levine, E. (2000) *Darkness over Denmark.* New York: Holiday House.

Levine, K. (2003) *Hana's Suitcase.* London: Evans Brothers.

Lindquist, D.H. (2011) Meeting a moral imperative: a rationale for teaching the Holocaust, *The Clearing House: A Journal of Educational Strategies, Issues and Ideas,* 84(1): 26–30.

Lister, R., Middleton, S. and Smith, N. (2001) *Young People's Voices.* Leicester: National Youth Agency.

Lower, W. (2014) *Hitler's Furies: German Women in the Nazi Killing Fields.* London: Vintage.

LTS (2000) *The Holocaust: A Teaching Pack for Primary Schools.* Dundee: Learning and Teaching Scotland.

LTS (2002a) *Education for Citizenship: A Paper for Discussion and Development.* Dundee: Learning and Teaching Scotland.

LTS (2002b) *The Holocaust: A Teaching Pack for Secondary Schools.* Dundee: Learning and Teaching Scotland.

Mail Online (2010) 'Primary Schoolchildren in Tears After They Are Told They Will Be Removed From Families As Part of Holocaust "Game"', 11 March. Available at <http://dailymail.co.uk/news/article-1256984/Primary-schoolchildren-tears-told-removed-families-Holocaust-game.html> (last accessed 3 June 2016).

Maitles, H. (1997) Never Again!, *International Socialism Journal,* 77: 103–10.

Maitles, H. (1998) 'Modern Studies'. In T. Bryce and W. Humes (eds), *Scottish Education.* Edinburgh: Edinburgh University Press.

Maitles, H. (2000) 'Thirty years of teaching political literacy in Scottish schools: how effective is Modern Studies?' In D. Lawton, J. Cairns and R. Gardner (eds), *Education for Citizenship.* London: Continuum. pp. 162–74.

Maitles, H. (2009) 'They're out to line their own pockets!': can the teaching of political literacy counter the democratic deficit?: the experience of Modern Studies in Scotland, *Scottish Educational Review,* 41: 46–61.

Maitles, H. (2010a) 'Why does wearing a yellow bib make us different'? A case study of explaining discrimination in a West of Scotland secondary (high) school, *Journal for Critical Education Policy Studies,* 8 (1): 246–261. Available at www.jceps.com/index.php ?pageID=article&articleID=183 (last accessed 3 June 2016).

Maitles, H. (2010b) Citizenship initiatives and pupil values: a case study of one Scottish school's experience, *Educational Review,* 62 (4): 391–406.

Maitles, H. (2012) 'Pedagogical issues in teaching the Holocaust'. In P. Cowan and H. Mailtes (eds), *Teaching Controversial Issues in the Classroom.* London: Continuum. p. 123.

Maitles, H. (2013) 'Modern Studies Education'. In T. Bryce and W. Humes (eds), *Scottish Education* (fourth edition). Edinburgh: Edinburgh University Press. pp. 528–33.

Maitles, H. and Cowan, P. (1999) Teaching the Holocaust in primary schools in Scotland: modes, methodology and content, *Educational Review,* 51 (3): 263–71.

Maitles, H., Cowan, P. and Butler, E. (2006) *Never Again! Does Holocaust Education Have An Effect On Pupils' Citizenship Values and Attitudes?* Available at www.gov.scot/Publications/2006/09/06133626/0 (last accessed 20 February 2015).

Maitles, H. and Gilchrist, I. (2003) 'Never too young to learn democracy!: A case study of a democratic approach to learning in a secondary class in the West of Scotland', paper presented at *SERA*, November 27–29, Perth. Available at: http://brs.leeds.ac.uk/cgi-bin/00003459.doc.

Maitles, H. and Gilchrist, I. (2006) 'Never too young to learn democracy!: A case study of a democratic approach to learning in a Religious and Moral Education secondary class in the West of Scotland', *Educational Review*, 58 (1), 67–85.

Marcus, A.S. (2007) Representing the past and reflecting the present: museums, memorials and the secondary History classroom, *The Social Studies*, May/June: 105–10.

Marrus, M. (1995) Jewish resistance to the Holocaust, *Journal of Contemporary History*, 30 (1): 83–110.

Megargee, G.P. (ed.) (2009) *The United States Holocaust Memorial Museum Encyclopedia of Camps and Ghettos, 1933–1945*, Vol. I. Indiana: Indiana University Press.

Megargee, G.P. and Dean, M. (eds) (2012) *The United States Holocaust Memorial Museum Encyclopedia of Camps and Ghettos, 1933–1945: Ghettos in German-Occupied Eastern Europe (Part A & B)*, Vol. II. Indiana: Indiana University Press.

Miles, W.F.S. (2004) Third World views of the Holocaust, *Journal of Genocide Research*, 6 (3): 371–93.

Moisan, S., Andor, E. and Strickler, C. (2012) Stories of Holocaust survivors as an educational tool – uses and challenges, *Oral History Forum d'histoire orale*, 32.

Morimoto, S. (2007) 'Democracy for teens: gender and becoming a good citizen'. Paper presented at the annual meeting of the American Sociological Association, 11 August, New York. Available at www.allacademic.com/meta/p184052_index.html (last accessed 9 December 2015).

Morpurgo, M. (2008) *The Mozart Question*. London: Walker.

Morrison, N. (2009) 'Eyes Wide Open', *TES Magazine*, 10 July, pp. 40–3.

MoTL (2016) 'March of the Living'. Available at <http://marchoftheliving.org.uk/> (last accessed 10 March 2016).

Mughal, F. and Rosen, E. (2010) *The Role of Righteous Muslims*. London: Faith Matters.

Myers, M. (2012) 'Gypsy and Roma families'. In P. Cowan and H. Maitles (eds), *Teaching Controversial Issues in the Classroom*. London: Continuum. pp. 200–10.

Narvaez, A. (1987) 'Role-playing Revives Holocaust horror', *New York Times*, 23 May.

Novick, P. (1999) *The Holocaust and Collective Memory*. London: Bloomsbury.

Orlenius, K. (2008) Tolerance of intolerance: values and virtues at stake in education, *Journal of Moral Education*, 37 (4): 467–84.

Ortloff, D.H. (2015) '"They Think It Is Funny to Call Us Nazis": Holocaust Education and Multicultural Education in a Diverse Germany?' In Z. Gross and D. Stevick (eds), *As the Witnesses Fall Silent: 21st Century Holocaust Education in Curriculum: Policy and Practice*. New York: Springer. pp. 209–23.

Osler, A. and Starkey, H. (2005) *Changing Citizenship Democracy and Inclusion in Education*. Maidenhead: Open University Press.

Oxford Dictionary Online (n.d.) Available at www.oxforddictionaries.com/definition/english/Nazi (last accessed 7 November 2015).

Pedersen, P. (1995) Simulations: a safe place to take risks in discussing cultural differences, *Simulation and Gaming*, 26: 201.

Peters, W. (1987) *A Class Divided: Then and Now*. New York: Yale University Press.

Pettigrew, A. (2010) Limited lessons from the Holocaust: critically considering the 'anti-racist' and citizenship potential, *Teaching History*, 141: 50–5.

Pinsker, L. (1882) Auto-emancipation, in L. Pinsker (ed.), *Roads to Freedom: The London News Chronicle: Writings and Addresses* (New York, 1944: pp. 83–4).

Power, F.C., Nezzi, R., Narvaez, D., Lapsley, D. and Hunt, T. (2007) *Moral Education: A Handbook*. Westport, CT: Praeger.

Prime Minister's Holocaust Commission Report (2015) *Britain's Promise to Remember*. London: The Cabinet Office.

Print, M. (2007) Citizenship education and youth participation in democracy, *British Journal of Educational Studies*, 55 (3): 325–45.

Prough, E. and Postic, R. (2008) 'Today's Dick and Jane: a look into the levels of political tolerance of adolescents in public and religious high school environments'. Paper presented at the 2008 Annual Meeting of the Midwest Political Science Association, 3–6 April, Chicago, Illinois. Available at www.allacademic.com//meta/p_mla_apa_research_citation/2/6/ 8/8/8/pages2688 (last accessed 9 December 2015).

Puolimatka, T. (1995) *Democracy and Education: the Critical Citizen as an Educational Aim*. Helsinki: Suomalainen Tiedeakatemia.

Rathenow, H.F. and Weber, N.H. (1998) 'Education for Auschwitz: a task for human rights education'. In C. Holden and N. Clough (eds), *Children as Citizens: Education for Participation*. London: Jessica Kingsley. pp. 95–112.

Rings, W. (1982) *Life with the Enemy: Collaboration and resistance in Hitler's Europe – 1939–1945*. New York: Doubleday.

Ritchie, A. (1999) *Our Lives Consultation: Final Report*. Edinburgh: Save the Children Scotland.

Rittner, C., Smith, S. and Steinfeldt, I. (2000) *The Holocaust and the Christian World*. Jerusalem: Yad Vashem.

Romi, S. and Lev, M. (2007) Experiential learning of history through youth journeys to Poland, *Research in Education*, 78 (1): 88–102.

Rooney, K. (2007) Citizenship education: making kids conform. Available at www.spiked-online.com/index.php?/site/printable/4023/ (last accessed on 25 May 2015).

Rosen, R. (2011) '"Jew" Used as a Term of Playground Abuse', *Jewish Chronicle*, 12 May. Available at www.thejc.com/news/uk-news/48828/jew-used-a-term-playground-abuse (last accessed 3 June 2016).

Ross, A. and Roland-Levy, C. (2003) 'Growing up politically in Europe today'. In C. Roland-Levy and A. Ross (eds), *Political Learning and Citizenship in Europe*. Stoke-on-Trent: Trentham. pp. 1–16.

Ruben, B. (1999) 'Simulations, games and experience-based learning: the quest for a new paradigm in teaching and learning', *Simulation and Gaming*, 30: 498–507.

Rudduck, J. and Flutter, J. (2004) *How To Improve Your School*. London: Continuum.

Russell, L. (2006) *Teaching the Holocaust in School History: Teachers or Preachers?* London: Continuum.

Rutland, S. (2015) 'Genocide or Holocaust education: exploring different Australian approaches for Muslim school children'. In Z. Gross and D. Stevick (eds), *As the Witnesses Fall Silent: 21st Century Holocaust Education in Curriculum, Policy and Practice*. London: Springer. pp. 225–44.

Sacks, J. (2014) 'Every religion must wrestle with its dark angels, and so today must we: Jews, Christians and Muslims alike'. Available at www.rabbisacks.org/every-religion-must-wrestle-dark-angels-today-must-jews-christians-muslims-alike/ (last accessed 29 April 2016).

Sagall, S. (2013) *Final Solutions: Human Nature, Capitalism and Genocide: A Psychohistorical Re-examination of the Holocaust*. London: Pluto.

Salmons, P. (2010) Universal meaning or historical understanding? The Holocaust in history and history in the curriculum, *Teaching History*, 141: 57–63.

Satloff, R. (2006) *Among the Righteous: Lost Stories from the Holocaust's Long Reach into Arab Lands*. New York: Public Affairs.

Save the Children (2000) *'It's our Education': Young people's views on improving their schools*. Edinburgh: Save the Children Scotland.

Save the Children (2001) *Education for Citizenship in Scotland: Perspectives of young people*. Edinburgh: Save the Children Scotland.

Schechter, H. and Salomon, G. (2005) Does vicarious experience of suffering affect empathy for an adversary? The effects of Israelis' visits to Auschwitz on their empathy for Palestinians, *Peace Education*, 2 (2): 125–38.

Schindler's List (1993) (DVD) USA: Steven Spielberg.

Schoenfeld, G. (2004) *The Return of Anti-Semitism*. San Francisco, CA: Encounter.

Schulz, W., Ainley, J., Fraillon, J., Kerr, D. and Losito, B. (2011) *Initial Findings from the IEA International Civic Education Study*. Amsterdam: IEA.

Schweber, S. (2003) Simulating survival, *Curriculum Inquiry*, 33 (2): 139–88.

Seaton, A.V. (1996) Guided by the dark: from thanatopsis to thanatourism, *International Journal of Heritage Studies*, 2 (4): 234–44.

Seixas, P. (1997) Mapping the terrain of historical significance, *Social Education*, 61: 22–7.

Shawn, K. (1999) What should they read, and when should they read it? A selective review of Holocaust literature for students in grades 2 through 6. In J.P. Robertson (ed.), *Teaching for a Tolerant World*. Urbana, IL: National Council of Teachers of English.

Short News (2006) 'Middle School Children Cry During Holocaust Role Play Simulation'. Available at www.shortnews.com/start.cfm?id=53762 (last accessed 17 November 2015).

Short, G. (2003) Holocaust education in the primary school: some reflections on an emergent debate, *London Review of Education*, 1 (2): 119–29.

Short, G. (2012) 'Teaching the Holocaust in the multicultural classroom'. In P. Cowan and H. Maitles (eds), *Teaching Controversial Issues in the Classroom: Key Issues and Debates*. London/New York: Continuum. pp. 130–41.

Short, G. (2013) Reluctant learners? Muslim youth confront the Holocaust, *Intercultural Education*, 24 (1–2): 121–32.

Short, G. (2015) 'Failing to learn from the Holocaust'. In Z. Gross and E.D. Stevick (eds), *As the Witnesses Fall Silent: 21st Century Holocaust Education in Curriculum, Policy and Practice*. Switzerland: Springer. pp. 455–68.

Short, G. and Carrington, B. (1991) Unfair discrimination: teaching the principles to children of primary school age, *Journal of Moral Education*, 20 (2): 157–77.

Short, G. and Carrington, B. (1995) Anti-Semitism and the primary school: children's perceptions of Jewish culture and identity, *Research in Education*, 54: 14–24.

Short, G. and Carrington, B. (1996) Antiracist education, multiculturalism and the new racism, *Educational Review*, 48: 65–77.

Short, G. and Reed, C.A. (2004) *Issues in Holocaust Education*. Hampshire: Ashgate.

Short, G., Supple, C. and Klinger, K. (1998) *The Holocaust in the School Curriculum: A European Perspective*. Strasbourg: Council of Europe.

Smetana, J. (2006) 'Social cognitive domain theory: consistencies and variations'. In M. Killen and J. Smetana (eds), *Handbook of Moral Development*. New Jersey: Lawrence Erlbaum. pp.119–54.

Snyder, T. (2011) *Bloodlands: Europe between Europe and Stalin*. London: Vintage.

Soule, S. and Nairne, J. (2006) 'Are girls checking out? Gender and political socialization in transitioning democracies'. Paper presented at the Midwestern Political Science Meeting, 19–23 April, Chicago, Illinois. Available at www.civiced.org/pdfs/research/GenderAndPolitical.pdf (last accessed 9 December 2015).

Spiegelman, A. (1987) *Maus 1: A Survivor's Tale: My Father Bleeds History*. London: Penguin.

Spiegelman, A. (1992) *Maus II: A Survivor's Tale – And Here My Troubles Began*. London: Penguin.

Stand Up To Racism (2016) http://standuptoracism.org.uk/2016/02/un-anti-racism-day-demonstration-march-19-2016-london (last accessed 29 April 2016).

Stanton, G.H. (2013) *The Ten Stages of Genocide*. Available at www.genocidewatch.org/genocide/tenstagesofgenocide.html (last accessed 2 May 2016).

Stenhouse, L. (1971) 'The Humanities Curriculum Project: The Rationale', *Theory into Practice*', 10 (3): 154–62.

Stevick, D. and Gross, Z. (2014) 'Research in Holocaust education: emerging themes and directions'. In K. Fracapane and M. Haß (eds), *Holocaust Education in a Global Context*. Paris: UNESCO. pp. 59–76.

Stone, D. (2010) Beyond the 'Auschwitz Syndrome': Holocaust historiography after the Cold War, *Patterns of Prejudice*, 44 (5): 454–68.

Supple, C. (1998) 'Issues and problems in teaching about the Holocaust'. In G. Short, C. Supple and K. Klinger (eds), *The Holocaust in the School Curriculum: A European Perspective*. Strasbourg: Council of Europe. pp. 17–58.

Taylor, M. (1999) *Faraway Home*. Dublin: O'Brien.

Telegraph Online (2010) 'Primary Schoolchildren "In Tears" Following Holocaust Role-Play'. Available at www.telegraph.co.uk/education/educationnews/7422641/Primary-schoolchildren-in-tears-following-Holocaust-role-play.html (last accessed 21 November 2015).

The Boy in the Striped Pyjamas (2009) DVD. Mark Herman (dir). USA: Miramax.

Tibi, B. (2008) Public policy and the combination of anti-Americanism and anti-semitism in contemporary Islamist ideology', *The Current*, 12 (1):123–46.

Times Educational Supplement (TES) (2015) 'My Secret? Let Pupils Lead, Says Teacher of the Year'. Available at www.tes.com/article.aspx?storycode=11007590 (last accessed 3 May 2016).

Toksvig, S. (2005) *Hitler's Canary*. London: Doubleday.

Torney-Purta, J., Lehmann, R., Oswald, H. and Shulz, W. (2001) *Citizenship and Education in Twenty-Eight Countries*. Amsterdam: IEA.

Totten, S. (1999) Should there be Holocaust education for K-4 students? The answer is no, *Social Studies and The Young Learner*, 12 (1): 36–9.

Totten, S. (2000a) Student misconceptions about the genesis of the Holocaust, *Canadian Social Studies*, 34 (4): 81–4.

Totten, S. (2000b) Diminishing the complexity and horror of the Holocaust: using simulations in an attempt to convey historical experience, *Social Education*, 64 (3): 165–71.

Totten, S. (2002) *Holocaust Education: Issues and Approaches*. Boston, MA: Allyn and Bacon.

Turner, B. (1993) 'Contemporary problems in the theory of citizenship'. In B. Turner (ed.), *Citizenship and Social Theory*. London: Sage.

UAF (2015) 'UAF and LMHR's Auschwitz educational trip'. Available at http://uaf.org.uk/2015/12/uaf-and-lmhrs-auschwitz-educational-trip/ (last accessed 20 March 2016).

UNESCO (United Nations Education, Scientific and Cultural Organisation) (1995) *Declaration of Principles on Tolerance*, Paris, 16 November. Available at www.unesco.org/cpp/uk/declarations/tolerance.pdf (last accessed 2 May 2016).

UNESCO (2015) 'The International Status of Education about the Holocaust: A Global Mapping of Textbooks and Curricula'. Paris: UNESCO. Available at: http://unesdoc.unesco.org/images/0022/002287/228776e.pdf (accessed 13 June 2016).

United Nations (1951) *Convention and Protocol Relating to the Status of Refugees*. Available at www.unhcr.org/3b66c2aa10.html (last accessed 4 December 2015).

United Nations (UN General Assembly) (1989) *A Summary of the Conventions on the Rights of the Child*, 20 November, United Treaty Series, Vol. 1577: 3. Available at www.unicef.org.uk/Documents/Publication-pdfs/UNCRC_summary.pdf (last accessed 2 May 2016).

United Nations (2005) '"Such An Evil Must Never Be Allowed To Happen Again", Secretary-General Tells General Assembly Session Commemorating Liberation of Nazi Death Camps', 24 Jan. Available at: www.un.org/press/en/2005/sgsm9686.doc.htm (last accessed 13 June 2016).

USC Shoah Foundation (n.d.) *Introducing IWitness*. Available at www.https://sfi.usc.edu/iwitness (last accessed 30 October 2015).

USHMM (2009) *Teaching about the Holocaust: A Resource Guide for Educators.* Washington, DC: USHMM.

USHMM (United States Holocaust Memorial Museum) (n.d.) *Killing Centers.* Available at www.ushmm.org/wlc/en/article.php?ModuleId=10007327 (last accessed 28 September 2015).

Vice, S. (2000) *Holocaust Fiction*. London: Routledge.

Welzer, H. (2010) *Das kommunikative Gedächtnis: Eine Theorie der Erinnerung* [*Communicative memory: a theory of remembering*]. Munich: Beck Verlag.

Werbner, P. (2009) Displaced enemies, displaced memories: diaspora memorial politics of partition and the Holocaust, *Ethnos*, 74 (4): 441–64.

Whiteley, P. (2005) 'Citizenship education longitudinal study second literature review. Citizenship education: The political science perspective'. DfES Research Report 631. Nottingham: DfES.

Wiedl, B. (2010) 'Laughing at the Beast: The Judensau'. In A. Classen (ed.), *Laughter in the Middle Ages and Early Modern Times*. Berlin and New York: Walter de Gruyter. pp. 325–64.

Wiesel, E. (1960) *Night*. New York: Hill and Wang.

Williams, P. (2007) *Memorial Museums: The Global Rush to Commemorate Atrocities.* New York: Berg.

Wistrich, R. (1994) *Antisemitism: The Longest Hatred*. New York: Schocken.

Wolfreton School (2014) 'Students visit Auschwitz'. Available at www.wolfreton.co.uk/students-visit-auschwitz/ (last accessed 15 May 2016).

Wollaston, I. (2005) Negotiating the marketplace: The role(s) of Holocaust museums today, *Journal of Modern Jewish Studies*, 4 (1): 63–80.

Wood, B. (2012) Scales of active citizenship: New Zealand teachers' diverse perceptions and practice, *International Journal of Progressive Education*, 8 (1): 77–93.

Wrigley, T. (2003) *Schools of Hope: a new agenda for school improvement*. Stoke-on-Trent: Trentham.

Xin, X. (2009) Holocaust education in China, *Discussion Paper Journal*, 1. New York: United Nations (Online). Available at www.un.org/en/holocaustremembrance/docs/paper2.shtml (last accessed 29 April 2015).

Yad Vashem (2015) *Women of Valor: Stories of Women Who Rescued Jews During the Holocaust.* Available at www.yadvashem.org/yv/en/exhibitions/righteous-women/ (last accessed 28 April 2016).

Yad Vashem/ODIHR (2006) *Preparing Holocaust Memorial Days: Suggestions for Educators.* Available at www.yadvashem.org/yv/en/education/ceremonies/guidelines_pdf/english.pdf (date of access 28 April 2016).

Zapruder, A. (2002) *Salvaged Pages: Young Writers' Diaries of the University.* New Haven, CT: Yale University Press.

Zembylas, M. and McGlynn, C. (2012) Discomforting pedagogies: emotional tensions, ethical dilemmas and transformative possibilities, *British Educational Research Journal*, 38 (1): 41–59.

Zick, A., Kupper, B. and Hovermann, A. (2011) *Intolerance, Prejudice and Discrimination: A European Report.* Berlin: Nora Langenbacher, Friedrich-Ebert-Stiftung, Forum Berlin.

INDEX